SOCIAL CONCERN AND SOCIAL ENTERPRISE

SOCIAL CONCERN AND SOCIAL ENTERPRISE

Kevin Gulliver

Edited by David Mullins,
University of Birmingham

First published by Brewin Books Ltd.
Studley, Warwickshire B80 7LG in 2000.

British Library Cataloguing on Publishing Data
A catalogue record for this book is available from
The British Library

ISBN: 1 85858 176 1 (Hardback)
ISBN: 1 85858 177 X (Paperback)

Typeset in Plantin
and made and printed in Great Britain
by Warwick Printing Company Limited
Theatre Street, Warwick CV34 4DR

Preface

The 75th Anniversary of the founding of Focus Housing has provided us with the perfect opportunity to look back critically at our heritage, our achievements and our failures. The 75 years have taught us that poverty cannot be effectively tackled solely by improving housing conditions. This was evident to the early Copec pioneers in 1925. It is a lesson that we have relearned in our recent history. The formation of the new Prime Focus group structure and identity are enabling us to go back to our roots when the importance of community was understood as a means of providing support to people in need. It is also preparing us to face the challenges of the 21st Century. I believe that 'Social Concern and Social Enterprise' successfully identifies the dominant ideas and key events that have shaped the significant Midlands Charity we have become today.

Dr. Peter Knight – Vice Chancellor, University of Central England, Chairman of Prime Focus

Copec Conference at Birmingham's Central Methodist Hall in 1924

Contents

★ Written in conjunction with David Mullins

vii

Foreword

by the Venerable John Duncan MBE, Archdeacon of Birmingham and Chairman of Birmingham Housing Trust, Copec and Focus Housing Associations (1965 to 1996)

'Forward', Birmingham's motto, pinpoints the city's characteristics of pragmatic and energetic response to changing times, and to the welfare of the city and its people. Certainly that spirit has been reflected in the voluntary housing movement in both Birmingham and the wider West Midlands region throughout the 20th century. This book seeks to describe and assess the achievements of this movement, and in particular, one of the oldest of its number in our region, Focus. Those who, like myself, have been involved in the voluntary housing movement since the mid-1960s right up until the millennium are very conscious of Focus' heritage and of our building on the work of those early pioneers, the Copec House Improvement Society. Founded in the mid-1920s, Copec's founders were drawn from the churches and leading people of Birmingham, and focussed on personal care for tenants in 'patched-up' properties in the city's central areas. They had a keen sense of Christian campaigning, publicising the scandal of slum housing. They also worked closely with Birmingham City Council to improve whole living environments for, and life chances of, local people.

This account of voluntary housing in the West Midlands builds on a previous history of Copec written by its first housing manager, Margaret Fenter, in 1960, and takes us 'forward' until 2000. The latter years of the 20th century have seen a rich variety of voluntary housing associations forming, with various emphases, in and around Birmingham, which then went on to merge with Copec and eventually to form Focus. These were Birmingham Housing Trust, Wolverhampton Housing Association, Shape Housing Association, Hestia Housing Association, St. Chad Housing Society and Harambee Housing Association (now Black Star). I pay tribute to all of those involved with these associations in the past. The rich variety locally was mirrored in the national trend, with substantial increases in the number and types of housing associations formed over the last 35 years. The funding and regulatory regimes, and the administrative and professional demands on housing associations, in the present day are highly complex. The pluralist, multi-ethnic and multi-faith community which Birmingham and the West Midlands now contains has demanded the development of just and non-discriminatory practices in housing associations. Christians, rather than being the majority, as they were at the time of Copec's formation, are now working in Focus with people from a range of faiths, convictions, backgrounds and cultures; an approach which reflects our time. Yet as Birmingham and its surrounding region moves into the 21st century, with ever changing demands, Focus' priorities still remain those of Copec's founders and their successors – caring for tenants, publicising housing injustice and working with statutory and voluntary sector partners, not only to house people properly – Focus' core business – but also to bring new opportunities to whole communities.

This book identifies many who, over the years, have been committed to taking these tasks 'forward' – as committee members, volunteers, officers and staff. Particularly I must pay tribute to those Chief Executives with whom I have been so pleased to be associated over 35 years – Janet Rushbrooke, David Mumford and Richard Clark. They have each brought high personal commitment and undoubted talent to the various phases of Focus' evolution.

Kevin Gulliver, who many will wish to thank for his demanding and detailed work as author, has presented a history of Focus Housing, and of those housing associations which came together to form it, in a way which illuminates and analyses howassociations have responded to changing circumstances. The book also clarifies and sharpens Focus' goals and tasks for today as it moves 'forward' to meet a new generation's needs. I commend this book to a wide readership.

Prime Minister Stanley Baldwin and Birmingham MP, Neville Chamberlain, Minister for Health and Housing in 1926, visit Copec properties at Pope Street in Birmingham's central ares.

Acknowledgements

So many different people from different walks of life have contributed to the writing of this book that a full list is not possible. I hope that those who are not mentioned will forgive me. First I wish to thank Richard Clark, Focus' Chief Executive, for asking me to write this book in the first place. It has not always been easy but I have learned a lot from the experience. I am grateful to him for the opportunity extended to me in late 1998 when the suggestion that I write this history, to mark Focus' 75th anniversary, was first made. It was Richard's idea to commission an 'academic' assessment of Focus' contribution to voluntary housing over the 75 years, and this has presented me with my greatest challenge and greatest satisfaction over the last 18 months. Richard also supplied useful comments on early drafts. Credit must also go to him for placing renewed emphasis on Focus' role in the inner city through the creation of the 'Social Investment Agency', now called Prime Focus of which Focus Housing is a subsidiary. The history shows that Focus' latest 'transformation' is very much in keeping with its heritage since 1925. And the present day emphasis on social enterprise enabled an easy choice for the book's title.

I should also like to extend my thanks to all present committee members and staff at Focus, and to those who are no longer involved with the housing association, but helped anyway. Of particular note are Tim Beavis, Dave Butchere, David Cairns, Basil Clark, Hilary Clark, Liz Clutton, Dick Empson, David Gregory, Chris Handy, Jim Hewitson, Kit Horton, Helen Hughes, Bert Massey, Pearl MacCauley, Aileen MacPherson, the Reverend Peter Mortlock, John Morris, Chris Patterson, Dawn Prentice, Heather Rhodes, Ruth Salton, Gillian Saunders, Terry Scarle, Professor Ken Spencer, James Tickell, Mark Tranter, Phyllis Turner, Paul Weston, Barbara Whitfield and Gill Winn. Special thanks should also go to Chris Wadhams, former Chief Executive of Shape, who provided many interesting insights into housing association development in the region. The staff at public libraries in Birmingham, Dudley, Sandwell and Wolverhampton were of great assistance in helping me to find historical material. The Birmingham Post and Mail, and the Wolverhampton Express and Star, supplied photographs. I must also thank staff at Focus' regional offices for supplying information at short notice. Special thanks go to those at the Snow Hill hostel for putting up with my constant rummaging in their basement archives for material.

Particular thanks must go to the history project's steering group who have read numerous drafts and have amended approaches, ideas and text with great patience for tight deadlines. I must especially thank John Duncan, the association's Chairman from 1965 to 1996, for his support throughout, for his gentle ribbing when I misinterpreted past events and for his contribution of the book's foreword. Also on the steering group, Rick Groves, previous chairman of Shape, made many valuable contributions, lent me books at short notice and gave insights into the development of Shape. Moyra Riseborough of the Centre for Urban and Regional Studies (CURS) at Birmingham University has commented on drafts and curtailed my tendency towards the verbose. Her constant reminders of the importance of people in the history have, I hope, made it less dry than it might otherwise have been. A late member joining the steering group was Philip James, Focus' strategic planning manager, who also read drafts at short notice and made many useful comments. David Mumford, ex-Chief Executive, also assisted with the book, which records his contribution to the association between 1965 and 1994.

The final steering group member who has been invaluable to me is David Mullins, Senior Lecturer in housing at CURS. He has managed the overall project with great patience, contributed ideas for the book's framework, suggested text; sub-editing all drafts, and rivalling me for sleep deprivation in those final few weeks of preparing the text for the publishers. He made a particular contribution in drafting chapters 7 and 8, drawing on his own work on mergers and organisational transformations, and many of the insights into Focus' evolution contained there are his. He also carried out some of the interviews, met me on many occasions in dangerous places, such as motorway service stations, and guided me constantly towards meeting even more dangerous and difficult deadlines.

I should also like to thank Focus' Regional Directors, John Morris and Kerry Bolister, for supplying the 'housing professionals' perspective', and for Research Officer Rachel Brocklehurst who commented on the first draft. Paul Bryan of Focus' finance department and Gordon Malcolm of the development department checked figures in tables and ensured greater accuracy than otherwise would have been possible. Paul Gallagher, my 'plain English guinea pig' made useful suggestions at the 'Jolly Crispin' on many a depressed Friday night.

A number of people unassociated with Focus have helped considerably. Chief amongst these are Professor Peter Malpass of the University of the West of England who pointed out flaws in an earlier draft and made suggestions for improvements. His seminal book on the history of housing associations, although published towards the end of my research (at almost the same time as Pat Garside's outstanding history of William Sutton Trust which also proved invaluable), enabled me to place some events in context, when previously there was little. Staff at Notting Hill Housing Trust, particularly Martin Prater, and those at the Howard Cottage Society supplied useful material and I should like to thank them too. John Glasby's book about the Birmingham Settlement also supplied many interesting insights into the history of the voluntary sector in Birmingham and the relationship between the Settlement and Copec. This relationship extends to the present day. I am also grateful to Brewin Books, publishers of this history, and Springboard, who designed the cover, for an excellent job to a tight deadline.

Last but not least I am grateful to my family for allowing me to use the spare bedroom as an office for this project. Material was often stacked from floor to ceiling and cannot have been easy to live with for the last 18 months.

List of tables

Glossary of terms and abbreviations

ADP
Approved Development Programme, the annual investment in housing association housing programmes, managed by the Housing Corporation

DETR
Department of the Environment, Transport and the Regions – Deputy Prime Minister John Prescott's 'super department' set up in 1997, formerly the DoE, responsible for housing in the English regions

DoE
Department of the Environment, central government department in England with responsibility for housing from 1970 to 1997

HAG
Housing Association Grant, a capital grant for housing association refurbishment and new house building, introduced by the Housing Act 1974

HC
The Housing Corporation, chief regulator of English housing associations (from 1996 RSLs) and main source of their funding, set up initially in 1964 but with an increased remit from 1974

HMP
Housing Market Package, a one-off funding package to housing associations in 1992/93 to acquire vacant and/or repossessed properties to stimulate the depressed owner-occupied housing market

I&P Societies
The majority of housing associations are Industrial and Provident Societies, registered with the Registrar of Friendly Societies

MoH
Ministry of Health which had responsibility for housing between 1919 and 1950

MoHLG
Ministry of Health and Local Government which had responsibility for housing from 1951 to 1970

NFHS
National Federation of Housing Societies, 1935 to 1973

NFHA
NFHS evolved into the National Federation of Housing Associations in 1973, lasting until 1996

NHF
The latest variant of the name for the trade body for housing associations – changed to the National Housing Federation to incorporate English RSLs following the Housing Act 1996

1

Introduction

Over the last few years, a number of quality histories of housing associations have been written. The histories of Bournville Village Trust (Hillman 1994, Harrison 1999), the Guinness Trust (Malpass 1998), Paddington Churches (Mantle 1995), Home (Malpass and Jones 1995), Friendship (Malpass and Jones 1996), Octavia Hill Housing Trust (Malpass 1999) and the William Sutton Trust (Garside 2000) are the most noteworthy of these histories. Most of these housing associations were founded either at the very end of the 19th Century, during the 1920s and 1930s, or in the 1960s and 1970s – three key eras of housing association development. Focus Housing is not as old as Bournville, William Sutton or Guinness – the great endowed Trusts of the late 19th Century. Its origins are in the 1920s. But through a series of mergers with other housing associations and development of its role, scope and structure over recent years, Focus is as much a product of the 1960s and 1970s as those more recently formed.

The story of Focus begins in 1924 as part of a philanthropic, predominantly Christian, response to the appalling housing conditions found in Birmingham, the country's major manufacturing centre and 19th Century Lord Mayor Joseph Chamberlain's 'best governed city in the world' (Upton 1997). Founded by a small number of Birmingham delegates to the landmark Christian Conference on Politics, Economics and Citizenship (COPEC), Focus has grown from a small, voluntary housing society reconditioning a few hundred slum houses to a major social enterprise with 12,000 homes across the West Midlands and assets in excess of £500 million. Despite these changes in scale, Focus has retained much of its early character. Throughout its history, it has been an organisation inspired by concern for the needs of local people. Yet it has also shown remarkable entrepreneurial skills in all eras since the 1920s, experimenting with new ways of meeting need through its development, housing management and wider community activities. The title of this celebration of Focus' 75th jubilee, then, seeks to show how the housing association has developed and adapted to changes in public policy over this period. Inspired by social concern but operating in a social entrepreneurial fashion sums up the Focus approach throughout its history.

This book grew out of the desire to commemorate all of those who have contributed to the success of Focus during its history – committee members, staff, tenants and others who have played a part. Earlier commemorations have been written (Fenter 1960, Thomas 1985). But as Focus' 75th anniversary falls in the millennium year, Focus' management committee decided to commission a new study of the association's history, which covers not only the early years but the most recent phase of the development of Focus into a 'Social Investment Agency' for the 21st Century. This history covers not only the principal changes in the association's approach to meeting housing need since the 1920s, but also seeks to place these changes within a wider context. It aims to contribute to the study of housing associations and their place in the development of 20th Century housing and social policy.

The Toll House at the intersection of Hamstead and Villa Roads in Handsworth, Birmingham. The first photograph shows it in 1885. The second shows Copec's north area office in 1987. This was where the Handsworth disturbances took place in 1985. Copec's office was used to house Inner City Contracts – a local building company founded by Copec, other housing associations and the local community to tackle unemployment in the area.

Opened in 1984, Flint Green House, Birmingham was developed as a rehabilitation unit for people with mental health problems; usually for people leaving a psychiatric unit at local hospitals. The scheme was funded by the Housing Corporation and Inner City Partnerships. Later in the 1980s, seven flats were provided in the large grounds of the scheme for residents wishing to have a 'halfway house' to independent living in the community. Called the 'Rookwood Project' and supported by Birmingham Social Services, the scheme was opened by David Edmonds, Chief Executive of the Housing Corporation in March 1989. Managed from Flint Green House, the scheme also had a designated Project Worker who visited and supported residents on a regular basis.

Housing associations have a unique heritage in this country's response to tackling poor housing conditions and poverty. The origins of housing associations can be traced back to the medieval almshouses, although perhaps more modern-day origins can be seen in the large endowed trusts of the late 19th Century. There has been a tendency to view modern housing associations from this long historical perspective, in part as a justification for their current prominence in English social housing policy. However, this is an incorrect assumption, with most of today's housing associations able to trace their history back to the mid-1960s at the earliest (Malpass 2000). Only a few of today's housing associations have existed since the 19th Century although a slightly larger number, including Focus, have their origins in the early decades of this century.

Some commentators (particularly Malpass 1999, 2000) have argued that modern housing associations are the result of housing policy changes over the last 100 years with new associations being formed in response to public policy in different eras. Even older associations have transformed themselves on a number of occasions to meet the policy challenges and opportunities of each new era (Mullins 2000a). Today, most housing associations are charities or operate under charitable rules. They provide housing for low income households and those with special housing needs. While they are constituted as independent bodies managed by committees of volunteers, housing associations have effectively been part of state housing provision since 1974 when they were provided with substantial public funding, although more limited public subsidies had been available since 1919. Now there are 2,300 associations registered with their public regulator, the Housing Corporation (1999). The majority are small concerns but some are large and sophisticated organisations, employing thousands of professional staff, managing thousands of homes with asset values running into £100's millions.

Figure (1) – Growth In The Focus Housing Stock 1965-2000

The association's housing stock grew to a highpoint in its early history of 339 properties in 1940 but declined thereafter to 241 in 1965. The graph shows a steady growth in rented housing after 1965, and particularly after 1985.

Focus is one of those rare housing associations which is a major player in the housing association 'movement' today, but with origins in the 1920s (Garside 2000, Malpass 2000). Originally called Copec, the association has a history which mirrors most of the key policy developments of the last 75 years. Over this period, however, Focus has transformed itself a number of times, often through mergers, or because changes in its organisational and legal structure more closely reflected the needs of the time concerned. Yet the history of Focus is also one of continuity and maintenance of core values, admittedly reinterpreted from time to time. At the heart of Focus' development has been a desire to meet housing need and tackle poverty, however these problems were defined in different eras. Focus now, and the housing associations which merged to create it over the last 75 years, have all exhibited the social concern which precipitated the formation of the original housing association – Copec in 1925. Similarly, the entrepreneurial approach to meeting need and developing new approaches to tackle poverty are all hallmarks of those housing associations which now make up Focus Housing.

Focus has developed over the last 75 years by adapting to change, placing the needs of inner city communities at the heart of its approach and by growing through mergers and the development of group structures. Over the period, the scale of the organisation has increased significantly, with 60 times the number of properties managed in 2000 than in the 1920s. Today's organisation comprises a group structure with a number of subsidiaries covering different areas and services. Focus' history is consequently complex.

'Typical' refurbished houses in Birmingham's middle ring.

How the book is structured

With different readers in mind the book has been divided into two parts. The first part will be of interest to those who need a chronological account of how Focus developed and responded to changing local and national circumstances. Readers will find descriptions of the key personalities and major housing schemes involved in Focus' history in this part. The second part will appeal to readers interested in what the history of Focus can tell us about wider themes in the development of today's non-profit housing sector. The role of mergers, emergence of new organisational forms, changes in governance and the important campaigning role of the voluntary housing sector are all discussed in the second part.

Part I of the history reviews in five chapters how Focus was founded and progressed over the next 75 years.

- **Chapter 2** covers the foundation of Copec in 1925 following a Christian conference about social problems held in Birmingham in 1924. It discusses early attempts to tackle slum housing in Britain's second city, how this was funded and how Copec grew in the 1930s.

- **Chapter 3** reviews the challenges faced by Copec during and after the war, particularly how it adjusted to a housing world increasingly dominated by local authority provision.

- **Chapter 4** deals with the re-discovery of social problems in the 1960s, the birth of Shelter, and the establishment of major public funding for housing associations in the 1970s. This chapter also describes the formation of several new housing associations in response to the above developments, which later merged with Copec.

- **Chapter 5** traces Copec's diversification in housing provision and rapid growth following the introduction of privately funded housing investment after 1988. It also recounts the formation of Focus, from a loose alliance of four associations in 1989 to the permanent merger of Copec, Hestia and St. Chad in 1991.

- **Chapter 6** shows how Focus adapted to the modern housing world and its latest transition into an agency – Prime Focus – concerned primarily with community renewal.

All of these chapters contain a number of photographic plates, chiefly of Focus' housing schemes and the people who made them possible. Detailed captions are provided in some cases to explain how housing was developed and about the people involved in Focus' success since 1925.

Part II is a thematic treatment of Focus' history. It deals with four key themes that have emerged out of the research for this history and shows how the housing association has been transformed by its interaction with the external environment.

- **Chapter 7** deals with the main organisational transformations from 1925 to 2000, showing how Copec and Focus have both responded to and sought to influence the policy environment in which they operated.

- **Chapter 8** concentrates on the key reasons for the mergers which have characterised Focus' development since the 1960s. First, the Copec and Birmingham Housing Trust merger is discussed, followed by that between Copec and Wolverhampton Housing Association. The formation of Focus from Copec and Hestia Housing Associations and the St. Chad Housing Society is then explained. Lastly, Focus' mergers with Shape and Harambee Housing Associations are described.

- **Chapter 9** discusses how Focus has been governed over the last 75 years and the extent to which it has been accountable to its tenants and key stakeholders.

- **Chapter 10** shows how Focus and its constituent housing associations have campaigned on poor housing conditions and the needs of homeless people.

How the research was carried out

Before moving on, a few sentences are required to explain to readers the research methods adopted and how the material on which the book is based was gathered. Attempts were made to 'triangulate' material as much as possible, checking facts, figures and opinions from a variety of sources. This has been possible for most of the book's content, except for some of the early history.

■ The main information sources were the records of the various housing associations which now make up Focus. These records were usually in the form of management committee minutes, annual reports, internal policy documents, newsletters and various correspondence. For the early days of the association, Margaret Fenter's history of Copec (1960) has also been of particular importance.

■ Secondary sources were also used extensively. Government, Housing Corporation and National Housing Federation policy documents are key examples. Cuttings from local and national newspapers added interesting detail. Literature about the history of housing associations, and housing generally, provided the backdrop to the study.

■ Lastly, interviews with current and previous committee members and staff enabled perspectives on key developments. Interviews with tenants provided the views of service users. Many other people outside the interviewees' group also contributed comments and opinions, some of which were used to fill in gaps.

Drafts have been checked by a variety of people – some from inside the association and others from outside. They all brought their particular perspectives to the final version, but not all comments have been included since there were many conflicting views on what were the most important aspects of Focus' history. I have tried to develop an approach which enabled sometimes conflicting views to be reconciled, but this has not always been possible. What follows is my interpretation of the key events of the last 75 years. Undoubtedly much has been left out.

PART I

Tenants at Hospital Street, Summer Lane Birmingham. This area saw Copec's early attempts at 'slum-patching' and was to remain a community closely connected with the housing association until the present day. Today, as Prime Focus, the association continues to help residents to regenerate the area with its long-term ally, the Birmingham Settlement.

2

Christians become slum landlords 1925-1938

'It was a good day for me when Copec came along, I have lived in this house for 12 years and not until the last two of them have I known what it is to enjoy a little decency and comfort. There are many people in this street who would like to change with me' (Copec Tenant, Birmingham Evening Mail 1927).

Copec was formed in response to the poor housing conditions in Birmingham's central areas such as those previously faced by the above tenant at Pope Street. Before moving on to explain how and why Copec was founded, it is appropriate to explain the backdrop which excluded many from decency and comfort.

In 1914, there were more than 40,000 'back-to-back' houses in Birmingham, which had mostly been built between 1821 and 1851. By 1924, at the time of the COPEC conference, most 'back-to-backs', while still in use, were deteriorating rapidly (Fenter 1960). Typically, these houses were arranged in terraces in double rows built back-to-back under a single roof. Either two or three stories high, they usually had one room on each floor (usually a kitchen or scullery on the ground floor, with a cellar below and a bedroom above and in some cases an attic in the roof). Normally up an entry and away from the street front, they were typically grouped six or more to a courtyard and were separated from their neighbours by a single brick wall. 'Courts' usually contained a 'brewhouse' (for washing) and water closets for communal use, where a solitary water tap might be located (Chinn 1999, Glasby 1999). Birmingham had more than 2,000 'courts' with between four and twenty 'back-to-backs' in each court. The density of 'back-to-backs' was often as high as eighty to the acre (Fenter 1960). An insight into life in the 'back-to-backs' was provided by Mrs. Scott who lived with her parents in Hockley in the 1920s:

'Wash day was usually on a Monday, which was done in the brewhouse up the yard where wood and coal was used to boil up water for washing. It was my job to start the fire and fill the boiler. I have watched my mother scrubbing collars and boiler suits 'til 10 o'clock at night. She used to take in washing for other people who paid her 1s. 9d. a bundle' (Quoted in Chinn 1999).

'Back-to-backs' were frequently infested by bugs and cockroaches, despite the sometimes considerable effort made by tenants to keep them clean. The problems of the houses themselves were compounded by the conditions in the surrounding neighbourhoods. Many courts and their yards had no clean water supply. Water was often drawn from wells which were contaminated by filth flowing into them from the open streets, overfull cesspits, sodden miskins (or rubbish heaps) and crammed graveyards. 'Back-to-backs' were located predominantly in Birmingham's central areas alongside butchers shops and slaughterhouses, adding to the problems of poor sanitation in the courts. Pig sties and heaps of manure meant further stench and a general assault on the health of people living there. The River Rea (running at the back of Focus' present-day Bradford Street office), the Hockley Brook and the canals were open sewers (Chinn 1999).

'Housing conditions were bad by today's standards, with houses clustered round courts, the lavatories being in a block in the yard (not outside each back door, as at council houses), and a long walk from the 'front houses'. (Interview with Hilary Clark 1999).

Typical wash houses at Long Acre Road, Nechells.

Poor housing contributed to health problems in a major way. High infant mortality rates and proportionately higher death rates amongst the adult population in courts meant that insanitary conditions were major killers. It has been estimated that each year in the late 19th century and the early decades of the 20th Century, about 3,000 people who lived in 'back-to-backs' died prematurely. The annual death rate in areas such as St Mary's ward, where Copec provided its first properties, averaged 27 per 1,000, whereas that for wealthier Edgbaston was 13 per 1,000. This is highlighted in a comment by Chinn (1999):

'Poverty murdered. The birth-right of the poor was a high death rate; their inheritance the dreadful conditions in which they struggled to live'.

Birmingham City Council had been trying to tackle housing and health problems since the 19th Century. The city's first Improvement Scheme in the 1870s had redeveloped 43 acres in Birmingham's central areas. In 1913, a Special Housing Committee, chaired by Neville Chamberlain, highlighted the scale of the city's housing problems (Glasby 1999).

After the Housing Act 1919 introduced subsidies for local authorities, the city council built 15,000 council homes by 1925 (Birmingham Post 1928). By 1939, the city council had built 55,000 homes. But most of this housing, aimed at 'good tenants earning more than £4 a week' was beyond the means of the many (Upton 1997).

It was against this backdrop that Copec was founded. This chapter looks at the formation of Copec and its early attempts in tackling slum conditions up until 1938 in relation to:

- **Baffling the enlightened conscience** – early responses to slum housing and the key people involved in Copec's philanthropic approach.

- **Christians as slum landlords** – the differences between Copec's housing management style and that of 'absentee' private landlords. An emphasis on management of the slums and the employment and training of staff.

- **Marrying the good with the bad** – Copec's early property acquisition strategy and the role of 'risk management'.

- **Dividends paid in heaven** – how Copec was funded from issuing of shares and loan stock, and by donations from charitable trusts and individuals.

- **Humanising the landlord/tenant relationship** – provides further consideration of the impact of Octavia Hill methods on the definition of the landlord role and some early examples of 'housing plus' activities in the 1920s.

- **Early diversification** – Copec's move into new geographical areas, and experiments with conversions of public houses and other properties into flats and maisonettes, and the first uses of limited public funding.

- **Housing societies at the crossroads** – how housing societies almost became part of housing's mainstream and their responses following disappointment at the consequences of the Housing Act 1935.

Baffling the enlightened conscience

Poverty, which had been ignored to a great extent during the Victorian era (although limited government and voluntary sector intervention was precipitated), began to be taken far more seriously in the early decades of the twentieth century. Both state intervention and philanthropic organisations attempted to tackle the problems of poor housing, environment and health:

> 'Under the influence of stark facts revealed by Booth, Rowntree and others, the Edwardians began to abandon Victorian attitudes towards the treatment of poverty and to accept the need for greater official intervention' (Reed 1973).

> 'The faulty construction of the whole central area of Birmingham has baffled the enlightened conscience and the progressive efforts of the last generation' (Tillyard 1926).

Just such a philanthropic organisation was established in Birmingham in 1925. Between 5th and 12th April 1924, a conference was held at the Central Methodist Hall in Birmingham. It was a landmark conference which brought together delegates from almost every Christian denomination in Britain to discuss and debate the need for social reform and 'for a response by Christians to the needs of the material world' (Fenter 1960). In the words of the day – 'it was recognised that an effort must be made to Christianise the corporate life of mankind in all its activities' (Tillyard 1926). The conference in Birmingham was named the Christian Conference on Politics, Economics and Citizenship – COPEC. In preparation for the conference, individual commissions of both clergy and lay members of various denominations were established to develop ideas and report upon a range of social problems from a Christian viewpoint. These included:

- The nature of God and His purpose for the World;
- The Home;
- The Relation of the Sexes;
- Politics and Citizenship;
- Leisure;
- Education.

The COPEC conference was chaired by the Right Reverend William Temple, the Bishop of Manchester. Temple was later to be Archbishop of both York and Canterbury. He was particularly known for his promotion of the relationship between Christian faith and public issues. In 1942, he wrote a seminal book – 'Christianity and Social Order'- which had a wide-ranging influence on the developing social awareness of the Christian Church.

Frontage of 'back-to-backs in Summer Lane.

What individuals can do

Following the conference, a small number of delegates from Birmingham, Manchester, Bangor and Altrincham (Garside 2000) established 'continuation committees' in their home cities and towns. In the two years following the conference these delegate groupings grew into housing societies. They were determined that the inspiration and findings of the COPEC conference should not be forgotten and that some practical social action should be developed based on the 'Home' report. In Birmingham, a small number of individuals were instrumental in ensuring that the continuation committee got off the ground. Two major themes were taken from the 'Home' report as a basis for action by the Birmingham continuation committee. The first was practical action to make housing improvements. The second was supporting the family. The 'Home' report, under the chapter heading 'What Individuals Can Do' had made a number of practical suggestions on what concerned Christian citizens might consider in tackling poor housing conditions:

> 'Those who have a certain amount of capital can unite with others to carry out housing schemes themselves through the formation of Public Utility Societies or they can purchase existing property which is not being well managed and initiate a better and more sympathetic management'.

So who were these individuals who took up the COPEC challenge in Birmingham? First was Anne Robinson, a local factory inspector aware of the effects of poor environments on peoples' health. She became the first Honorary Secretary of Copec's management committee. Then there was Professor Frank Tillyard, head of the Faculty of Commerce at

Councillor Norman Tiptaft laid the foundation stone at the corner of Percy Road and Fernley Road, Sparkhill. Ten three-bedroomed houses were built here in 1934 using funding from the Rotary Club. Members of the Copec management committee can also be seen.

Birmingham University and also a lawyer; another was Bishop Hamilton Baynes, Provost of Birmingham Cathedral.   Another key individual was Florence Barrow. She was already very active in the Settlement movement, which had been established in the late 19th century by social reformers who were shocked at the living conditions of the poor in urban settings. Miss Barrow was working at Aston's Birmingham Settlement at the time of the COPEC conference and had recently returned from Poland where she was in charge of the Quaker Relief Unit which was offering support to refugees from Russia. The living conditions she saw in Birmingham's Summer Lane area, still the base of the Birmingham Settlement today, motivated her to become involved in the COPEC committee.

Two other leading members of the 'Home' commission had a great deal of practical experience in establishing and managing housing for the poor. These were Dame Elizabeth Cadbury, who was Chairman of the Bournville Village Trust, and Miss M. Jeffery, Manager of Property for the Commissioners of Crown Lands in north-west London and a supporter of the St. Pancras House Improvement Society. These individuals worked through Copec's continuation committee to set up a Public Utility Society (PUS) under the Industrial and Provident Societies Acts. On 5th November 1925, a public meeting was held and the outcome was the establishment of the Birmingham Copec House Improvement Society. On 16th November, the inaugural meeting of the new PUS was held at which draft rules were produced, a seal was adopted and a management committee appointed. The Chairman was Frank Tillyard with Secretaries being Frank Hickinbotham and Corbyn Barrow, two local solicitors (Corbyn Barrow resigned as Secretary in 1928 was succeeded by his sister Florence). Councillor Miss M. Wilson, who represented St Mary's Ward and was an active campaigner against Birmingham's poor housing conditions, and Miss M. Hillsdon of Birmingham's Public Health Department, were also appointed. Other committee members were appointed over time. Chapter 7 discusses further the significance of the social status and networks of these key individuals who founded Copec, but as Garside (2000) has noted:

'Christian congregations were very active in promoting housing trusts in the 1920s.....support was widely drawn, and sponsors included church denominations, political parties, women's groups, chambers of commerce, Masonic Lodges and councils of social service'.

COPEC's MANAGEMENT COMMITTEE (1927)

Chairman
Professor Frank Tillyard

Honorary Secretary	**Honorary Secretary**	**Secretary**
F. Hickinbotham	G. Corbyn Barrow	Mrs A. Robinson

General Committee

Miss F.M Barrow	Councillor J.E Willmott J.P
Bishop A. Hamilton Baynes	Mrs Lidderdale
Frank W. Coffey	Mrs A.E. Robinson
Miss Hillsdon	Sidney Shipway
H.F. Keep J.P	Eric Vincent
J. Keyte	Councillor Miss Wilson

General Manager
F. Margaret Fenter

Christians as slum landlords

As with many housing societies of the time, Copec adopted a housing management approach based on Christian values and social concern. Copec's first secretary Frank Hickinbotham summed-up the approach:

> 'We believe that housing improvement comes before social improvement. After the houses have been rebuilt we shall start to improve social conditions' (Daily Chronicle 1927).

Copec's committee members were influenced by the views expressed by Lord Balfour of Burleigh (Chairman of Kensington Housing Trust and later a leading figure in the National Federation of Housing Societies) (Malpass 2000) at Copec's Annual General Meeting in 1934 – 'slumdom, whatever form it took, was due to a failure of management'. There is no evidence of a wider debate about the root causes of poverty and slum living by Copec's management committee members. Copec was thus wedded to management solutions to the problems of Birmingham's slums. As Fenter (1960) pointed out:

> 'Christians had become slum landlords but they had no intention of becoming absentee landlords. From the first the intention was to do something more than recondition. Some houses had been neglected for so long that many tenants had become apathetic, and in their own words it 'gave them no heart' to try to keep them decent. The committee considered that continuous help and encouragement were necessary to remedy this state of affairs'.

It was usual in Copec's early days for women committee members to collect rents and to take a personal interest in tenants and their wellbeing. Copec's members also involved themselves in day-to-day disputes amongst tenants to ensure that properties and their amenities were not abused but used fairly by all tenants living within a court environment.

Children's sand-pit and shelter provided by Copec at Tower Street, Summer Lane.

It was considered at the time that scrupulous fairness and attention to detail in arbitrating amongst tenants and dealing with those tenants who abused facilities were essential in order to provide an 'orderly' life within Copec's properties. Other members also visited particular properties while they were being refurbished to ensure that adequate progress was being made with the reconditioning work. This approach to housing and tenant management was inspired by Octavia Hill, who had worked in London's slums in the late 19th Century (Clapham 1997). The advantages of close personal contact with tenants and attention to detail with a careful balance between landlord and tenant were appreciated by Copec's members to deal with 'problems arising from tenancies' (Annual Report 1928).

Ultimately this concern for management solutions and a growth in the number of properties to be managed led to the employment and training of professional managers to take on the duties initially performed by committee members. In 1927, Miss Margaret Fenter began work as General Manager. She came to Copec after gaining a Social Studies Diploma at the Birmingham Settlement and undertaking a period of training at St. Pancras House Improvement Society. She was a member of the Society of Housing Managers, and strongly influenced by Octavia Hill. Her tutor was Miss Jeffrey, one of the original commissioners of the COPEC conference 'Home' report. In her youth, Miss Jeffrey had been a pupil of Octavia Hill in London.

From the beginning of Copec, attempts were made to publicise Octavia Hill's ideas. In 1930, the National Council of Women and the Soroptimist Club of Birmingham, combined to form a study circle to discuss Hill's approach. Margaret Fenter was an active member of these groups, and established a housing management training scheme, chiefly for women. In 1929, Copec's first housing management trainee was appointed and this practice was to continue until 1960. In recognition of Hill's commitment to training women for the housing service 14 women were trained as housing managers during the 1930s:

> 'The value of having trained women workers cannot be too strongly emphasised. The fact that there is such a satisfactory high percentage of rents paid, in spite of the present hard times, and that there is such a good feeling between tenants and Copec, shows conclusively that good business management and friendliness can be most successfully combined. It is greatly to be desired that more landlords should place their property under such management on the lines advocated by Octavia Hill' (Annual Report 1930).

Fenter later said (1960) about her devotion to the Octavia Hill method that she wanted:

> 'To make known the interest and value of property management as a career for women and to create an informed public opinion in favour of the employment of trained women on city estates'.

Margaret Fenter's own duties were wide and varied. They included rent collection, supervising repairs, helping tenants with their problems, keeping Copec's records and accounts and general office management. Fenter also performed a company secretarial role by administering share and loan certificates, maintaining a register of members and shareholders, and reporting to Copec's management committee. In 1929 she became responsible for committee business, including minute taking. Copec's rent collection and arrears policy was typical of many housing societies at the time. Tenants with problems could make arrangements to clear their arrears, although a number were given Notice to Quit if arrangements to clear arrears had broken down. Keeping properties maintained was not linked to tenants' ability to pay the rent. Copec's policy was to keep properties up to scratch irrespective of tenants' rent payments record. This led to more systematic property maintenance including regular redecoration of homes.

Interior of Gee Street before reconditioning. Notice the hole in the ceiling.

Marrying the good with the bad

Copec's property acquisition strategy reflected its mission to improve the worst slum housing in Birmingham's inner areas. As Garside (2000) has noted, this was the 'gap' in housing provision, not being met by the newly expanding local authority landlords, where the new societies offering Octavia Hill style management found their greatest role in the inter-war period.

When Copec was established in 1925, Birmingham City Council was concentrating its housing efforts on developing new housing on the outskirts of the city to relieve overcrowding in the central areas and to house new migrants to the city (there had been a major influx of munitions workers during the First World War). In common with other 'front-line housing societies' of the time (Garside 2000), Copec agreed that its priority must be the clusters of 'back-to-back' slum housing and made a deliberate decision to focus on the housing conditions in Birmingham's central wards. Management committee members were aware that their contribution to tackling the housing problems of the day were a drop in the ocean (at the time, it was thought that Birmingham needed around

50,000 new homes and there were 40,000 'back-to-back' properties which required urgent action) (Chinn 1999). With so much poor housing in the target areas the problem was where to start. While Copec began to acquire properties from 1925, the first major refurbishment scheme did not begin until 1926. Fortunately for the tenant quoted at the start of the chapter this was at Pope Street. The costs of early refurbishment schemes ranged from £107 to £188 per property (Annual Reports 1925,1926) in contrast to the costs of building a council house, which could be as high as £600 (Upton 1997).

Copec's First Major Housing Scheme

Florence Barrow was one of the first to contribute in a concrete fashion and sold a house which she owned to provide an initial loan to Copec (this was later transferred to a donation). With the funds raised through this sale, nineteen back-to-back houses were bought in Pope St – numbers 24 to 30 and their rear houses arranged around a court. Refurbishment began in 1927 with re-roofing, new floors, replastering, repair of stairs, new grates and installation in each house of gas and a cold water supply. The washhouses in the court areas were completely rebuilt and each home was provided with an individual toilet. Costs of acquisition and refurbishment were £3,569. The reconditioning of Pope St was extremely popular with tenants. It had an immediate effect on the neighbourhood since it showed the local community what could be done to improve living conditions. Valuable lessons were also learned from the Pope St work. For example, the Pope St properties were refurbished to a high standard and Copec's management committee felt that such standards were not replicable if it was to tackle poor housing conditions in a wide-ranging way.

Encouraged by their first success, Copec's management committee began to search for other properties that could be improved. But with the Pope St experience behind them, they established property appraisal criteria for potential acquisitions and improvements. Considerable thought was given by the management committee to how its limited resources could be best used. Their approach is summarised below.

- Copec did not wish to use its resources for reconditioning a relatively small number of properties in the worst condition. The management committee therefore devised a policy which it called 'marrying the good with the bad' (Fenter 1960). In this early example of what would now be called risk management, Copec spread the costs of acquisition and the impact of improvements through a judicious mix of better and poorer quality housing. Further it was decided that only freehold property or houses which were able to be acquired freehold were considered for acquisition; and that properties had to be structurally sound with adequate outbuildings.

- The management committee's second aim was to prevent properties declining into slums, as well as rescuing those which had serious problems and were already classified as slums. It was well known, and was widely reported in the local press at the time, that slum landlords could purchase property, avoid doing any repairs, make more money from these properties and generate profits on their purchase price even after considerable deterioration. Copec was not prepared to subsidise slum 'absentee' landlords for neglect of their properties.

- The management committee wished to spread its housing investment across different neighbourhoods within Birmingham's central areas as part of a strategy to encourage other landlords to improve their own properties. This can be seen as a means of promoting what could be achieved by reasonable landlords in contrast to those who neglected their properties. It also highlighted to tenants, the community and policy-makers on Birmingham's Housing Committee what could be achieved in slum areas (Annual Reports 1926-1935). (See map on page 49).

Properties were acquired in the 1920s in various ways. Often, searches by individual committee members and later office staff were undertaken in Copec's main activity areas. Auctions were sometimes used to acquire property. Offers were occasionally made by individuals and concerned private landlords who thought that more could be done for their tenants through a cooperative effort than they could manage alone. 1928 saw a flurry of acquisitions, mainly in Nechells. Some of these properties had open spaces at their rear, which Copec used to provide communal gardens for tenants. Refurbishment followed a broad plan. Interior work, including installing gas and water, and improvements to structure and outhouses were the most common features, although variations existed according to the quality of properties.

Sturge House in Hospital Street – Copec's first newbuild scheme.

Dividends paid in heaven

With the momentum from the creation of Copec and the pressing need to tackle local housing problems, Copec set about establishing a sound financial footing on which to base its housing investment. However, the precariousness of Copec's early financial position was demonstrated by a bank clerk who commented – 'this is the concern where the dividends are paid in heaven isn't it?' when Copec deposited its first rent payments! While the goal of Copec's management committee was to provide better housing and social care, like other housing societies of the time, Copec wished to provide a high standard of refurbishment, repairs and management in comparison with private landlords. From the start there was a strong emphasis on charity and philanthropy, with Copec issuing a series of appeals for funds both for specific schemes and for wider purposes. Margaret Fenter captures the importance of charitable motivations in supporting Copec's early development. Voluntary donations of time and amenities (such as office space and a typewriter) were seen as significant:

> 'The financial contributions of many public-spirited people were essential to Copec's foundation, but it could not have functioned without the generous help received in numerous other ways from a large number of people' (Fenter 1960).

During the 1920s and 1930s, many donations were received by Copec from individuals and grant-making trusts for use in improving existing housing, developing new housing schemes and providing community amenities and support to tenants. There were also some cases of loans where lenders did not take the interest but enabled Copec to keep the interest income for expenditure on gardens and other community amenities.

Lord Mayor Alderman Grey and Copec Secretary Florence Barrow seen inspecting slum properties in 1935.

Donations To Copec In The 1920s And 1930s

- Alderman Lloyd for the refurbishment of the 'Queen Adelaide' public house and development of the Long Acre allotments;

- The Misses Rushton for the Rushton House public house conversion;

- Florence Barrow for the Pope St. refurbishment and office expenses;

- Alderman W. Cadbury for the development of community amenities;

- The Feeney Trust and the Graham St Trust for Tower St Gardens;

- The Common Good Trust for rehabilitation of gardens;

- Joseph Sturge as a legacy for part development of Sturge House;

- The Birmingham Rotary Club for the Percy Rd refurbishment;

- Mr. H. Payne for furniture for tenants in need.

Source: Fenter (1960)

However, the main source of Copec's funds at this time came from issuing shares and loan stock rather than from charitable donations. The first appeal for support was made towards the end of 1926. Following this appeal, share and loan stock was issued with an initial 4 per cent interest rate, although dividends were not paid in Copec's first year. As a visiting German academic to Birmingham at the time commented in a later article:

> 'The social achievements which Copec has accomplished must not lead one to the supposition that this is purely a charitable enterprise. It must be emphasised that Copec conducts its enterprise strictly on business lines. It is a PUS and has the right to issue shares and loan stock. The shares have the nominal value of £1, and no member may hold more than £200 worth of shares. The loan stock must not exceed £250,000' (Asch 1932).

In 1933, the issue of 4 per cent loan stock was discontinued and investors were encouraged to convert their holdings from 4 per cent to 3 per cent by 1936. Copec undertook that the 1 percent saved through this conversion would be used solely for investment in the housing stock. This extra income was allocated to Copec's repairs and alterations fund which was used for both day-to-day repairs, and later, modernisation. Copec operated on the basis that neither its shares nor loan stock were tradeable on the open market and all were redeemable by option of the management committee, except for a special loan stock issue of 2.5 per cent in 1938. As time went by, executors of wills and others who did not want to receive dividends or interest sold their holdings. From Copec's early days, some individual members also converted their share and loan stock into donations. Interest-earning loans, where the lender enabled Copec to keep the interest income, were used for expenditure on gardens and other community amenities. Thus Copec was already beginning to move away from the financial model of '5 per cent philanthropy' towards a more charitable model (see chapter 7).

Table (1) – Copec's Financial Circumstances 1926-1938 (£)

Year	Shares Issued	4% Loan Stock	3% Loan Stock	Total Stock	Ann. Profit/ Surplus
1926	4138	4405	–	4405	218
1927	6033	7370	–	7370	477
1928	7471	14310	–	14310	638
1929	8705	21845	–	21845	553
1930	9713	25955	–	25955	773
1931	10228	28485	–	28485	704
1932	10662	33525	–	33525	1027
1933	12231	35020	4070	39090	1040
1934	12480	34920	9330	44250	1044
1935	13068	34920	12270	47190	1973
1936	13477	15740	33690	49430	1414
1937	13648	13845	37045	50890	1164
1938	13979	13145	38155	51300	1329

Source: Copec annual reports and accounts 1926-1939

Notes
1. In 1936 close to half of 4 percent Copec loan stock holders transferred their stock to 3 percent return on their investment. Transfer from 4 percent to 3 percent returns continued throughout the late 1930s. By 1939, two thirds had transferred.
2. In 1938 and 1939, small tranches of loan stock (£220 and £275 in each case) were issued at a return of 2.5 percent. This loan stock is shown in the 3 percent column.
3. The column for profit and surplus shows the sum in the Copec accounts after investment in property and interest on loan stock had been paid. The annual profit accumulated was shown in the accounts as a surplus following Copec's conversion into a charitable organisation in 1939.

The other main source of Copec's income was through rents charged on acquired and improved properties. Usually, weekly rents varied from 3s. 6d. to 12s. 6d. Rents on new properties through much of the 1920s and early 1930s (but not between 1933 and 1939) were controlled by the Rent Acts, which limited the ability of most housing societies to raise extra income via rents. However, rents on unimproved acquired properties were less likely to be affected and in many cases Copec's tenants would have been unable to afford rents set at the level determined by the Acts. Copec was able to raise rents by about 8 per cent per annum to cover the costs of capital works on improvement and refurbishment (Fenter 1960). Even so, the costs of day-to-day repairs, which were generally more expensive than improvements made to properties after acquisition, had to be borne by Copec. Quite often rents had to be substantially adjusted after reconditioning and improvement. Rents were sometimes raised to the maximum allowed by the Rent Acts although often they were reduced where the previous private landlord had illegally exceeded the statutory maximum.

Table (2) – Copec's Income And Costs 1927-1938 (£)						
Year	Gross Rents	Outgoings	Net Rents	Repairs Reserve	Management costs	Recovery Of Tax/ Bank Int.
1927	1453	393	1059	327	109	114
1928	2835	963	1872	638	212	131
1929	3330	1313	2017	749	249	383
1930	4395	1699	2695	769	438	272
1931	4820	1999	2821	819	482	387
1932	5174	2140	3034	776	517	589
1933	5837	2540	3296	875	582	684
1934	6576	2775	3800	986	657	607
1935	6983	2871	4111	1047	697	1356
1936	7164	2945	4219	1074	715	808
1937	7489	3228	4261	1123	748	660
1938	7878	3496	4382	1181	786	855

Source: Copec annual reports and account 1927-1938

Notes
1. Column 2 shows outgoings from gross rental income. These outgoings include taxes and local rates. Column 3 shows rental income after these costs.
2. Columns 4 shows the amounts transferred to the repairs reserve for major maintenance expenditure (ie a maintenance 'sinking fund'). Column 5 outlines Copec's annual management costs, including salaries, administration and publicity.
3. The final column is recovery of income tax on claims for maintenance, and interest from a bank deposit account.

For its long-term financial strategy, Copec aimed to build-up a substantial financial reserve. While Copec's housing had a considerable potential value, the amount which could be raised in practice was negligible because the sale of land and properties was not envisaged. Investment in day-to-day repairs was not considered to be retrievable in terms of the added value to properties. Indeed, the actual value of individual properties was expected to depreciate over time. The housing stock's value appeared in the balance sheet at original costs for many years except where donations were received which were offset against these amounts. Only relatively small proportions of income from rents were used to build the repairs reserve (this ranged from 22.5 per cent in 1927 to 15 per cent in 1936). The amounts from rents moved to the depreciation and general reserves varied year-on-year according to overall surpluses generated in the profit and loss account. Some repairs were paid for out of general income but larger repairs works were met from Copec's reserves. New acquisitions of properties and modernisation were paid out of reserves throughout the 1920s and 1930s. Investments in banks and government securities were made later to build up funds for future housing investment (Annual Reports 1927-1939). As the Manchester Guardian commented in 1937:

'Copec is a relatively wealthy society – at least alongside Manchester Housing (1926) Limited – which is the only comparable PUS in Manchester'.

It must be said that Copec's ability to respond to problems of slum housing in this period was severely limited by the relatively small funds it was able to raise by these means. The absence of public subsidy for reconditioning activity rendered the committee's independent stance in relation to its core business fairly academic. However, as time went on some opportunities were taken to access public funding for new construction activity, an option which had in fact been available to Copec, under the Housing Act 1924 and subsequent legislation, since its formation. The Gee Street flats in 1936 were the first scheme to be funded with support from Birmingham City Council. This involved payments under the 1930 Slum Clearance Act for the rehousing of people displaced by demolition activity. A second opportunity to access subsidy occurred in 1937 for part of the Sturge House scheme built on the site of demolished properties in Hospital Street. This scheme of nine flatlets for older people provides a good early example of 'mixed funding'. Payments towards three of the tenancies were provided by the city council under the Housing Act 1935 as the occupants were rehoused from overcrowded accommodation. The scheme was also supported by a substantial legacy from Joseph Sturge who had a particular interest in the needs of older people. This enabled the flats to be let at very low rents for the time.

Humanising the landlord-tenant relationship

From its inception Copec saw itself as providing a qualitative rather than quantitative response to Birmingham's seemingly intractable housing problems:

'One of the aims of Copec is to humanise the relationship of landlord and tenant. The relations between Copec and its tenants are most friendly. Further, our voluntary workers, who either as rent collectors or club leaders know the circumstances of tenants, have been able to visit them in time of illness, and by sympathy and friendly interest have helped to keep them from apathy and despair' (Annual Reports 1926-1933).

The spirit of Octavia Hill lived on in Copec's approach to housing management services. Fenter (1960) and Copec annual reports over the 1925 to 1939 period refer to many activities involving welfare and community services which today we might call 'housing plus'. The philosophical basis underlying the provision of these various services is indicated by the following quotation:

'Circumstances did not permit the personal activities on the scale practised by Octavia Hill but what was done was carried out in a similar spirit and with the same ends in view' (Fenter 1960).

Copec sponsored initiatives for young people and established tenants' savings institutions rather like today's credit unions with the assistance of philanthropic trusts and management help from the Birmingham Settlement:

'A derelict workshop was repaired and decorated, a gas fire installed and some furniture provided....clubs for boys and girls were started....at first administered from the office but....in 1934 responsibility was taken by Bournville Youth Club' (Annual Reports 1928-1939).

Activities like these were helped along by a donation of £1,000 from the Boeke Trust. This was the start of Copec's 'Amenities Fund'. Income from donors and the interest accrued were spent on amenities 'not usually expected from landlords' and for the benefit of whole communities:

'It is not intended to use this Fund for the individual benefit of tenants, but for shrub planting, window boxes and other amenities which may be enjoyed by tenants as a group.....an activity started by the manager and assistants was a savings club.....it was considered to be well worth while to encourage tenants in habits of thrift even if the money was drawn out from time to time.....owing to a generous gift.....we have been able to start a scheme for helping tenants, who need it, to buy furniture, chiefly beds.....the scheme proved useful.....and the loans made are being steadily repaid' (Annual Reports 1928-1939).

Early diversification

Copec planned to extend its housing work across all of Birmingham's central areas. The 1930s saw Copec achieving this aim in some measure with further properties being acquired in Nechells, Small Heath, Moseley and Sparkbrook. It was at this time that Copec decided to carry out its first demolitions, which, although reducing the numbers of houses available for letting, enabled improved transmission of air and light to adjacent properties. Urban densities were also reduced. Copec became the landlord of retail property: the 'Mosse Houses' in Tower Street (something it was to do in its later incarnations). Included were a drysalters (a dealer in dyes, gums, pickles and tinned meat), a greengrocers, a cooked meat shop and a small grocers. From 1929 to 1939, 68 further properties were acquired in the Summer Lane area, including Tower Street, Farm Street, New John Street, Brearly Street and Hospital Street. Copec raised funding from the Feeney Trust, the Graham Street Trust and from an appeal instigated by Florence Barrow to buy 750 sq. ft. at the back of Tower Street. This land was transformed into seventeen gardens, a sandpit and a shelter for local children. Copec provided its first flatted refurbishment at this time, with six flats provided at Tower Street. Other refurbishment experiments were undertaken at Hospital Street in 1933 by converting ten 'back-to-backs' into what was termed 'throughs' with each house given two rooms downstairs, four bedrooms and bathroom and inside toilet.

Last orders at the bar

At the suggestion of Copec's secretary Florence Barrow, local brewers were approached to see if deteriorating and sometimes empty public houses could be de-licensed to provide temporary accommodation for tenants displaced by refurbishment elsewhere. The approach was linked to two aims of Copec's predominantly tea-total management committee – to improve housing conditions and reduce the sale of alcohol in working class neighbourhoods. Fenter (1960) gently summarised the popular linkage of the day between social problems, poor housing conditions and the consumption of alcohol:

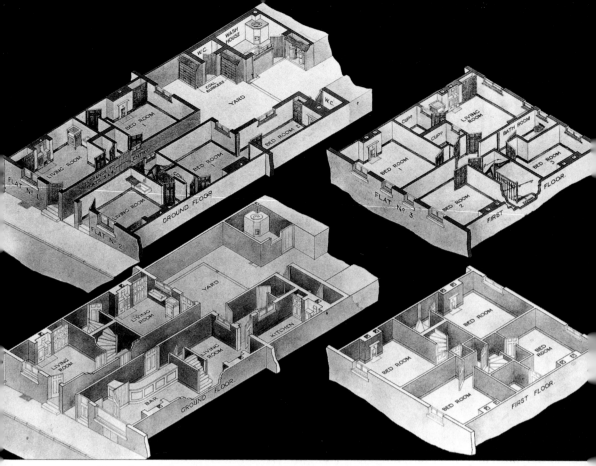

Plans showing how the 'Jolly Brewer', a de-licensed public house was converted into flats.

'Only a person who has been obliged to live in a back-to-back house can really know what it means. Those more fortunate must use their imagination. The drama of birth, life and death in a family must be enacted in three rooms. Any leisure occupations that are possible at all must be carried out in one room or one of the bedrooms must be sacrificed. Small wonder that young children are all too often found in the street, teenagers hanging around street corners, and father in the public house'.

This moralistic theme had also appealed to philanthropic housing reformers elsewhere, for example the Alexander sisters who were involved in the conversion of public houses into flats in the Notting Dale area of Kensington (Malpass 1999). But it should also be noted that many public houses were already used by private landlords as 'doss-houses' for itinerant workers with no other housing option. They were often in extremely poor condition with no proper facilities for healthy living. Refurbishing public houses became a central Copec activity between 1928 and 1931. In December 1928 the 'Queen Adelaide' off Hospital Street was bought together with an adjoining house. The 'Queen Adelaide' was converted into three flats with a new oak staircase constructed and a wash-room provided for tenants.

The second public house refurbishment experiment was in 1930 on the corner of Farm Street and Great Russell Street, called the 'Royal Oak'. Renamed Rushton House because furbishment had been subsidised by the two Rushton sisters (patrons of Copec's early work) in memory of their mother, this refurbishment consisted of flatted conversion in the public house and provision of four refurbished houses in adjoining 'back-to-backs'.

A further public house – the 'Jolly Brewer' in Wheeler Street, Summer Lane – was refurbished in 1931. Flats were provided in the upper stories with extra accommodation produced by refurbishment of back-to-backs acquired at the same time. The Birmingham Post wrote an article about the refurbishment in 1931 which said:

> 'Copec's architect had turned it inside out. Old doors leading to the bar and smoke room had been bricked-up, and a new one had been built in an enclosed area, which is brightened in the Summer by window boxes of flowers. An inviting entrance this, with gas over the door'.

However, while such schemes had clear attractions for the moral conscience of the management committee, they turned out not to have such beneficial use value for Copec or its tenants. These conversion schemes were discontinued after the 1930s because they had generally produced low quality accommodation. Flats were unpopular and the costs associated for tenants and Copec were high.

Further experiments with flats

A new phase of housing development began in 1933. This involved partial demolition and conversion of properties into flats and maisonettes. This was piloted in Summer Lane's Milton and Great Russell Street properties where an internal staircase had to be built to upstairs flats with room borrowed from the ground floor. The first and second floors were transformed into maisonettes. The approach was also used to refurbish Farm Street and Gee Street in the same area. Houses were demolished to provide better throughput of light and air. Staircases were constructed to provide good access to upper floors. While electric light was installed in these schemes, washing facilities remained in the back yards. The development of flats and maisonettes in this period can be seen as a precursor of later periods where Copec's increased flatted refurbishment, and that by other housing associations, replaced much of the family housing in Birmingham's central areas.

At Summer Lane's Gee and Frankfort Streets, unfit houses and a public house were demolished. In consultation with the city council's Estates and Public Works Committees, it was decided to build ten flats in two storeys – six with three bedrooms and four with two bedrooms. Families on Birmingham's municipal waiting list, displaced by the city council's 1930s clearance scheme and others from property being reconstructed by Copec became the first tenants. For the first time, Copec used public funding for its work:

> 'A subsidy under the 1930 Act was obtained for each flat under an agreement with the city – the first subsidy to be obtained by a housing society in Birmingham' (Fenter 1960).

Four of the original tenants were still in the flats in 1985. Brother and sister Mary and John Mitchell were among the first to move into what were for the time innovatively designed flats. Sixty-four year old Mary, who was 14 years when she moved in with her parents in 1936 made the following comment which highlights how fortunate her family felt when they moved into the flats:

> 'They were beautiful. We were one of the first in the area to have an inside bathroom and toilet. People used to knock on the door and ask if they could have a bath' (Tenants Newsletter 1985).

Mayfield Road scheme in Moseley, Birmingham.

Housing societies at the crossroads

The Ministry of Health's Departmental Committee on Housing, under the chairmanship of Lord Moyne, deserves some attention here. This is because Moyne explored different, and potentially radical, approaches to providing housing for the poor which were ultimately rejected. Garside (2000) notes that:

> 'In the early 1930s it was even argued that the voluntary housing sector should supplant elected authorities at both central and local level in all kinds of low cost housing provision. By 1939 however, local authorities had emerged with their power reinforced, deemed the only agencies to whom urban reconstruction, including slum clearance and rebuilding could be entrusted' (Garside 2000).

Copec was visited by the Moyne Committee and gave evidence. The importance of the Moyne Committee's report in 1933, which led to the Housing Act 1935, is that it:

'Effectively marked the triumph of local authorities as the main provides of new rented housing for the working class, with the result that the voluntary organisations remained on the margins of housing policy for the next forty years' (Malpass 2000).

The Moyne Committee 1933 – Radical Proposals

- Central Public Utility Council (CPUC) to approve housing societies and their housing projects (similar to the Housing Corporation today).

- Local people should be encouraged to form housing societies, but where they could not, local authorities would be expected to establish local housing management commissions (LHMC's).

- Local authorities were to be encouraged to make use of the proposed powers of compulsory purchase for reconditioning and managing property. Where they declined to do so, PUSs could appeal to the Minister of Health to obtain similar purchase rights as local authorities.

- Proposed subsidy available to PUSs for the relief of overcrowding through new building, but reconditioning work should not be subsidised.

Source: Malpass 2000

The Moyne Committee's suggestions were largely rejected. As negotiations on the draft of the 1935 Act progressed it became clear that local authorities had strong reservations about any expanded role for PUSs. Their opposition to Moyne's proposed local housing management commissions (similar to local housing companies today) was great. This meant that the spotlight on PUSs faded. As it did so attention moved away from policies relating to refurbishment to those tackling overcrowding and the redevelopment of inner city areas. Policies to combat overcrowding subsequently became the main target thrust of the Housing Act 1935 (Malpass 2000). While Copec's management committee welcomed the attack on overcrowding, there was some scepticism about the 1935 Act's effectiveness:

'The Housing Act 1935 represents an important step in overcoming the evils of bad housing: though the standard of overcrowding adopted is a low one, it is a step in the right direction. Birmingham City Council are conducting a survey at the present time to discover the extent to which overcrowding exists and we are awaiting their report with interest' (Annual Report 1936).

However, some small victories were won by housing societies. The 1935 Act restated the powers of local authorities to make loans to housing societies and to subscribe to their share capital. It also increased the proportion of costs that could be borrowed from the Public Works Loan Board. However, inner urban redevelopment, the mainstay of Copec's work, was left to local authorities. Housing societies received small subsidies to tackle overcrowding on the same terms as local authorities, except that any rate fund contribution was at the discretion of local authorities. But the 1935 Act did not introduce

Copec's first use of public funding to build flats at Gee Street, Summer Lane. They are shown under construction in 1936.

the CPUC nor LHMCs, which would have radically changed the provision of social housing and probably brought housing societies like Copec into the mainstream of housing provision. Instead, the Act set up only an advisory body to the Ministry (the Central Housing Advisory Committee) (Malpass 2000).

Some voluntary housing bodies responded to the 1935 Act by setting up their own trade association – the National Federation of Housing Societies (NFHS) (Garside 2000). The NFHS was founded following regional conferences in Birmingham, Manchester and Newcastle. Copec was one of the 75 founding members, which comprised mainly newer 'front line' housing societies or garden city societies like the largest founder member, the Great Western (London) Garden Village Society (Malpass, 2000). Very few 19th century voluntary housing bodies joined at this time. The NFHS was acknowledged in the Housing Act 1935 and obtained status as a central agency for government to channel funds to housing societies (NFHA 1985). A year later, 92 of the 226 active housing societies had joined this new trade agency. Of the original membership, only about one third are today identifiable as modern housing associations. As Malpass (2000) has commented:

'Some of today's well-known associations were founder members........although only a few became large players: only three original members [(Copec, now part of Focus HA), Liverpool Improved Houses (now Riverside HA) and Church Army] were represented in the largest 50 associations in the late 1990s'.

While housing societies were marginalised by the 1935 Act, Copec took advantage of limited subsidies. Government subsidy and some assistance from the rates were used in re-housing people displaced under slum clearance schemes. To qualify for subsidy, Copec had to enter into an agreement with Birmingham City Council as to type of house, rents chargeable and tenants (Annual Report 1935). The first subsidies obtained for new building were in 1936. These were granted for re-housing of people displaced from demolished property under the Act and enabled Copec to re-house not only tenants from some of the city's clearance areas but a few from its own demolished houses. Further subsidy was later obtained under the 1935 Act for rehousing people from overcrowded accommodation. However the absence of public subsidy for reconditioning, which was Copec's core business, remained the major constraint to its growth.

End of term report – before the war

Despite the disappointments brought by the Moyne Committee, Copec had made a creditable start in the first thirteen years of its existence. From an entirely voluntary enterprise dependent only on resources that could be raised from fellow citizens, Copec had grown to employ paid staff and had brought improvements to over 300 properties, bringing decency and comfort to an increasing number of tenants. It had moved from reconditioning existing properties to strategic demolitions and conversions and had begun to dip its toe in the water of public funding, with Birmingham City Council support for rehousing people displaced from demolished properties and for new construction of flats. Nevertheless it remained relatively small by today's standards, and its growth was severely constrained by the funding model it had adopted and the lack of public subsidy for its core business of 'slum-patching'. Moreover, its activity was still a drop in the ocean compared with the scale of the problem it had set out to address.

At the outbreak of war in 1939, Copec converted to a charity which marked a key change in its development (see chapters 3 and 7). The Second World War was to present Copec with new challenges as it sought to maintain a service to its tenants and protect its fragile financial position. The next chapter discusses how a new 'charitable' Copec rose to these challenges and emerged into a new environment after the war's end. This environment was one in which local authorities were established as the main providers of new housing for working class people and where Copec was forced to redefine its role before it could begin to grow again.

Table (3) – Birmingham Copec House Improvement Society Key Developments 1925-1939		
Year	**Key Developments**	**Homes**
1925	Birmingham Copec House Improvement Society founded. First properties at Pope St, Ladywood reconditioned, with bathing washhouse provided.	19
1926	Pamphlet published. 'A Call To Christians To Become Slum Landlords'. Met with good response in investment and donations. Sets up amenities fund from donations to provide community initiatives such as gardens/ fencing.	67
1927	Margaret Fenter, trained in Octavia Hill methods, appointed as housing manager.	111
1928	Purchase of de-licensed public house and converted into flats.	167
1929	Some of the re-conditioned properties provided with bathrooms and hot water supply. Housing survey entitled 'Five Hundred Birmingham Houses', undertaken (see chapter 10).	202
1930	'Mosse Houses' reconditioned with funds raised by St Anne's Church, Moseley, and an old workshop converted into a club and playroom.	243
1931	Five plots of land provided by special gift for gardens. Increased attention given to gardens and provision of window boxes. Exhibition of furnished flats.	249
1932	'New Homes For Old' exhibition held at the Birmingham Art Gallery (see chapter 10).	255
1933	Experiments in conversion of 'back-to-backs' into maisonettes, 'through' houses and flats with inside sanitation, baths and hot water supply.	313
1934	Erection of 10 new houses in conjunction with the Rotary club.	339
1935	Plans for demolition of 'back-to back' housing in bad condition and erection of new maisonettes. Copec becomes founder member of NFHS.	359
1936	Gee St and Pope St new build scheme using subsidy under the 1930 Act for rehousing families displaced by clearance activity.	363
1937	Sturge House built with a legacy from Joseph Sturge and public subsidy under 1935 Act for relieving overcrowding.	373
1938	Reconditioning ceases as World War Two approaches.	373
1939	Copec becomes a charity – decreased reliance on loan stock.	373

3

New challenges:
the war and its aftermath
1939-1959

The Second World War saw Copec facing new challenges as well as continuing to tackle the long-term problems of poor housing conditions in Birmingham's central areas. Copec had to deal with specific problems, such as bomb damage to its properties and the provision of air raid shelters. There were labour and materials shortages in most industries, and particular shortages in the construction industry. Finances to buy land and properties, and to do refurbishment, were short. And Copec had to reduce the interest on its loan stock in the early years of the war because of a reduced income from rents. In 1941, Copec's influential Chairman, Professor Frank Tillyard resigned. This marked a new era in the association's management with Chistopher Taylor taking the chair, which he was to hold until 1972.

The immediate postwar period was one of consolidation. Life for Copec after the war was not easy as the public sector became increasingly involved in meeting need as part of the Labour government's new welfare state. However, there were still some opportunities for the voluntary sector in the changed environment. This chapter traces how closer collaboration with Birmingham City Council, managing properties on behalf of other agencies, and providing new schemes for people with special needs became key elements of Copec's work in the 1940s and 1950s.

- **Things will never be the same again: the war years** – Copec's housing programme was halted and its existing housing was damaged during the war. How it responded is discussed. The war's impact on finances and tenants is also discussed. Early thinking about a postwar role is reviewed.

- **New efforts hedged in: 1945-1950** – some of Copec's plans formulated during the war were discarded as local authorities took the postwar lead in housing provision. Copec decided to work as a junior partner with Birmingham City Council.

- **The desirable outcome of Copec's efforts: welcoming central area redevelopment** – the late 1940s and early 1950s saw the wholesale redevelopment of Birmingham's central areas. Copec's relationship with Birmingham City Council became even closer as it took on the role of management agent in these areas.

- **Strictly incomparable to a commercial undertaking: conversion to charitable status** – new approaches to housing management and financing housing projects were developed in line with Copec's charitable status.

- **Pioneering new services** – as refurbishment of slum housing became less of a priority in the late 1950s, Copec branched out into new housing and services for people with special needs. Copec began to realise its role as a housing provider for ethnic minorities.

Things will never be the same again: the war years

'Things will never be the same again.....war brings sweeping and rapid changes, sometimes unforeseen'. (Fenter 1960)

During the war, Birmingham's already inadequate housing was severely damaged. From the beginning of the 'Blitz' in 1940 until 1945, more than 2,000 tons of bombs were dropped on the city, destroying more than 12,000 houses and damaging thousands more. Copec's chief area of activity, in the Summer Lane district, was particularly badly hit because of its proximity to munitions factories (Glasby 1999). Copec was concerned for its housing and tenants and encouraged women and children to evacuate Birmingham during the 'Blitz'. Copec also expressed concern at the slow progress in providing tenants with adequate protection against air raids. Many had no form of air raid shelter until the end of 1940. While brick surface shelters were provided in many backyards, Copec felt that more up-to-date shelters were needed, which was possible in the following year. However, Copec's management committee saw this as having detrimental effects on the ability of Copec to manage its properties effectively (Fenter 1960).

Bomb damage to Copec's properties at Hospital Street during the 'Blitz' 1940.
They were subsequently demolished.

On 19th September 1940, an air raid made 36 Copec properties temporarily uninhabitable. Others received minor damage. With the evacuation of a small number of whole families to the countryside, Copec was able to offer rehousing options to tenants who stayed behind and who experienced bomb damage to their homes. Also, rehousing was offered to other landlords whose tenants' homes had been 'bombed out'. Thirty-three Copec properties were completely destroyed during the war; predominantly in Lord St, Percy Road, Talfourd Street, Hospital Street, and Hampton Street. in Birmingham's central areas. By the end of the most intensive period of bombing in Birmingham in late 1941, the total cost of damage to Copec properties was estimated to be £10,000 (Fenter 1960).

Maintaining services

Attempts were made to maintain an adequate repairs service throughout the war, although this proved difficult. Maintenance was undertaken when labour became available with building materials often salvaged from war damaged properties. A small labour force was retained, supported by gifts in kind from charitable organisations (eg the Quaker Friends' Relief Service). The 1942 Copec annual report summarised repairs work at this time:

'Work has been going steadily during the year, and Copec is greatly indebted to its contractors, who have worked well in spite of severe handicaps due to shortage of labour and materials. It has been possible to replace all broken glass in inhabited rooms and a certain amount of redecoration has been carried out. There are still a good many repairs to finish, but they are of a more permanent character, and it will not be possible to carry them out until after the war'.

The Boys Club at Canal Street during the war.

Amongst others, Barrow Cadbury, one of the Bournville Cadbury family, made donations to assist with repairs to war damaged properties. As the war progressed, the management committee had to accept that those properties which had previously been earmarked for demolition or major reconditioning were rapidly deteriorating. Copec found it difficult to keep these properties up to a satisfactory standard and was resigned to managing this problem as best it could through emergency repairs only.

Facing-up to financial anxieties

Copec's anxieties about finances increased during the war. Rents were immediately reduced on properties once appreciable bomb damage had been sustained with a scale of reductions for particular damage put into operation.

Scale Of Copec Rent Reductions Due To Bomb Damage

- houses definitely dangerous – all rent remitted;
- houses temporarily uninhabitable but can be used for storage – small storage rent charged;
- houses partly inhabitable – rent charged on basis of number of habitable rooms;
- houses damaged but inhabitable – full rent.

Source: Annual Report 1941

In 1941 the loss of rental income due to damaged properties and reduced rent levels was around £1,000 but fell to £500 in 1942 as properties were gradually repaired and air raids became less frequent. Copec's income was also reduced by growing rent arrears, often caused by tenants' difficulties in providing for families which were split due to evacuation. Even so, some tenants who now served in the armed services found it easier to pay their rent because they formerly relied on unemployment allowances and casual work. On the other hand Copec's finances were strengthened during 1940 and 1941 when the interest on its loan stock was reduced from 3 per cent to 2.5 per cent, although the full interest charge was reinstated in 1942. As Malpass (2000) has commented on the war's effects on housing societies and tenants:

> 'The mobilisation of millions of young men and women into the forces, and the evacuation of women and children caused massive disruption to established ways of life. The poor organisation of (the evacuation) meant that nearly everyone drifted back home. From the point of view of landlords evacuation created problems of rent arrears, which added to the management problems of letting certain types of dwelling' (Malpass 2000).

Copec's rental income was also affected by the introduction of the Rent and Mortgage Interest (War Restrictions) Act 1939. Rents for landlords, such as housing societies, but not for local authorities, were frozen at 1939 levels, thereby reducing their freedom to raise income in line with the war's rising costs (Malpass 2000). Management costs increased due to rises in salaries and the introduction of a pension scheme sponsored by

Table (4) – Copec's Income And Costs 1939-1949 (£)

Year	Gross Rents	Outgoings	Net Rents	Repairs Reserve	Manage-ment costs	Income From Invest-ments
1939	7883	2899	4983	1182	788	880
1940	7837	2666	5170	1175	782	548
1941	6844	2328	4515	1026	685	250
1942	7255	2338	4917	1088	726	332
1943	7143	2321	4822	1285	899	405
1944	7339	2306	5033	1315	1027	473
1945	7822	2784	5038	1173	992	404
1946	8099	2867	5231	1214	1297	507
1947	9299	4743	4555	1394	1533	705
1948	8791	4384	4405	1319	1628	572
1949	6056	2748	3307	908	1181	472

Source: Copec annual reports and accounts 1939-1949

Notes
1. Column 2 shows outgoings from gross rental income. These outgoings include taxes and local rates. Column 3 shows rental income after these costs.
2. Columns 4 shows the amounts transferred to the repairs reserve for major maintenance expenditure (ie a maintenance 'sinking fund'). Column 5 describes Copec's annual management costs, including salaries, administration and publicity.
3. The final column is interest from a bank deposit account and dividends from investment.

the National Federation of Housing Societies. At the same time, other outgoings were increasing due to rising wartime costs (Annual Report 1940). Some redress of lost income came in 1949 when War Damage payments were received for all Copec properties which were demolished because of bomb damage (Annual Report 1949).

Another financial change came about when Copec's management committee realised that the accounts did not properly represent the true value of the housing stock. Consequently, changes were made in the way the accounts were presented. In particular, the capital value of Copec's housing stock was depreciated by £18,000 giving a more realistic value of its housing. A further change was made in the amounts being carried to reserves. Credit balances were maintained by the end of the war despite the difficulties Copec had in maintaining a service equal to the pre-war period, the level of repairs required and the resulting reduction in income. Conversions of shares to loan stock resulted from the Copec's transformation to charitable status in 1939 (discussed below in the section headed 'strictly incomparable to a commercial undertaking').

Table (5) – Copec's Financial Circumstances 1939-1949 (£)

Year	Shares Transfer To Loan Stock	4% Loan Stock	3% Loan Stock	2.5% Loan Stock	Total Loan Stock	Annual Profit/ Surplus
1939	13172	12730	40940	495	67337	1888
1940	11462	12330	40990	595	65377	1761
1941	11462	12325	40650	575	65012	1071
1942	11462	12325	40550	575	64912	1379
1943	11462	12310	40600	575	64947	1275
1944	11462	12310	41085	1250	66107	1316
1945	11462	12310	41085	1250	66107	1454
1946	11462	12310	41085	1300	66157	1434
1947	11462	12310	41085	1900	66757	525
1948	11462	12310	41085	2000	66857	223
1949	11462	12310	41085	2000	66857	119

Source: Copec annual reports and account 1939-1949

Notes
1. The first column shows income loan stock issued in exchange for shares converted after Copec converted to charitable status.
2. Virtually no new loan stock was issued throughout the 1940s except for small amounts at 2.5% return.

Supporting tenants

The war had placed a considerable extra strain on tenants, on top of the grinding poverty of 'normal life'.   As Chinn (1999) has commented about the 'normal life' of Birmingham's central areas dwellers:

> 'They were in poverty because of low wages, irregular earnings, illness, disability and widowhood, and they battled daily to overcome the harsh circumstances in which they found themselves'.

Although the war provided better employment opportunities than the 1930s, many of Copec's tenants were more vulnerable because of the war's effects. Because of this, Copec decided to provide extra support to those who had stayed in Birmingham, especially women and children. While this support was limited, it provided some relief from the deteriorating conditions in Birmingham's central areas. It can also be seen as a continuation of Copec's philanthropic approach (today's 'housing plus') in practice. The number of overcrowded families in Copec properties living in overcrowded conditions, under the definitions of the Housing Act, 1935, was reduced from 6 to 4 percent (3 percent if those temporarily away due to the war were deducted) (Annual Report 1940). Copec was also able to arrange for some women and children to take short holidays in both 1943 and 1944. The Holiday Fellowship Centre in Derbyshire was used to provide a week's holiday in both years. This was made possible by the Charles Henry Foyle Trust. Other holidays were arranged by the Quaker Friends Relief Service at Ullenhall, Warwickshire and Glasshampton, near Stourport, Worcestershire. Tenants were required to cover two thirds of their holidays' costs which were supplemented by the two organisations above and by the Rotary and Soroptimist Clubs through specific appeals. Other approaches to tenant support were offered:

> 'During the year tenants have been helped to obtain furniture and bedding, mostly in cases where, owing to bombing or increases in the number or ages of the family, the number of beds was hopelessly inadequate. In some cases, however, tenants have been able to acquire utility furniture on their own account where easy payments on a reasonable basis could be arranged. This increase in self-reliance is the end to which the manager is always working' (Annual Report 1944).

Along with Summer Lane-based Birmingham Settlement, Copec established a housewives' scheme to organise help during air raids. Copec's management committee commended the way in which its tenants assisted with putting out fires created by incendiary bombs which fell on or near to Copec properties. Other support schemes were begun during the war, including a knitting group to provide activities mainly for women and children while producing much needed new clothing. A savings group was also set up amongst tenants. The group managed to save £40 in a few months in 1941. By 1942 this amount had grown to £245 with an increasing number of tenants taking part. As the management committee said in its 1940 annual report:

> 'It is one of our principles of management to stir up a sense of independence and thrift amongst the tenants'.

Copec maintained its communal amenities where possible, despite the need for land for air raid shelters. Grants from the Common Good Trust and the Boeke Trust assisted with these communal amenities. Bulbs and seeds for both flowers and vegetables were provided throughout the war by the Gardeners' Guild. A pressing need during this period was for manual washing machines (wringers) and a number were supplied with assistance from individual donations with further donations providing repairs to machines later in the war. The various clubs and societies, established by Copec before the war were also continued for the early years of the conflict. These clubs met in the communal room at Canal St with Senior and Junior boys clubs. A girls club was also provided, offering gymnastics, fretwork and games. These activities were supported by Bournville Youth Club staff (Fenter 1960).

Planning for the post-war period

The final years of the war saw the management committee trying to come to grips with an uncertain future for Copec. It had already made a significant contribution to Bournville Village Trust's report – 'When We Build Again', (1941) which had laid out ideas for Birmingham's postwar redevelopment. Against the backdrop of this report, planning meetings in 1943 and 1944 came up with some proposals for new directions. Potential directions included continuing refurbishment of 'back-to-backs' in the central areas of the city; tackling poor property in the middle ring of the city; catering for specific 'special groups' such as older people; establishing a Neighbourhood Unit (pre-dating the association's later urban renewal work) to consolidate work in the Farm St area of Aston; and experimenting with new construction approaches with industrial firms (Annual Report 1943). After the war, Copec had some success in raising new funds to complete repairs to damaged properties and to begin new housing schemes. The Housing Act 1946 provided Exchequer subsidies to housing associations on the same terms as local authorities, although associations in practice had to overcome considerable hurdles before subsidy was granted; not least the goodwill of local authorities in sharing subsidies with them (Malpass 2000). Copec did not apply for these subsidies and activity remained on a small scale. The growth in the public sector's role after the war, exemplified by Birmingham City Council's redevelopment of the city's central districts, was also to pose challenges to the role of the voluntary housing sector, including Copec.

Copec's Policy Priorities in 1944

■ The completion of pre-war schemes where possible, particularly the planned provision of accommodation for single women;

■ An immediate repairs drive to return properties to at least pre-war standards;

■ The erection of temporary accommodation or adaptation of existing properties unsuitable for permanent use which might be used to meet the housing shortage;

■ An experiment in building a few houses with prefabricated units;

■ Attention to particular areas in which Copec had large numbers of properties with the idea being to develop community life generally beyond the provision of housing alone.

New efforts hedged in: 1945-1950

Former Copec Chairman Frank Tillyard, guest speaker at the 1946 Annual General Meeting said that 'Copec had the spirit, the personnel and the money for new work, but efforts were hedged in by external restrictions'. The prophetic nature of his statement is discussed here.

'Big Brother': partnership with Birmingham City Council

From its inception, Copec had a close relationship with Birmingham City Council and was not as independent as its status and funding suggested. Copec coordinated its efforts with those of the council to meet housing need in the city. Copec's management committee included two or more councillors during this period, as it had done from its foundation in 1925. Their presence enabled the council to comment on Copec schemes and Copec's management committee to respond to council policy. For example, the City Surveyor and the Health Department were consulted about properties before purchase and reconditioning. This early example of partnership with Birmingham City Council

One of Birmingham's five redevelopment areas in Long Acre Street, Nechells in the late 1940s. The city council's clearance policy was to have major effects on how Copec developed in the 1950s.

pre-figured close relations between Birmingham Housing Trust and the city council in the 1960s and more recent good working relationships between Focus, Birmingham City Council and other local authorities in the West Midlands. Postwar expansion of the city council's role, however, fundamentally changed its relationship with Copec. In 1947, the Minister of Health confirmed Birmingham's compulsory purchase order on its redevelopment areas. As Chinn (1999) has observed:

> 'Birmingham's postwar redevelopment was influenced by three significant prewar events: the 1935 Housing Act; the city's 1938 Housing Conference; and the appointment of Herbert Manzoni as City Engineer and Surveyor......the scene was set for slum clearance and rehousing on a scale never before witnessed in the city, and there was little doubt that it was needed desperately'.

Under the direction of the influential Herbert Manzoni, the city council announced in 1946 its intention to acquire under the Town and Country Planning Act 1944 some 33,000 houses in Birmingham's central areas. This was the first part of its redevelopment plan for the five core areas of the city. Manzoni's aim was to create a series of neighbourhoods of about 10,000 people in areas which were strictly zoned, with land divided into different uses, such as housing, industry and open spaces (Glasby 1999). There were 29,000 'back-to-backs' left in Birmingham, almost 60 percent of which were in the redevelopment areas. There were still 6,500 dwellings without individual water supply. Of these, 60 percent again were in Birmingham's five blighted redevelopment areas (Chinn 1999). The redevelopment plan heralded a major change in Copec's affairs with the issuing of Compulsory Purchase Orders (CPO's) for all the land and buildings in these five areas covering four-fifths of Copec's properties.

Table (6) –	Housing Conditions In Birmingham's Redevelopment Areas In 1945 (At The Time Of Approval Of CPO)					
Redevelopment Areas	No. Of Houses	No. Of Unfit Houses	No. Of Back-To-Backs'	No. Without Internal Water Supply	No. Without Separate W.C.	No. Without Bath
Duddeston And Nechells	5,277	3,961	2,492	1,059	3,067	4,094
Summer Lane	8,804	7,038	4,982	1,210	4,978	6,395
Ladywood	7,313	5,998	4,585	549	4,953	6,028
Bath Row	4,207	4,064	2,858	506	3,094	2,524
Gooch Street	4,162	3,609	2,033	529	2,499	3,218
All Areas	29,763	24,670	16,950	3,853	18,591	22,259

Source: Birmingham City Council Public Works Department Publication (1951)

Notes
1. New names were chosen by Birmingham Evening Mail readers for the redevelopment districts. Ladywood and Nechells retained their old names. Gooch Street became known as Highgate, Bathrow became Lee Bank and Summer lane was renamed Newtown (Glasby 1999).

A public enquiry was held at which Copec objected to some of the compulsory purchases of its property (particularly Sturge House). Copec's management committee was concerned about possible capital losses on properties and the resulting loss of rental income. However, the public enquiry praised Copec's housing management record and the subsequent compulsory purchase of Copec properties resulted in gains as well as losses (Fenter 1960). In particular, Copec obtained the status of a management agency with the city council's Central Areas Management Department which enabled it to manage a wider range of property owned by landlords working in these areas:

'This year is a landmark in the history of Copec, for many of our properties have been taken over by the city and will be dealt with in the redevelopment areas. While regretting having to part from so many tenants who have become our friends, we are thankful that more people may look forward to better housing conditions and healthier surroundings. Our thoughts go back to the early days of Copec when the properties which have been acquired (by the city) were shockingly overcrowded and in wretched condition' (Annual Report 1949).

Copec's new role in the redevelopment areas may be seen as an early example of acting as 'an agent of the state' (as many housing associations were later to do). For the remainder of the 1940s, Copec shared in the work to redevelop the central areas. It became one of eighty-two agents empowered by Birmingham City Council to collect rent on behalf of the city's Central Areas Management Department. Some building and renovation work was undertaken using improvement grants introduced by the

Housing Act 1949 (as Copec had insufficient funds at this time to undertake all but minor refurbishment work). Some thirty-two properties were improved using these grants. By the end of 1949, Copec managed 90 tenancies in the Ladywood area and 330 in the Summer Lane district on behalf of the Department. As a result, Copec managed a total of 450 properties, including retail units (Annual Reports 1946-1949). It was at this time that Janet Rushbrooke took up her post as Deputy Housing Manager to Margaret Fenter (she was later to become manager when Margaret Fenter retired in the mid-1950s).

While the immediate postwar period saw Copec loosing rental income as some of its properties were purchased by the city council, in compensation, the association received fees for its services from the city council as a leading management agency in the redevelopment areas. Income for agency services grew from £84 per year in the late 1940s to more than £1,500 in 1955 when the arrangement was brought to an end. At the height of Copec's work as a management agent, this income represented between 20 and 25 percent of rental income from its own properties (Annual Reports 1948-1956).

A former Copec property in Tower Street, Summer Lane. One of the last areas in Birmingham to see redevelopment in the 1950s.

The desirable outcome of Copec's efforts: welcoming central area redevelopment

While its traditional work had changed appreciably, Copec's management committee welcomed the wholesale redevelopment of the areas for which it had campaigned so long. Committee members were pleased to think that they had made some contribution to shaping public and municipal opinion during the 1930s which had influenced postwar redevelopment in Birmingham (see chapter 10). As Fenter (1960) and the 1949 annual report remarked:

> 'Such a redevelopment was not unforeseen and when it came was welcomed by Copec's management committee, since it has meant a much more comprehensive attack on conditions in the central areas.....it is the desirable outcome of the efforts of Copec to secure better housing conditions therein.....the committee considers that Copec has had some share in shaping of public opinion now resulting in the great changes being made in the central areas of the city'.

The worst blocks of property were being steadily dealt with and planning was taking place to demolish worn-out properties and to redevelop large areas on new and better design lines (as it was thought at the time, although the desirability of tower blocks in subsequent years was to be questioned with the benefit of hindsight). However, when the redevelopment scheme was initially implemented, the Central Areas Management Department was still being established so early purchases of properties by the city council meant that urgent repair work had to be done. The properties were in a similar condition to those bought by Copec in the 1920s and 1930s. Years of poor landlordism had left a legacy of disrepair.

Copec had some difficulty in accommodating its new role as the city council's management agency. It was only responsible for undertaking minor repairs and thereafter reported repairs to a City Inspector. While Copec collected rents, the chasing of rent arrears was the responsibility of the Department . There was little coordination of these two closely related functions. In addition, the work of Copec's housing management staff (3 at the time) was no lighter because more properties were managed. Copec's view was that the housing management functions should not be divided. Its management committee felt that this division of housing management duties did not fit well with Copec's established approach and its very close relationship with tenants and their concerns (still based on Octavia Hill methods) (Fenter 1960). Copec's 1949 annual report reveals a certain concern about the role the association was to take on, although it clearly decided that it should 'take the plunge':

> 'After careful consideration the management committee entered into an agreement with Birmingham's Central Areas Management Committee under which Copec becomes an agent for the city council for properties in Sheepcote Lane, King Edwards's Road, Nelson Street and two adjoining properties. Although it is too early to judge how the arrangement will work out, the management committee is glad that its experience should be of service in the collosal but urgent task which has been undertaken'.

Blending the old with the new

With the advent of new management arrangements for Copec's properties in Birmingham's central areas, especially the compulsory purchase of Copec properties by the city council and the division of housing management functions between the city council and Copec, Copec developed new management approaches. Accommodating tenants nominated by the city council meant that it became more difficult to assist tenants on an individual and personal basis. Larger numbers of tenants who were more mobile challenged the idea that long term relationships could be made with tenants. Views amongst housing professionals on the level of interaction between tenants and housing officers were also changing nationally. In addition, Copec had been used to reconditioning housing with sitting tenants who often stayed for long periods (Fenter 1960). No evidence is available about whether tenants preferred previous management arrangements or welcomed new ones.

Copec's former Secretary Florence Barrow receiving a 'Good Citizen's' award after her retirement in 1955.

Despite these changes in circumstances, Copec remained devoted to the Octavia Hill tradition during the 1950s, as Janet Rushbrooke, Copec's new Housing Manager, was as committed to Hill's approach as her predecessor, Margaret Fenter:

'The friendly contact with tenants continues to be greatly appreciated, and they in their turn become increasingly responsive to the help given, pay their rent regularly and show an interest in the care of the properties. The Octavia Hill methods, after thirty years of experience, show this lasting benefit and indicate a type of 'landlordism' which could with much advantage be adopted by more municipal authorities' (Annual Report 1955).

The continued importance of the approaches developed by Octavia Hill, who had died in 1912, was reflected in Copec's commitment to its housing management training scheme, aimed chiefly at women. However, the training scheme also represented the increasing professionalisation of housing management with professional trade institutions growing over this period (eg the Society of Housing Managers which became the Institute of Housing in the 1970s). Copec's training scheme had a throughput of 41 trainees between 1931 and 1959, with on-the-job training supplemented by theoretical aspects with trainees studying for the Housing Managers' Certificate of the Royal Institution of Chartered Surveyors. Hilary Clark, a trainee in 1945, and later Housing Director of Wolverhampton local authority and a Copec committee member, gives a fascinating insight to the training provided:

> 'My training was in the Octavia Hill tradition; for a generic housing manager. We collected rents three days a week, keeping meticulous records, by hand, of every penny. On Fridays we went out 'spraying'. Most of the old houses were alive with bedbugs, and we used a hand spray and paraffin-based liquid to combat them. Most of our work was done on bicycle, except for spraying, for which we borrowed an Austin Seven from Florence Barrow, an elderly Quaker, to carry the gear' (Interview 1999).

Strictly incomparable to a commercial undertaking: conversion to charitable status

Copec's management committee had long felt that its work was not 'strictly comparable with a commercial undertaking' (Fenter 1960). Copec had previously been run on business lines, raising capital through shares and loan stock and paying dividends to share holders and low rates of interest to loan stock holders (see chapter 2). It also extensively used its committee members' professional skills. In March 1939 the management committee put a resolution to a special meeting of shareholders that Copec should become an Industrial and Provident Society with charitable status (see chapter 7 for a detailed discussion). This was an early example of such a conversion, and occurred before the war time excess profits tax, which stimulated other housing societies (for example Kensington Housing Trust, St. Pancras House Improvement Society and the Howard Cottage Society) to convert (Malpass 2000). Two propositions were put to loan stock shareholders:

- inviting them to offer their holding of loan stock to the committee to finance housing for special needs groups (see below).

- reducing the loan stock, by enabling shareholders who wished to redeem their holdings at a price determined by Copec's accountants, to do so.

The result was that some shareholders with holdings of around £8,000 in nominal value allowed this amount to be donated to Bryony House (see over). Holders of loan stock of the nominal value of £12,000 sold their stock back to Copec. In this way, Copec strengthened its finances at a time of great change. Some of the advantages of the conversion were summarised in a paper put to Copec shareholders in March 1939:

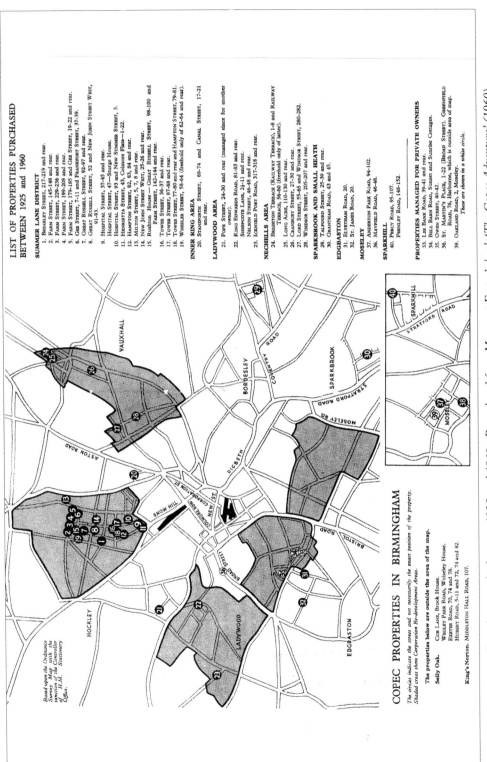

A map of Copec's properties between 1925 and 1960. Reproduced from Margaret Fenter's book 'The Copec Adventure' (1960). She was Copec's first housing manager.

'Copec, like any trading company or private individual, is subject to payment of Income Tax, Schedule 'A', on the annual value of the properties it owns, and owing to the improvements made by the Society to its properties the assessments upon Schedule 'A' tax are showing a tendency to increase. By means of detailed claims for all sums spent on repairs above the statutory allowances the tax actually paid is reduced to some £140 a year. This outgoing and the labour of preparing the elaborate maintenance claims could be saved if the Society were converted into a legal charity. In the opinion of the committee this would also bring Copec's constitution more into line with its professed objects to provide houses without profit and with a low rate of interest on the capital invested'.

Thus the shareholders' decision to convert to charitable status reflected a win:win combination of moral principle (through moving to non-profit status) and pragmatic advantage (through administration and tax savings). These changes can be seen in hindsight as a major shift in the way Copec's management committee and staff saw themselves. In particular, Copec was moving away from the '5% philanthropy' philosophy to an organisational model based on charitable foundations (this was the first key transformation in Copec's organisational structure and philosophy over the next fifty years – chapter 7 provides a more detailed account). Returns on investment, although below market rates, had been viewed in commercial terms by share and loan stock holders. Copec had now begun to highlight its charitable status and links with municipal authorities as the key driving forces behind its work. In this way, Copec showed signs of being more like the modern social enterprise it was later to become – one of Garside's (2000) 'commercial philanthropists' – mixing business acumen with charitable aims, while maintaining good links with the public sector.

Pioneering new services

Housing associations, despite postwar disappointments, remained active, and new services were pioneered, particularly for older people (Malpass 2000). From early times, Copec wished to meet the needs of groups of people who had little provision made for them by Birmingham City Council:

'One of the acknowledged roles of housing societies has been to meet the needs of those individual people or classes of people for whom very little provision is made by the local authority, because it is considered that families have prior claims' (Fenter 1960).

In the 1950s Copec paid growing attention to this role. It also noted the increasing proportion of the population who were 'elderly or infirm'. At the same time, Copec had always been interested in housing single women. While some provision was made for these groups prior to the war, it was small and incidental to Copec's main housing work. Copec's management committee decided alongside its new role as a managing agent in Birmingham's central areas for family accommodation, it would also increase its housing provision for special needs groups.

The opening of Brook House in 1951. This scheme, built on land leased from Bournville Village Trust, provided flats for single working women. Seen here at the opening are (from left to right), well-known Birmingham philanthropist Margery Fry, who opened the scheme, Dame Elizabeth Cadbury, Chairwoman of the Bournville Village Trust, Florence Barrow, Copec's Secretary, Paddon Smith, Lord Mayor of Birmingham and Mr. C. B. Parkes, architect of the scheme and head of Bournville's architectural department.

Single women and the 'city of a thousand trades'

Copec found that applications for its small number of flats from single women were so numerous that it needed to expand this provision urgently in the late 1940s and 1950s. Birmingham, the so-called 'city of a thousand trades', (Upton 1997) traditionally had a large number of female workers during the 20th Century's early decades, but the influx of women workers into essential industries during the war meant that this trend was extended and became an important factor in the local employment market.

Early provision for single women began immediately after the war with the purchase of two large houses in Mayfield Road, Moseley. These were reconditioned and converted into eighteen one room bedsits with an additional room for a warden and one furnished room for guests. Four shared bathrooms and toilets were provided alongside a tenants' laundry. With the help of German prisoners of war and a firm of garden contractors, the large garden at the back of the property was cleared and an air raid shelter was made into a garden room. Single women tenants could have a small plot in the garden of their own. Rents ranged from 18s. 1d to 29s. 7d. per week, including charges for services and local rates (considerably higher than council rents at this time). Nevertheless, properties were much sought after by women with limited means.

Further properties were bought in Anderton Park Road in Moseley with two detached houses being joined by a bridge on the top floor. Fire doors and smoke screens were provided to improve safety and the result was five self-contained flats, although they had shared washing and bathing facilities. Numbers 94 and 96 Anderton Park Road were bought in 1956 which were converted into eight self-contained flats for single women. Number 98, which adjoined number 100, was bought in 1957 with four bedsits provided. A major scheme developed by Copec in the 1950s was Brook House, Cob Lane located within the boundaries of Bournville village in Selly Oak. Brook House had 20 self-contained flats in two storeys. Brook House was partly funded by the Birmingham Soroptimist Club and was built on land leased from Bournville Village Trust (BVT) and designed by BVT's in-house architects. However, the scheme would probably not have been completed without public subsidy under the Housing Act 1936. As Birmingham City Council's Public Works Department publication (1951) explained, this was rare public funding for housing association work in the city:

> 'In approved cases the Exchequer grant was paid to the local authority who passed it on to the association. An arrangement was agreed with Bournville Village Trust for the erection of 208 houses, the city councl passing on to the Trust the subsidy and making the maximum advance in their power. No additional contribution from the rate fund was made. Similar arrangements were made with Copec for 20 flats for single women at Bournville'.

Brook House was a popular scheme. Its flats were let to women office and factory workers, teachers, hospital workers and post office workers. Brook House was pleasantly located with a large communal lawn and rear gardens provided for individual tenants. The flats were hidden from the busy Bristol Rd by a belt of trees. For a few years after the scheme's opening in 1951, tenants could see cows grazing on nearby Woodbrooke Farm!

Another housing scheme was developed in 1955 called Wolseley House. Funded by a legacy from Arthur Wolseley and designed by BVT architects, the scheme provided accommodation for single women and women with physical disabilities. Later, bungalows for disabled people were built in the five and a half acre grounds. Oak doors and panelled walls were preserved in the scheme. One flat was occupied by a resident caretaker. With a view of the Lickey Hills, Wolseley House was extremely popular amongst single women working in the city centre. Another reconstruction scheme was developed in Elvetham Road, Edgbaston with seven bedsits provided. The scheme was close to the redevelopment area established by the city council and housed single women with limited means. The last scheme for this client group was developed in 1959 when a property conversion in Middleton Hall Road, Kings Norton provided eight self-contained flats.

Adding life to years: housing older people

The term 'adding life to years' was coined by Lord Amulree from his book of the same name. He was a consultant at the Birmingham University College Hospital and his book promoted housing in the community as an effective means of meeting the needs of older people. Lord Amulree later laid the foundation stone of Copec's Bryony House scheme as a mark of his conviction (see below).

However, Bryony House was not the first Copec scheme for older people. This had been Sturge House (see chapter 2). The management committee decided to add to its older peoples' provision with a range of developments throughout the 1950s. Florence

Bryony House in Selly Oak. Opened in 1955, the innovative scheme provided flats for elderly people. Funded entirely through charitable donations from the Soroptimists and the Birmingham Council for Old People amongst others, it cost £53,000 to build. In memory of Gertrude Humpidge, Birmingham's first almoner, Florence Barrow and friends furnished a room in her honour.

Barrow in particular championed the needs of older people. She envisaged the provision of well-equipped homes with some nursing supervision for older people who were no longer able to remain independent. She was also interested in helping relatives who were responsible for elderly parents or grandparents. Largely through Florence Barrow's efforts, a sub-committee was established between Copec, the Birmingham Soroptimist Club, the Birmingham Council for Old People and other interested parties in the city.

BVT assisted Copec with the provision of a site in Bryony Rd, Weoley Hill. Plans were drawn-up by BVT's architects and an appeal was made to Copec shareholders for extra funding in 1952. This appeal was supplemented by a co-appeal by the Soroptimists and the Birmingham Council for Old People in early 1953. Building work started later that year and by 1954, £48,000 had been raised towards the cost of the scheme. Copec's management committee decided to establish a unique management arrangement for for the scheme, which they called Bryony House. A non-profit making company was set-up which would lease the scheme from Copec at a nominal fee. General supervision of Bryony House was placed in the hands of the new management committee whose membership was drawn from the major organisations which had raised funds for the project. Bryony House was finally opened in June 1955. It was believed to be the first scheme of its kind in the country, specially built for older people who required nursing services but who would find an 'ordinary' old peoples' home unsuitable. Bryony House accommodated thirty-five residents in rooms for one or two people. A self-contained flat

Shown here is Bryony House's fully fitted kitchen.

Wolseley House in Weoley Park Road, Selly Oak. Developed on Bournville Village Trust Land it provided 13 flats. Named after Arthur Wolseley, who left the residue of his estate to Copec in 1942, it was opened by local MP Harold Gurden in 1958.

was also provided for a matron with further accommodation for residential staff. In addition, the scheme included bathrooms, a well-equipped kitchen, a lounge, a dining room and an office.

Taking their place in the normal life of the community: refugees and new migrants

The Birmingham Council for Refugees was responsible for assisting people in Germany and central Europe wishing to move to Birmingham after the war. Two Copec committee members, Mr. H. Gosling and Mr. G Church, were active members of the Council for Refugees, and they asked Copec to assist them with housing refugee families. Copec, therefore, leased two properties – one in Grantham, Rd., Sparkbrook and one in St James Rd, Edgbaston. The first property was let to families from Austria and Czechoslovakia who came to Birmingham sponsored by Miss Dorothy Cadbury (another member of the well-known Quaker family). Copec's chief duty was to keep the properties in an adequate state of repair. St James Rd. was run as a hostel with six refugees occupying one or two rooms each with shared bathrooms and toilets (Fenter 1960, Annual Reports, Minutes of the Management Committee 1955). As Fenter commented in 1960:

> 'They (refugees) have now, happily, largely taken their place in the normal life of the community'.

Copec's commitment to rehousing refugees at this time anticipated its approach in the 1980s and 1990s when it housed asylum seekers from Vietnam and the former Yugoslavia (see chapters 5 and 6). Working with excluded groups has always been a hallmark of Copec's approach. This was shown when, during the 1950s, the first post-war wave of immigration from the New Commonwealth (predominantly the West Indies) began. Many of the new migrants settled in areas where Copec managed housing. Copec responded to the needs of migrants in partnership with a new housing association, Birmingham Friendship, that had been set up to 'house and befriend immigrants and to help them to integrate into the British way of life' (Malpass and Jones 1996). Fenter (1960) summarised the situation faced by migrants to Britain at this time:

> 'There is an urgent need for better housing for immigrants from overseas territories. At present their necessity is frequently exploited by unscrupulous landlords with gross overcrowding and insanitary conditions the result. A beginning has been made by the Friendship Housing Association and Copec in tackling this problem but there is scope for more activity of this sort'.

Copec lent Friendship £1,000 in 1956 to assist with improving properties in Sparkbrook. Over the next few years, a close relationship developed between Copec and Friendship with Copec providing financial and management support to the new association. By the end of the 1950s, three Copec committee members had been invited onto Friendship's management committee. In later years, both housing associations would place the housing of communities with roots in the West Indies, Africa, and South Asia central to their housing role in Birmingham and the areas beyond the city (see chapters 4 and 5).

Becoming housing's 'third arm'

At the end of the 1950s, it is clear from looking at Copec's records that it could not easily shake off the effects of the war and postwar re-construction. Several of its early leaders had stood down. The first Copec manager, Margaret Fenter, had retired in 1953. The loss of Copec's original role as a 'slum patcher' as Birmingham City Council expanded its work in the central areas had long-term effects on how the association developed. In short, Copec's committee members were not prepared for the huge social and economic changes which were to follow the war. Thus the future seemed uncertain. This situation was not unusual at the time as the voluntary sector as a whole was trying to come to terms with the expanding welfare state in the early post-war period in which charities were viewed in some quarters as anachronistic and somewhat distasteful. Garside (2000) captures the mood when she notes that:

> 'In the Brave New World ushered in by the postwar Labour government, local authorities held the key and housing societies remained largely excluded. Subjected to rent controls and denied public sector finance, they retreated to mend their damaged property and manage their existing estates'.

As we shall see in chapter 4, however, Copec was able to develop a new housing role in the 1960s and 1970s as housing associations became housing's 'third arm'. Through merger with other, newer organisations Copec's aims evolved to meet social problems which were being 'rediscovered' in the 1960s.

4

The re-discovery of poverty: housing responses 1960-1979

The 1960s and 1970s saw a range of initiatives, policies and developments, which enabled housing associations to become major providers of publicly funded housing. This was a period when the wider voluntary sector grew in importance in social policy. For example, housing associations became the 'third arm' of British housing (the other two being council housing and owner-occupation) (Malpass 2000). Housing associations also became known collectively as the 'voluntary housing movement'. The position of associations as major providers of social rented housing was expanded and 'formalised' in the 1970s with both Labour and Conservative governments supporting their development as part of a diversifying social housing sector (Copec 1999). Copec provides an example of how housing associations developed in this period, especially after the Housing Act 1974 which enabled more substantial growth through generous public funding. Copec's development over the two decades was also fuelled by mergers with other, younger housing associations (see chapter 8 for greater detail), incorporating new ideas and approaches and its expansion from Birmingham into the rest of the West Midlands conurbation.

The first mergers were with Birmingham Housing Trust in 1970 and with Wolverhampton Housing Association in 1976. These mergers enabled Copec to develop increasing numbers of rented homes across the West Midlands. Other local housing associations were being established in response to the 'rediscovery' of social problems from the 1960s onwards. The birth of Shelter in 1966 was bound-up with the formation of these new associations at this time, particularly those formed to tackle housing problems in inner city areas. Several had Christian roots. Four such new associations (Shape, Hestia, St. Chad and Harambee), formed around this time, were all to merge with Copec in future years to form a new housing association – Focus. This chapter continues the story of Copec but also considers the circumstances surrounding the formation of these new associations and finds out how they became involved with Copec.

- **The swinging '60s: housing associations 'in-and-out' of housing policy** – looks at Copec's approach in the early 1960s and how it reacted to the public's 're-discovery of poverty' through the foundation of Shelter and the broadcast of 'Cathy Come Home'.

- **Creating new housing associations in the 1960s** – two new housing associations (Birmingham Housing Trust and Wolverhampton Housing Association), later to merge with Copec, were formed as part of the renewed attack on poor housing conditions by the voluntary sector.

- **The 1970s watershed** – this section discusses the effects on Copec of the new public funding regime introduced by the Housing Act 1974 and charts its progress as a growing social housing provider and an agent for area renewal.

- **Creating new housing organisations in the 1970s** – traces the creation of Shape and Hestia Housing Associations, and St. Chad Housing Society, which were to merge with Copec to form Focus in the 1990s. This section also describes how Copec supported an independent advice service in Birmingham.

Reimproved Copec properties in Hubert Street, Selly Oak. One of the few refurbishment schemes carried out by Copec in the early 1960s.

The 'swinging 60s': housing associations 'in-and-out' of housing policy

Under the Housing Act 1961, housing associations were given access to Exchequer loans at a cheap rate of interest. The 1961 Act also launched new-style cost-rent and co-ownership housing societies. By 1963, 39 such housing societies had delivered 88 schemes with 5,540 homes (Malpass). This brief flirtation with housing societies was seen as a success by the Conservative government which wished to see a 'third arm' of housing between the owner-occupied sector and local authority housing. This 'new' housing sector was seen as helping to replace the private rented sector which had failed to respond to policies to revive it in the previous ten years (Cope 1999).

The Housing Act 1964 extended support to housing associations by allocating more Treasury funds and securing lending arrangements with building societies. The same Act also established the Housing Corporation to act as a clearing house for government funds and to promote the overall development of housing associations. Between 1965 and 1972, the Corporation financed the construction of more than 5,000 homes which were let at cost rents. These rents were too high for the poorest members of society, who were generally trapped in the private rented sector. While the Housing Corporation secured central government funds for the cost-rent housing societies, existing and older housing associations, such as Copec, remained predominantly reliant on local authority subsidies, their own fundraising efforts and donations from Shelter (see below) until the Housing Act 1974 set up a proper public funding stream (Cope 1999). Copec received limited public funding through the Housing Subsidies Act 1967 for a small number of improvement schemes in the late 1960s. Birmingham Housing Trust made more use of this public funding stream, which was a main part of its growth during 1968-1970.

'Cathy' and the rediscovery of social problems

Shelter (the campaign for homeless people) was launched on 1st December 1966 in the crypt of St. Martins-in-the-Fields Church in London. A few evenings earlier, the BBC had broadcast a drama documentary, 'Cathy Come Home', depicting the devastating effects of homelessness on a family's life. Although the documentary did not mention Birmingham by name, recordings of the city's slum dwellers highlighted specific complaints, including houses overrun by rats, chronic dampness, overcrowding, poor living conditions and the track record of private landlords. Jeremy Sandford, the documentary's author, said that he specifically had Birmingham in mind when he wrote it. Tony Garnett, the Birmingham-born producer of the documentary later denied that 'Cathy Come Home' was an attack on the housing authorities in the city. However, he indicted the overall housing system and society which had allowed such housing conditions to arise:

> 'We think that viewers may find it difficult to believe some of the conditions we filmed – they have been recreated from the times of Dickens' (Birmingham Post and Mail 1966).

The new Shelter charity and the documentary quickly became linked in the nation's mind. It should also be noted that public awareness of poor housing had been stimulated by publicity in the national press surrounding poor treatment of tenants by private landlords like Peter Rachman, whose name had become an emblem for exploitation of tenants (Garside 2000). As a Birmingham paper said at the time:

> 'Rachmanism of excessive rents charged to those in urgent need of homes exists widely in Birmingham' (Birmingham Post and Mail 1966).

Shelter was formed by organisations to 'publicise the emergency situation that exists within the housing problem, and appeal for money to carry out a rescue operation'. The day after its launch, Shelter took out a full page advertisement in the Times, showing a child in a slum kitchen with the slogan 'Home Sweet Hell'. The public responded by donating £50,000 in the first month after the launch (Evening Post And Mail 1966). In the next seven years £5.3 million was raised by Shelter with close to half channelled to housing associations (Malpass 2000). Public concern was further stimulated in Birmingham when Canon Norman Power, vicar of St John's Ladywood, wrote an influential book – 'The Forgotten People'. Sponsored by Copec, Canon Power's book highlighted the plight of people still living in the city's redevelopment areas (Annual Report 1968).

Some of the appalling housing conditions in which many people lived in the 1960s. A new spotlight was directed at these problems with the birth of housing charity Shelter in 1966 and the broadcast of the drama-documentary 'Cathy Come Home' in the same year.

Shelter and the scene in Birmingham

Shelter initially concentrated its efforts on areas of acute need including Birmingham, Glasgow, Liverpool and London. It worked closely with existing housing associations, such as Copec in Birmingham, to increase housing provision and improve existing homes. Shelter also helped newly formed housing associations, such as Birmingham Housing Trust, to become established. As a Shelter memorandum (1989) explained:

> 'The next natural step was to form a national housing trust which would raise money at the Oxfam level.....one of the main objects being the raising of large sums of money to finance staffing and capital expenditure of housing trusts in different parts of the Britain.....we provided initial advice and finance to enable other housing trusts to start in districts of really great need.....we started trusts in Liverpool, Birmingham, Nottingham and East Lothian'.

Shelter's local launch was organised 6 days after the main launch in London, with Birmingham's Deputy Lord Mayor and former Copec committee member Corbyn Barrow as Chairman of the launch. To mark the launch a service was held in Birmingham Cathedral. Shelter's key objectives were to publicise the needs of the homeless and those living in poor housing conditions and to raise funds for housing associations to provide housing to alleviate these problems (Copec Annual Report 1966).

Shelter's original trustees included the Housing Societies Charitable Trust, the British Churches Housing Trust, Christian Action, Housing the Homeless Central Fund, Notting Hill Housing Trust and Catholic Housing Aid Society (Malpass 2000). Chaired by the Reverend Bruce Kenrick, Shelter began to donate funds raised from its ongoing appeal to designated associations in the four cities which were prioritised for action. Kenrick was an influential figure of the time and had established Notting Hill Housing Trust in the early 1960s, partly as a result of his experiences with slum housing in Harlem, New York. His experiences had been published in an influential book – 'Come Out The Wilderness' in 1963.

Economic crises but local authorities remain dominant

A Labour Government was elected in 1964. Richard Crossman, Minister of Housing and Local Government, was determined to achieve his party's pledge to build 500,000 houses per year by 1970, with an increased emphasis on council housebuilding. The actual number of completions was less than this target (at 2.7 million of which 1.3 million were council houses). Following the devaluation of Sterling by Labour Chancellor Roy Jenkins in 1967, the number of council homes completed declined. This was due to public expenditure cuts being used to combat inflation resulting from that year's currency devaluation. Even so, levels of owner-occupation and council house occupation in England increased to 51% and 30% respectively over the period (Malpass and Murie 1994).

In Birmingham, the local authority role in providing new council accommodation reached a height in the late 1960s with 30,000 council homes produced between 1965 and 1969. The city council was able to rehouse around 17,000 people per year over this period and to cut its huge waiting list. The leap in council housebuilding in Birmingham involved huge changes to the environment of some inner areas with industrialised buildings and prefabricated high-rise flats replacing terraced housing and courts. It also led to further growth in the suburbs with more new council estates in Birmingham's outskirts. By the turn of the 1970s the majority of residents in 'back-to-backs' had been rehoused following extensive clearance, although some tracts of pre-1919 housing existed in the central areas and middle ring of the city. Much of this housing was left to the private sector and increasingly to housing associations who began to acquire and rehabilitate such properties on a significant scale in the late 1970s. As Garside (2000) has commented:

> 'From the early 1960s, housing associations were singled out to tackle an aspect of the housing problem somewhat reminiscent of the 1930s. These were the 'twilight areas' or 'stress areas' suffering a combination of environmental and social problems, untouched by postwar slum clearance schemes'.

During the 1960s, Copec was only carrying out small scale refurbishment schemes, mainly in Birmingham's 'middle ring'. Refurbishment projects were producing around 4 to 10 new homes each year. Some of this work was supported by public funding from the Housing Act 1949 for improvement work. In the late 1960s, however, the Housing Subsidies Act 1967 provided housing associations with new funding to cover acquisition and refurbishment costs. Rehabilitation was becoming a much more important aspect of associations' work. Although the 1970s would see the zenith of refurbishment of 'stress area' properties, the foundations upon which the growth was built can be traced back to the 1967 Act (Malpass). Copec received this new public funding and was able to keep rents low by topping-up scheme costs with Shelter donations.

An early housing refurbishment by Copec Housing Trust in Stirling Road, Edgbaston.

Creating new housing associations in the 1960s

During the 1960s the fortunes of Copec became entwined with Birmingham Housing Trust (BHT) and Wolverhampton Housing Association (WHA). These new housing associations were formed as part of the response to the Shelter campaign, and later merged with Copec to form a large voluntary housing grouping to meet housing needs in Birmingham, Wolverhampton and Sandwell (see chapter 8). BHT and Copec were the two Birmingham housing associations which received support from Shelter. BHT in particular was very close to Shelter. Shelter gave advice and support to BHT as it had similar aims and approaches to the chief beneficiary of Shelter support in London – Notting Hill Housing Trust. WHA was established in conjunction with a local Shelter group but also received financial support from the national Shelter campaign.

Christian and council activism: forming Birmingham Housing Trust

BHT was formed on 9th August 1965 by a group of concerned people who came together to help tackle poor housing conditions endured by many people who lived in Birmingham's inner ring. The people involved in setting up BHT were connected with the University of Birmingham, including its Chaplain Reverend John Duncan, and two students from the Faculty of Social Science and Geography, Liz Clutton and Kit Horton. Neither Liz Clutton nor Kit Horton had seen housing problems like those they encountered in Birmingham. Liz Clutton said:

'I have never seen anything quite like this before and I was appalled by the contrast of affluent areas existing on the fringe of extremely poor ones' (Birmingham Post and Mail 1965).

**BIRMINGHAM HOUSING TRUST
MANAGEMENT COMMITTEE 1965**

Chairman
Reverend John Duncan

Honorary Treasurer   **Honorary Secretary**   **Manager**
Ronald Ind   Peter Loose   Cllr. David Mumford

Committee Members

Mrs Diana Cumberland   Miss A. Clutton
Mrs Kit Deeney   Miss Constance Evason
Miss Muriel Evason   Robert Hope
Reverend C.P. Hutchinson   Brian Leake
Andrew Reddy   Victor Russell
Philip Wiener

Both students were involved in the Student Christian Movement and they attended a housing conference in Liverpool in early 1965, chaired by Bruce Kenrick, because they wanted to do something to help. They approached Kenrick with a view to getting some advice and he suggested setting up a housing association similar in approach to that of the Notting Hill Housing Trust, of which he was Chairman. An initial meeting was held in a cafe in central Birmingham. Attending the meeting were Liz Clutton, Kit Horton, John Duncan and David Mumford, who became the first manager of BHT and later Chief Executive of Copec and Focus. The two Evason sisters, Connie and Muriel, also attended and became management committee members when BHT was established. Connie Evason was a Birmingham social worker who had a keen interest in housing problems in the city. BHT developed strong links with Shelter from its inception with both Bruce Kenrick and Shelter's Director Des Wilson (later the Liberal Democrats' campaigns advisor) providing advice and financial support. Kit Horton commented at the time:

> 'Actually we did not believe we could get it started but with John Duncan and David Mumford's backing and some financial assistance from Shelter we eventually got things moving' (Birmingham Post and Mail 1966).

The group's initial decision to set up a new organisation rather than work through existing bodies such as Copec is an interesting indication that this was part of a new social movement. It drew in new individuals with different values and outlook who would not

Birmingham Housing Trust catered for people in the severest need in the late 1960s. This tranquil scene is at the rear of one of the Trust's projects for 'battered women'.

have had social contact with those involved in Copec. The first formal BHT meeting was held in the front room of the Evason sisters' home. John Duncan was elected as BHT's Chairman. David Mumford, who was also a city councillor and heavily involved in anti-race discrimination work in Birmingham, became the first paid employee. His salary was partly paid for from a Shelter grant. David Mumford was particularly close to Shelter founders Bruce Kenrick and Des Wilson and this relationship enabled BHT to fund its first housing developments. Being a local councillor and prominent member of the local Labour Party also placed David Mumford in a good position to influence city housing policy. To this end and because of a good relationship with the Town Clerk, Walter Wood, and Harry Watton, the Labour Leader of the council, David Mumford was able to persuade the council to lend BHT enough to cover start-up costs and to underwrite BHT's first properties acquisition. BHT was officially launched in September 1965. It was registered as a wholly non-profit making body under the Charities Act 1960 and the Industrial and Provident Societies Act 1965. Its principal aim was to provide alternative housing to people in the city who were living in overcrowded or inadequate housing conditions. As well as Shelter donations and loans from the city council, BHT also received a £3,000 donation from the Notting Hill Housing Trust.

BHT's early work consisted of buying large properties and converting them into self-contained flats. BHT not only hoped to meet housing need but believed that it could make a significant contribution to halting the decline of older parts of the city. The first properties were bought by BHT in February 1966. Its first completed housing scheme was in College Road, Edgbaston. During its five year history before merger with Copec in 1970, BHT showed remarkable tenacity in raising funds for housing investment. BHT's last accounts show that it had received £112,000 in grants from Shelter. During its final year, BHT received £13,000 in subsidies from Birmingham City Council but had

Soho Road, Handsworth. One of the last Birmingham Housing Trust schemes to be developed before the association's merger with Copec in 1970.

a bank overdraft of £32,000. In addition to raising funds from the city council and Shelter, BHT made appeals to the general public through the local media and by issuing stark promotional literature about Birmingham's housing conditions. The public appeal in BHT's last year raised £2,000. Public appeals aimed to raise sufficient funds to top-up loans from Birmingham city council and mortgages from BHT's bank (it claimed to be able to borrow £7-8 for every donation of £1 made). It wished to keep rents as low as possible and envisaged charging between £3 and £4 per week. Over the next five years, BHT acquired and renovated almost 200 homes in Birmingham's central areas. This achievement contrasts favourably with the portfolio of 260 properties Copec retained in its management after its first 45 years!

Tangible assets and overdrafts: a marriage made in heaven

After the merger between Copec and BHT in 1970 (the new housing association became the Birmingham Copec Housing Trust – BCHT – see chapter 8 for a detailed description of the merger), the new housing association had more than 500 rented homes in management or development with an asset value of £1,332,174. As the merger document said at the time:

> 'A merged organisation should be capable of playing a much more effective part in solving the housing problems of Birmingham than the two separate associations could hope to do on their own, and the pooling of resources should make us better able to meet the commitments of an expanding organisation'.

The new association had revenue reserves of £198,000. Its rent roll was £48,000 of which £28,000 of rents were from Copec's properties. The association still had the legacy provided by early issues of share capital, donations and bequests made to Copec in the 1920s and 1930s as well as grants from Shelter in more recent years. David Mumford commented:

> 'Financially, Copec was well positioned; it had about £60,000 sitting in a current account while BHT had a growing debt' (Interview 1999).

Sundry Donations To Copec Totalling £263,014 (1970)	
Organisation	**Amount (£)**
Grants from Shelter	168,863
Wolseley Bequest	44,379
Appeal for Homes for 'Handicapped' People	11,565
Sturge Bequest and Memorial	3,677
Hackett Bequest	2,657
Mrs. W. M. Copeman – Gift of Property	1,250
Cob Lane Sinking Fund	1,273
Common Good Trust	1,000
Reserve for Purchase of Land	700
Dr F. Braid – Gift of Property	500
Peake Trust for Amenities	100
Foyle Trust for Social Needs of Tenants	50

The majority of homes owned were traditional inner city rehabilitated houses in Birmingham's central areas. However, as chapter 3 indicated, Copec had developed a range of 'special needs' housing, mainly for older people and single women. In the late 1960s BHT was also involved in special needs housing; most notably meeting the needs of women experiencing domestic violence. David Mumford commented about the reasons why these groups of people were targeted:

> 'BHT saw itself as working with those who no-one else would. BHT dealt with the excluded – battered wives as they were called then – people who needed rehousing quickly. This was the real purpose of the voluntary sector' (Interview 1999).

Responding to the Shelter call: Wolverhampton Housing Association

Wolverhampton Housing Association (WHA) was formed in April 1967 by a group of the town's citizens as a response to the growing problem of overcrowding, poor housing conditions and neighbourhood decline, exemplified in the 'Cathy Come Home' documentary. WHA was also driven by concern for the town's growing ethnic minority communities and the housing conditions in which they were living. Jim Hewitson, a local estate agent, Keith Berry, Rector of Beckminister Church, and Dudley local authority Councillor David Gregory, joined forces with other local citizens who had connections to the Methodist Church. David Gregory remembers:

> 'We were concerned about the 'monumental forms of tenure' – local authorities and private renting – in the central areas of Wolverhampton giving people little choice. We new of the problems of immigrant communities shown by the Rex and Moore study in Birmingham a year or so before. I was personally interested in forming what was known as 'the third arm' in housing and learning from the European experience (Interview 2000).

They decided to act after inviting Des Wilson of Shelter to explain the options for developing a community-based housing association. A local Shelter group was formed. Supported by Jeremy Riches, a local solicitor, Councillor Bill Clark, Ram Aithal, a local Asian businessman, and the town's Council for Community Relations, WHA was launched and began acquiring and converting property in Pennfields, a predominantly pre-1919 area of terraced housing close to the town centre. WHA's first scheme was a refurbished property called St. George's House on Wolverhampton's Penn Road with ex-offenders referred by the Probation Service as its first tenants (Interview with Jim Hewitson).

WHA's early work was supported by local authority, bank mortgages and from charitable donations from the Methodist Church (£50,000 of investment was a typical annual sum). A fund-raising and membership appeal were also launched in late 1968. Registered as an Industrial and Provident Society under the relevant Acts, WHA was one of only a handful of housing associations working in Wolverhampton at this time. With fifty members initially, the association grew over the next year or so by attracting new members and obtaining further funds through its charitable appeal. It also obtained the support of the Wolverhampton Shelter Group, the Wolverhampton Council of Churches as well as the Probation Service. David Gregory became WHA's first Chairman with Jeremy Riches becoming the Secretary. Staff were employed in 1970 with a full-time manager, John Murray-Barton and an administrative assistant being appointed. Staff costs were subsidised by a grant from Shelter. Over the next five years, WHA grew with about 20-30 properties acquired and converted (Interview with David Gregory 2000), receiving a boost with the grant provisions introduced by the Housing Act 1974. By the end of 1975, despite 'flying by the seat of our pants' (Interview with Bert Massey 1999), WHA had close to 100 homes in management, had begun to work in General Improvement Areas (GIAs) in the town and was seen as the lead association to work in the proposed Housing Action Areas (HAAs) in Wolverhampton's Steelhouse Lane and Pennfields districts.

Arms-length allies: Shelter and Copec

As a longstanding member of the National Federation of Housing Societies and as the main voluntary sector landlord in Birmingham, Copec was invited to receive and spend Shelter funds allocated to Birmingham alongside BHT. Copec's management committee was pleased to receive the invitation to the national Shelter launch and played a prominent role in launching the Shelter initiative locally. While Copec did not take part in the Shelter fundraising appeal, which was taken up in the city by BHT, it received substantial grants throughout the 1960s as the senior 'partner' of Shelter in Birmingham. For example, it received £8,640 from Shelter in 1966 and a further £796 from donations made directly to Copec from concerned individuals locally who had been affected by Shelter's national campaign. It received a further £12,347 and £958 respectively in 1967 and £14,233 and £1,069 in 1968.

Copec's Chief Executive David Mumford and Chairman the Venerable John Duncan with Housing Corporation Chairman Lord Sherman planting a tree to celebrate a housing scheme. The Housing Corporation was established in 1964 but was granted extended powers under the Housing Act 1974 to regulate and fund housing associations.

The 1970s watershed

A prelude to the development of a system of extensive public subsidy for housing associations in 1974 was represented by the Cohen Committee. Set up in 1968 as a sub-committee of the Central Housing Advisory Committee (CHAC), Sir Karl Cohen's committee was asked to review the activities of housing associations and make recommendations (Malpass 2000). Some of the difficulties facing the housing association movement would probably have been resolved by the Cohen Committee had there been more government interest. However, the Labour government had no interest in 'this funny little sector' and Cohen was a leading local authority protagonist (Cullingworth 1979). Copec amongst many housing associations gave evidence to the Cohen Committee and research for the study (DoE 1971) was carried out by Birmingham University's Barry Cullingworth (a Copec management committee member at the time). In actuality, the Cohen Committee never produced its report, although Cullingworth's research report was later published by the Central Housing Advisory Committee (CHAC). (The incoming Conservative government had disbanded the Cohen Committee and passed its responsibilities to CHAC under the Ministry of Housing and Local Government). Despite this, Cohen had performed a valuable function in characterising the housing association sector in 1970 and prepared 'much of the ground for reforms implemented via the Housing Act 1974' (Malpass 2000).

Housing associations: the first funding watershed

The Housing Act 1974 was a watershed in the development of housing associations. The Act enlarged the powers of the Housing Corporation to assist housing associations to develop housing let on fair rents. Fair rents were moderated market rents intended to be fair to both landlord and tenant. They were established by the Housing Act 1974 (Alder and Handy 1985) and set by an independent Rent Officer Service. This effectively removed the right from landlords to exercise any real control over the rents charged. The Housing Corporation was also given the statutory duty to register and supervise those housing associations which wished to be allocated the new grant (Housing Association Grant or HAG). The Housing Corporation's supervisory powers enabled it to conduct enquiries into the running of associations, to wind them up or to freeze their assets. The 1974 Act paved the way for an effective deficit subsidy system to enable associations to make an enlarged contribution to meeting housing need. The 1974 Act did not significantly challenge the local authority monopoly on the provision of 'social housing', but left associations to 'fill the gaps' in housing need (Cope 1999). Both Copec and BHT took up this challenge as we shall see.

The 1974 Act, through its generous new subsidy system and new policies for dealing with older housing, provided the basis for growth in housing association activity throughout the 1970s and laid the foundation for bringing housing associations to the centre of housing policy in the 1980s. The new HAG system was designed to support housing associations during the development process recognising the limited ability to cross-subsidise rents on new housing schemes. HAG funding was restricted to housing associations which were registered with the Housing Corporation. The 1974 Act also introduced Revenue Deficit Grant (RDG) and Hostel Deficit Grant (HDG). This was done in recognition of the vulnerability of association balance sheets and covered a wide range of circumstances in which associations could not reconcile their income and expenditure. Although RDG and HDG were discretionary grants, paid annually to support housing associations' revenue expenditure, they proved to be a lifeline for the majority of housing associations, especially those with financial commitments for housing developed in the 1960s.

Financial strength through merger

The BHT/Copec merger provided the new association with an operational surplus for the early years of the 1970s with reserves averaging £350,000. However, this reserve reduced over the next few years as it was used to subsidise Copec's housing development before mainstream public funding came into being with the Housing Act 1974. The reserve subsidised the costs of growing overheads of a rapidly developing organisation and funding extra support services to tenants and communities (for example, Birmingham Housing Aid Service – see below).

Table (7) – Copec's Financial Growth In The 1970s

Year	Fixed Assets	Mortgage Loans	Share Capital	Loan Stock	Subsidies/ Donations	Gross Rents
1971	1,333,174	853,562	9,700	46,404	34,963	83,036
1972	1,832,057	1,205,593	9,701	46,404	52,155	109,794
1973	2,477,009	1,771,232	9,701	46,404	74,181	167,807
1974	3,053,848	2,367,218	9,702	46,204	95,718	219,222
1975	4,191,061	3,491,960	9,702	46,154	93,792	259,057
1976	6,055,241	5,132,014	6,547	35,760	80,358	348,198
1977	9,753,861	8,141,703	6,508	32,879	86,387	500,721
1978	13,134,096	9,493,825	6,080	31,632	91,210	665,827
1979	18,604,290	10,303,236	6,080	31,632	87,120	743,209

Notes
1. Column 1 – fixed assets – shows the insurance value of Copec's housing.
2. Column 2 – mortgage loans – describes borrowings from local authorities and banks. From 1975, Copec received Housing Association Grant to subsidise housing projects.
3. Columns 3 and 4 – share capital and loan stock – show the decreasing importance of these sources of income. In the late 1970s, some shares and loan stock were surrendered and their value was attributed to reserves.

From 1976, Copec was eligible for the Housing Corporations' RDG and HDG. Copec's reserve position declined rapidly in the late-1970s as it used its funds developed historically to subsidise its new housing development. The association became wholly deficit-funded for the next ten years or so, reliant upon RDG and HDG to cover its growing management costs and costs associated with its increasing number of special projects (see below). However, Copec's asset base grew appreciably (by a factor of thirteen between 1970 and 1979). By the end of the 1970s, Copec managed property with a value of almost £19 million. The rent roll of £83,000 in 1971 grew to stand at £743,000 by 1979 – an increase of close to 800 percent. Copec Treasurer David Corney remarked in 1977:

'The increased scale of Copec's activities is reflected in the Accounts; expenditure of more than £3 million on building, acquiring, converting and improving properties, and a rent roll higher than £500,000 are indications that Copec is now making a substantial impact on the housing scene throughout the West Midlands' (Copec Annual Report 1977).

This scale of activity, of course, was only brought about through the subsidies of the 1974 Act. For example, in 1977 Copec received £509,000 in HAG and £400,000 in RDG (although this latter sum was backdated two years). HDG also enabled the association to expand its provision for 'special needs' groups.

The road to regeneration

In 1969 the government specified a number of key requirements for the formulation of local renewal strategies, including a comprehensive review of older housing, a consideration of the balance between redevelopment and improvement, and the development of area-based improvement. These resulted in the development of the concept of the General Improvement Area (GIA). GIAs had to be located in predominantly residential areas and criteria for selection of GIAs included a secure planning future, the physical potential of the properties involved and residents' and owners' views. Eventually, areas with 300-500 dwellings were suggested as the norm. By 1971, most local authorities had at least one GIA in the pipeline with some formulating a rolling programme of GIA declarations. From 1969 to 1979, 1,300 GIAs were declared in England covering more than 400,000 homes (Gibson and Landstaff 1982).

Steelhouse Lane, Wolverhampton. This so-called 'twilight area' was the subject of major regeneration when a Housing Action Area was declared in the mid 1970s. Wolverhampton Housing Association had already refurbished a handful of properties in the area by 1975, but more housing was improved there after WHA's merger with Copec in 1976 and following the Housing Act 1974. The Act provided substantial public funding to housing associations for the first time from this date. Today, Focus manages more than 300 properties in the area.

The Housing Act 1974 ushered in a different approach to housing renewal. It was a major shift in policy away from the slum clearance programmes of the 1960s (Groves 2000). Local authorities' renewal strategies could include Housing Action Areas (HAAs) and Priority Neighbourhoods as well as more generous grant aid in existing GIAs. Within local authorities' overall renewal strategies, specific factors were to be taken into account including the level of 'social' stress, local attitudes, the physical condition of the housing stock, environmental factors, displacement of local people, the resources required and the prevailing trends in the local housing market. HAAs were seen as the major innovation in area renewal policy and tended to cover about 300-400 homes each. Between 1975 and 1979, 450 HAAs were declared incorporating improvement of 154,000 homes. The majority were in the conurbations, particularly inner city areas (Gibson and Langstaff 1982).

HAAs were to assist in the development of Copec and the Wolverhampton Housing Association with a number of HAAs declared in Birmingham, Wolverhampton and Sandwell containing a significant number of these associations' homes. By 1979, the number of rented homes managed by Copec grew by nearly 600%. The association managed almost 3,500 homes. Most of the growth was achieved after the Housing Act 1974 put financial aid for housing associations on a proper footing for the first time. Between 1970 and 1974, growth had been at about 20-25 percent per year. After 1974, the growth rate increased to 40-50 percent per year. In terms of actual homes produced, the growth in homes in the early 1970s was about 120 per year, whereas post-1974 Act, the growth rate was 400 homes per year. Initially, these homes were provided in Birmingham's central areas, especially in Aston and Small Heath, but increasingly in the middle ring districts of Handsworth, Sparkbrook and Saltley. In the mid-1970s, Copec expanded into Wolverhampton and Sandwell, partly through its merger with WHA, and partly due to its increasing role in urban renewal represented by GIAs and HAAs. Copec began work in the All Saints HAA in Wolverhampton and the Beeches Rd HAA in Sandwell in 1976. As Professor Ken Spencer of the University of Birmingham and a Copec management committee member recalls:

> 'I was asked by the management committee to set-up an area committee in Sandwell to develop links with local people in the HAAs and with the local authority. It took me about 3 years to get off the ground effectively. At this time Chris Patterson, a local Probation Officer took over as the Chairman of the Sandwell area committee'.

It should be noted, however, that despite these successes in Copec's growth, it remained a minor player in stress area renewal. The numbers of properties improved in stress areas at this time by Copec were small in comparison to the totality of properties which needed refurbishment. While Copec carried out a vital job on a small scale, the problems of stress areas remained largely untouched and were to re-emerge as major policy imperatives in the 1990s. However, Copec was playing an increasing part during this period in meeting the needs of 'special groups'. This provision, as in the immediate postwar period, was to be central to Copec's housing development throughout the 1970s and beyond.

Growing emphasis on special needs

Copec's growing portfolio of supported housing schemes for people 'with special needs' meant that a new department was needed – Special Projects. Set-up in 1975 the Special Projects department began to develop and manage a range of schemes, primarily for women experiencing domestic violence, homeless people, the elderly, those with mental health problems and the physically disabled. Managed by Derek Marks throughout the 1970s, the Special Projects department developed a number of innovative schemes. Of particular note are Ashley House, the Clarence Hotel and Tillyard Croft, all in Birmingham. Ashley House provided accommodation for women and children suffering from domestic violence. The Clarence Hotel was a project for homeless men and women. Tillyard Croft, named after the first Copec Chairman, Frank Tillyard, was a mixed scheme for older people, single people living with and caring for elderly relatives and people with physical disabilities.

An early example of a Copec project for people with special needs. This project on the Hagley Road was developed in partnership with the Royal National Institute for the Blind.

The increasing importance of race

Racial discrimination in the private rented sector had been identified by a number of key studies in the 1960s (Rex and Moore 1967). By the 1970s, identification of racial discrimination in the lettings activities of local authorities and housing associations began to emerge (Parker and Dusmore 1976). The 1974-1979 Labour Government enacted the Race Relations Act in 1976 to tackle direct and indirect discrimination on the grounds of race, colour, nationality or ethnic/national origins. As a result, the housing provisions of the Act made it unlawful for housing organisations to discriminate on racial grounds in their provision of accommodation, including the quality of accommodation provided. The Act imposed a duty on the Housing Corporation and local authorities:

> 'To make appropriate arrangements with a view to securing that their various functions are carried out in due regard to the need to eliminate unlawful discrimination and to promote equality of opportunity and good relations between persons of different racial groups' (CRE 1991).

The Commission for Racial Equality (CRE) was established to administer the Act and to investigate cases of racial discrimination reported to it, including conducting formal investigations and issuing of non-discrimination notices on organisations found to be in contravention of the Act. The CRE could, in certain cases, institute legal proceedings against organisations who persisted in discriminatory practices. The 1976 Act was to have major effects on how Copec developed in the next decade (see chapter 5).

Creating new housing organisations in the 1970s

Four housing associations which later merged with Copec to form Focus in the 1990s were founded at this time. They varied considerably in their approaches. Hestia was based in north Birmingham initially and provided general needs housing and housing for special needs groups. St. Chad was an association originating in Staffordshire which sought to provide housing for the people of Lichfield and Tamworth, particularly older people. Shape was established to provide housing and urban renewal in south Birmingham to excluded groups, primarily through shortlife housing (ie housing identified for demolition but improved with minimal funding to provide a 'short life' of about two to five years). Harambee Housing Association was formed in response to the needs of African-Caribbeans in Handsworth, Birmingham. Another organisation was also formed at this time, the Birmingham Housing Aid Service (BHAS), which merged with Copec in 1973. Later still, BHAS merged with Shelter's housing aid service (see chapter 6).

Hestia Housing Association

Hestia Housing Association was formed in 1970 by a group of local businessmen who were committed to improving housing conditions for people on low incomes in Birmingham. Taking its name from the Greek Goddess of health, the new association began its housing work with funding from the local authority and from banks. Members had a breadth of experience in local government and business, both of which proved to be assets in establishing a housing association at that time. At the first meeting of the group on 21st January 1970, it was proposed that the new association should seek registration as an Industrial and Provident Society. The minutes state that:

> 'Since three names are required by the National Federation of Housing Societies for consideration, the following were proposed: Hestia, Goodwill and Focus' (a prophetic choice).

Hestia grew quite quickly and had 65 homes in management by the time the 1974 Act came into being. When undergoing the registration process with the Housing Corporation, Hestia had to restructure its Committee of Management since its Chairman was a local estate agent. New Housing Corporation rules prevented participation by those with conflicting commercial interests. Finally registered in March 1976, Hestia briefly became New Hestia (although 'New' was subsequently dropped). The new Chairman and Chief Executive were Jim Marsh and David Ranceford-Hadley respectively. David Ranceford-Hadley was a local councillor in Dudley. By this time, Hestia had grown to manage 180 properties in Birmingham, the majority in the Handsworth area. Following registration, Hestia became eligible for HAG and over the next few years expanded into Birmingham's Bordesley Green and Erdington districts. Hestia was initially based at Soho Road in Handsworth with six full-time staff. In 1977, the association moved down the road to Soho Hill in Handsworth, an area where the density of housing association activity was high (including Copec and Midland Area). By the end of the 1970s, Hestia managed more than 400 rented homes and had begun to develop housing schemes in Coventry and Dudley.

St Chad Housing Society

St. Chad emerged out of voluntary activities amongst a group of people who had an interest in the housing problems and care needs of older people and people with disabilities in Lichfield and Tamworth. These people formed the first management committee of the St. Chad Housing Society in 1973, which was initially based in Lichfield. St. Chad was strongly linked to the Methodist Church and collaborated on providing a volunteering and visiting scheme as a result of the 'Stay At Home Strategy' produced by an organisation close to it – Methodist Homes. A pilot for this scheme was undertaken first in Lichfield and then expanded to cover the surrounding rural areas of Staffordshire. Primary movers in establishing St. Chad were the Reverend James Hutchens, a Methodist Minister, and John Haggert, also a member of the Methodist Church. St. Chad registered as an Industrial and Provident Society and began with schemes in Lichfield, but later developed schemes in Birmingham, Warwickshire and Tamworth.

Like many small associations established in the early 1970s, committee members undertook housing management tasks. This went on until 1977, when the committee appointed its first staff member, Barbara Whitfield. She had been running the Lichfield Counselling Service and was asked by the Reverend James Hutchens if she would like to become involved. At this time, St. Chad had 24 completed properties and was on site with Merton Court and Avery Court. Barbara Whitfield became Secretary and General Manager. As the stock grew, more staff were appointed, although St. Chad remained a small association.

St. Chad had its first housing developments at Green and Forrest Courts in Lichfield.

These schemes provided flats for rent with care and support for elderly residents of the city. St Chad grew slowly at first since it depended on members to provide the time and effort to organise housing management duties and to administer contractors for its first schemes. Registration with the Housing Corporation followed the 1974 Act and enabled a small amount of HAG to be obtained to supplement funds from the city council, charitable donations and mortgages. By the end of the 1970s St Chad still only had 35 rented homes in management.

However, by working with local authorities, particularly in Lichfield and Tamworth, where close relationships were developed with the Conservative-led councils, and with the probation service and voluntary agencies, St. Chad was able to grow slowly. Taking advantage of HAG from the Housing Corporation after 1974, St Chad built homes for older people, couples of all ages and single homeless people. Housing with support became a major component of the St. Chad's work, and by the time merger discussions began with Copec and Hestia to form Focus, St. Chad managed 300 properties, 90% of which were purpose-built. More than half were located in Lichfield, with the majority of the remaining properties spread out over Staffordshire and Warwickshire.

Shape Housing Association

Shape was formed in the 1970s to meet the needs of inner city dwellers, predominantly in the southern and central areas of Birmingham. The housing association specialised in shortlife housing in it early days (this is housing designated for demolition within 5 to 10 years but is refurbished with minimal finding to provide temporary housing for people in need). As Shape Chairman Rick Groves explains:

> 'Shape had the very simple idea of working with young people on the streets and teaching them to acquire skills such as bricklaying, carpentry and plastering. At the same time they were renovating shortlife housing which was to become their home. It was fraught with difficulty, but from its origins, Shape always linked the two ideas of housing and employment for the very poorest groups' (Interview 1998).

From its early days, Shape was concerned with the life chances of tenants and other residents in the neighbourhoods where it operated. In 1982, its committee called for a report on the unemployment levels amongst its tenants and the opportunities for the organisation to tackle this problem. The consequences of this report were to further affect Shape's development into an agency dedicated to community renewal (see chapters 6 and 7). Shape also developed a range of supported housing schemes in Birmingham such, as South Road House and the Snow Hill hostel, which was acquired from the private sector and refurbished. Shape grew throughout the 1980s and early 1990s to manage more than 600 homes, most notably for single people and ethnic minorities.

Harambee Housing Association

The origins of Harambee can be traced to the growing African-Caribbean community in Handsworth in north Birmingham. Community groups such as the Afro-Caribbean Self-Help organisation came together after the 1974 Act to obtain public funds for investment in local housing, but controlled by the community. Harambee, as an 'umbrella' agency for community organisations, was formed in 1975. It registered as a housing association with the Housing Corporation a year later. Key individuals were Maurice Andrews, a local solicitor, and Beany Brown, a community activist. During the 1970s, Harambee grew slowly. A small number of refurbishment schemes were completed in Handsworth over the decade and Harambee became an influential housing agency in the local community (Interview with Dave Butchere 2000).

Birmingham Housing Aid Service

Birmingham Housing Aid Service (BHAS), funded through the Urban Programme and via the city council, was established in 1970 as a small voluntary organisation providing independent housing advice. By 1973, its was facing financial difficulties after its three year grant ran out and the city council was unable to continue funding. Copec came to its assistance, since Copec's Chief Executive David Mumford recognised the need for housing advice services in Birmingham. In 1974, BHAS moved to Copec's offices in Colmore Row. Throughout the 1970s, Copec grant-aided BHAS. Although BHAS was funded by Copec it remained an independent advice service providing advocacy services to Copec tenants as well as to the general public. Throughout the 1970s BHAS was a main source for referring potential tenants to Copec since Copec had closed waiting lists at the time. Publicising BHAS in its Tenants Newsletter (August 1974), Copec stated:

> 'The Birmingham Housing Aid Service goes into peoples' problems in great detail and can sometimes come up with an alternative or temporary solution while our waiting list is closed'.

This meant that Copec agreed to accept onto to its waiting list a proportion of BHAS' clients as well as nominated households from local authorities. As Chairman John Duncan remarked in the 1974 Annual Report:

> 'BHAS, offering housing aid and advice to people, regardless of whether they are to be helped by Copec, continues to work under our auspices, seeing about twenty new applicants each week. We welcome this new organisation as a reminder that people in their suffering are our central concern'.

During the 1970s, BHAS was one of Birmingham's major housing advice centres and worked closely with other agencies, such as Shelter Housing Aid, the Trinity Advice Centre in Handsworth and various Citizens Advice Bureaux. Copec, like other housing associations, had a non-political stance on housing and related issues, which made it difficult for it to take sides on particular issues. Over the next few years, BHAS was able to amass a large database of Birmingham's housing needs and used this information to lobby local government. For example, BHAS research reports on housing needs in Birmingham were extensively quoted in the city's Housing Investment Programme (HIP) submissions to the Department of the Environment. The BHAS mission said:

> 'We also seek, by way of reports, campaigns and the media to raise public awareness of current housing issues and to highlight the increasing difficulties faced by many who are in housing need'.

BHAS dealt with 8,000 enquiries from people each year and staff there interviewed and gave in-depth advice to around 1,500. Of all people interviewed by BHAS in the 1970s, 50 percent were provided with general advice, twenty-five percent were referred to Copec for rehousing and twenty-five percent were referred to other housing associations, hostels for the homeless or other housing schemes in the area.

Copec expanded its operations into Saltley and West Bromwich in the late 1970s. Shown here are two of its area housing offices right in the communities they served. The first (left) is in Alum Rock Road Saltley. The second (below) is the West Bromwich office in the town's High Street.

Looking towards the 1980s

The associations who later made up Focus had developed significantly in the 1960s and 1970s, with many of the key elements of the later enlarged association actually coming into being in this period. But changes to the housing system and to the housing association movement in particular, which followed the election of Mrs. Thatcher's Conservative government in 1979, were unprecedented. It was the 1980s and early 1990s which were to enable Focus to come into being and for the housing associations which existed in 1979 to become part of a larger and more diverse voluntary housing sector.

5

Diversification and the push for growth 1980-1993

The 1980s brought radical change for housing associations like Copec as Conservative governments sought to transform the welfare state, and with it, social housing (Cope 1999). Copec's previous concentration on refurbished housing for rent in inner city areas, its reliance on public deficit funding, and its small although valuable contribution to meeting needs in the West Midlands were all transformed in this era. Between 1980 and 1993, Copec grew considerably as housing associations became the major providers of new social housing. Copec reorganised itself into a group structure with subsidiaries providing housing for sale for non-traditional groups and new services to tenants in flatted schemes. The funding regime in this period enabled Copec to move from an organisation run on deficit to one which made a surplus on its rents. Millions of pounds of private finance were raised for new housing developments, including developments outside of the West Midlands conurbation. The association continued to meet housing needs, however, including those of people with care and support requirements. The 1980s also saw the end of the Copec name itself. Copec merged with two other associations – Hestia and St. Chad (see chapter 8 for more detail) and became known as Focus. Issues dealt with in this chapter can be grouped under six key headings:

- **A move to the right** – shows how the Conservative governments of the 1980s incorporated housing associations into an increasingly commercial environment.

- **A growing social enterprise** – traces the growth of Copec in the 1980s as it became the largest housing association in the West Midlands and set about urban renewal on an increased scale – also describes how the ethnic minority communities, established in inner areas in earlier decades, began to increasingly shape the development of some aspects of the association's housing service.

- **More than bricks and mortar** – Copec, and its later merger partner, Shape, developed people-centred initiatives and approaches which mirrored moves towards social investment in the late 1990s.

- **One, two, three ..... developing group structures** – Copec, Hestia and Shape developed distinctive group structures for their organisations as housing associations extended their operations in many different directions.

- **Sheltering under the Focus 'umbrella'** – Focus was formed from a strategic alliance of Copec, Hestia, St. Chad and Midland Area Housing Associations. Shortly after, all but Midland Area merged into a unitary housing association – Focus.

- **Responding to the housing market** – completes the final years of Conservative administrations when Focus became a large social enterprise, and reacted to market-driven housing policy initiatives.

The opening of Ralph Barlow Gardens in 1982. Seen here (from left to right) are Sir George Young MP, Housing Minster in the late 1980s, who opened the scheme, Copec Chairman John Duncan and local MP Geoff Rooker (Labour's Housing Spokesman in the 1980s and later a Minister in the Department of Agriculture). Ralph Barlow Gardens was a sheltered scheme for older people in Kingstanding, Birmingham, named after former committee member and housing manager Ralph Barlow.

A move to the right

A Conservative government headed by Prime Minister Mrs Thatcher came to power in 1979. The new government set about tackling the country's housing system from a market-oriented position. The Housing Act 1980 embodied the approach of the new government. The government sought to promote owner-occupation as the 'natural' tenure, it wanted to reduce the role of local housing authorities in providing housing and it tried to stimulate the private rented sector. The aspect of the 1980 Act which covered all of these policy themes was the introduction of the Right To Buy (RTB) for council tenants. The RTB effectively meant that most council tenants, and tenants of non-charitable housing associations, were entitled to purchase their homes at substantial discounts from their council landlords. Over the next nine years RTB reduced local authority housing stock by 1.1 million. By 1989, the council sector had fallen as proportion of all housing from 30 to 24 per cent (Malpass and Murie 1994).

The 1980 Act also introduced new tenancy arrangements for public and private tenants and implemented a new funding regime for public housing (with general reductions in assistance for local authorities to provide new housing or to replace that housing lost through the RTB). In the wake of the Act some new funding types for housing associations were introduced (particularly Improvement for Sale and Sale on Shared Ownership). Charitable housing associations like Copec and Hestia established non-charitable subsidiaries to carry out these activities because it was not clear whether housing for sale could be deemed as a charitable purpose.

Mr. and Mrs. Faulkner in 1984. They were winners of the Copec 'best garden' award. Copec established the award in the late 1970s to encourage tenants to improve their gardens. This mirrors Copec's approach in the 1920s and 1930s when the association saw the importance of gardens and greenery to tenants living in Birmingham's central areas.

The Housing Act 1988

Larger changes for housing associations came in the Conservative government's third term when it sought to extend private sector influences on social housing. This was the key principle of the Housing 1988 Act, which sought to increase the volume of housing that could be provided for a given amount of public money by mixing public and private funds. This principle still applies today (Cope 1999). Only the amount of grant awarded and not the amount borrowed privately was counted as public expenditure. The down side of the policy was that it meant that rents rose to cover the costs of repaying private loans, usually raised from banks and building societies, and the housing benefit system 'took the strain'. Consequently, the affordability of associations' rents became compromised and the housing benefit bill inexorably rose (Malpass 2000).

A second objective of the 1988 Act was to increase value for money in the funding of associations by requiring them to take on a greater proportion of the risk of housing development. The phasing-out of the Revenue Deficit Grant system was related to the riskier financial environment being introduced. Instead, the Rent Surplus Fund was introduced whereby housing associations could build-up reserves on their rent accounts to support future borrowings for housing investment from private lenders. The result of this overall framework, which came into being in April 1989, was that associations had to operate in an increasingly commercial environment, having to ensure value for money at all stages of the development process and in their operations generally (Cope 1999).

Trafalgar Road, Balsall Heath. The large newbuild houses, designed to meet the needs of extended families were designed to fit in with the rest of the Moseley Village Conservation area. This is a prime example of one of Copec's 'mini-communities' with newbuild and refurbished housing developed to meet community as well as individual needs.

A growing social enterprise

The 1980s were a decade of substantial growth for Copec. At the beginning of the 1980s, Copec managed 2,746 rented homes and had a development programme of 834 homes. It also managed around 250 'bedspaces' for people with special needs. Over the next 10 years, the rented housing stock in management grew by 73 per cent, although the number of homes in development declined by more than 50 per cent from a highpoint in 1980 to a low point in 1987, before picking up again after the introduction of private finance. The association was still housing people in the severest housing need in predominantly refurbished housing. The majority of Copec's tenants were unemployed, one third were lone parent families and close to half were from an ethnic minority group (Gulliver 1989). The combination of disadvantaged tenants and an ageing housing stock made Copec's housing management task a difficult one, as was recognised by the Glasgow University national study in 1988, in which Copec was a case study landlord:

'Less advantaged groups and stocks of poor quality dwellings may create a more complex, and potentially more costly, management task than more advantaged tenants and better quality dwellings'.

Opened in April 1985 by HRH Princess Diana, the Good Shepherd Centre was an innovative scheme for homeless men in Wolverhampton replacing the existing low standard night shelter situated opposite. The 54 bedspace scheme, with total scheme costs of £860,000, was developed using funding from the local authority and the Housing Corporation. A special committee to oversee the development of the project was established comprising the Corporation, Wolverhampton Council and Copec representatives. Seen here are Copec's Wolverhampton area committee members and staff alongside the Little Brothers of the Good Shepherd, a Catholic Brotherhood of monks, who managed the scheme.

A range of supported housing schemes continued to be developed, including those for people with mental health problems, the disabled and what previous decades had called 'battered women'. The insured value of Copec's rented stock increased from £29 million to £145 million over the same period – a growth in the asset base of 400 per cent, reflecting the growth in house prices, particularly in the late 1980s (Copec Annual Reports and Accounts 1980s). In 1989, Copec received its largest ever cash allocation from the Housing Corporation of £13 million, equivalent to 14 per cent of the West Midlands total Approved Development Programme. David Edmonds, Housing Corporation Chief Executive of the time, said:

'This large allocation of housing funds reflects the high esteem in which Copec is regarded by the Housing Corporation' (Tenants Newsletter 1989).

Diversification and the development of communities

Many of the schemes developed by Copec in the 1980s, and Focus in the early 1990s, were newbuild. A key aim was to develop 'mini self-contained communities' in the inner areas of Birmingham, Wolverhampton and Sandwell (and later Dudley). Schemes were typically of 20 to 60 units, and often included a supported housing element. Most of these schemes were developed on in-fill sites in inner areas and were developed with a range of partners, including local authorities, health authorities and voluntary agencies. Of particular note were Copec's newbuild estates at Trafalgar Road, Brighton Road, Kitts Green, Wilkes Green and O'Keefe Close in Birmingham, and Avery Road and Petford Street in Sandwell.   Major projects for special needs groups were also continually developed in this period, such as the Good Shepherd Centre in Wolverhampton for homeless men, and Flint Green House in Birmingham, established to offer rehabilitation services for people with mental health problems. A further project for homeless people – Rolfe House – was refurbished in Smethwick in the 1980s.   Stanley Lodge, in Wednesbury, was an additional project for people recovering from mental illness. Copec was also a major provider of housing for women and children experiencing domestic violence. In partnership with the Haven (one of the country's leading charities for this group of people), the association developed a number of refurbished and newbuild projects, including those for Asian women. In the early 1990s, after the formation of Focus, the association refurbished a former council tower block in Wolverhampton renamed Phoenix Rise.

Table (8) – Growth In Rented Homes In the 1980s			
Year	**Rented Homes Managed**	**Rented Homes In Development**	**Total Homes**
1980	2746	834	3580
1981	3057	628	3685
1982	3312	532	3844
1983	3576	474	4050
1984	3710	495	4205
1985	3931	498	4429
1986	4173	518	4691
1987	4455	414	4880
1988	4587	473	5060
1989	4764	630	5394

'Bread and butter' work

Copec had a decentralised housing management structure throughout the 1980s, with an office opening in Handsworth in 1982 to house its north housing management team. In the mid-1980s, a further housing management team was established in Birmingham – West – so that the association had housing offices adjacent to the majority of its stock holdings. A final office in the south of the city was opened in 1990. Copec also had branch offices in Wolverhampton and Sandwell.

As the 1980s progressed, funds allocated by the Housing Corporation increasingly centred upon newbuild housing rather than the traditional refurbishment work which Copec had undertaken for the previous sixty years. 'Typical' funding from the Housing Corporation in this period was £6 million of which one third was for newbuild housing. Even so, Copec managed to obtain funding for its 'bread and butter' refurbishment work throughout the 1980s. For example, 150 homes were refurbished in 1986/87 before funding for this type of housing work began to decline more steeply. The Housing Corporation's funding for major repairs also dried-up during this period. Copec only received £70,000 in 1987/88 and £80,000 in 1988/89, although the amounts awarded for this type of work were often topped-up at the end of the financial year if resources allowed. Funding for shortlife housing became one of the few ways in which Copec could sustain a 'meaningful' refurbishment programme with the number of shortlife homes in management increasing to 150 by the end of the 1980s. The majority of these shortlife homes were local authority properties due to be demolished for road widening purposes with 'lives' from 5 to 10 years.

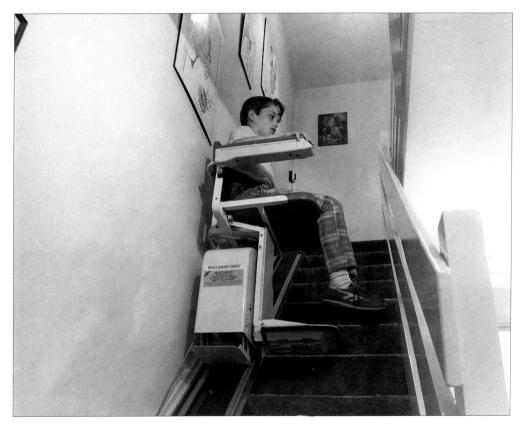

Copec's 'aids and adaptations' programme.

Qualitative improvements to the Copec housing stock were also signalled in 1987 and 1988 with a small number of 'deconversions' of so-called 'large over small' flats in larger houses being reconverted back into large family houses for letting to extended Asian families. By 1989, Copec was investing considerable resources in rehabilitating homes which had been in management for some time or which were owned but had never been improved. In the last year of the decade, Copec invested more than £2 million in housing renovation. Sixty percent of this investment was used to lengthen the lives of existing housing. Lillian Cope House, a hostel in Washwood Heath, received £300,000 of investment. In 1993 the 'Warm Homes' initiative was started whereby tenants living in some of the oldest properties received new heating and improved insulation.

Renovation work on one of Birmingham's few remaining Georgian Terraces was launched by Clare Short MP in March 1989. Copec bought the Grade II listed buildings from the Gooch Estates who had owned them since before the First World War. Ten of the homes were tenanted but the other eight were derelict and required total refurbishment. Many of the sitting tenants had lived in these homes for many years including one who was born in George St West in 1908. Copec's 'aids and adaptations' programme began in the early 1980s with tenants' homes being converted to meet the needs of tenants with disabilities. Grabrails, stair lifts, lower worktops and wider doorways were provided in about 10 homes per year on average over this period. During the 1980s, Hestia and St. Chad, later to merge with Copec to form Focus, developed a range of housing schemes for special needs groups, particularly sheltered schemes for the elderly. By the time Hestia and St. Chad joined Focus, they managed 2,000 and 350 rented properties respectively (Annual Reports and Accounts 1980s and 1990s). A later merger partner, Shape, also developed housing for 'special needs' groups in this period, especially schemes for homeless men.

Bosnia-Herzgovina House. Focus provided this scheme for refugees from the former Yugoslavia. Throughout the 1980s and into the 1990s, the association housed hundred of refugees, mainly from the world's chief trouble spots. Vietnamese 'boat people', Somalians and Yemenis were housed in Wolverhampton and Birmingham. Coventry received refugees from Bosnia. Today, Focus is assiting the Home Office with dispersal of asylum seekers from Kent and is working closely with the Midlands Refugee Council.

Racial discrimination – shaping the service

Racial discrimination in housing and responses by housing associations and their representative bodies (for example the NFHA) had major effects on the way Copec operated from the early 1980s onwards. Although there had been evidence of racial inequality in housing going back to the 1960s (eg Rex and Moore 1967), it was not until the 1980s that it became 'central in debates about housing management' (Morris and Winn 1990). Professional organisations in housing (eg CIH, NFHA) had issued various codes of practice. The Housing Corporation had published a range of strategies and the Commission for Racial Equality (CRE) later produced a code specifically for rented housing. These publications were underpinned by the Race Relations Act 1976 and housing legislation in the 1980s.

Willie Salmon and Souad Akbur outside Copec's head office in Paradise Circus, Birmingham. They were two in a long line of graduate housing management trainees. Copec established its in-house scheme in the mid-1980s to attract more people from ethnic minorities into housing.

Research at this time showed that black and minority ethnic (BME) groups were more likely to be living in poorer quality housing with fewer amenities than their white counterparts (Brown 1984). They were disproportionately located in inner city areas (for example in Copec's areas of operation such as Birmingham, Sandwell and Wolverhampton), and dispersal policies allegedly adopted by Birmingham City Council were found to be racially discriminatory (Henderson and Karn 1987). Asian households were more likely to be living in older, terraced housing and African-Caribbeans were most often living in council flats. Overcrowding and lack of basic amenities were more prevalent in housing occupied by BME groups (Brown 1984). Research concluded that BME groups experienced greater housing stress because of their average lower incomes, their higher unemployment rates, the circumstances in which they arrived in England and because of racial discrimination in the housing market. Racial discrimination was found in all major tenures, including housing associations (Morris and Winn 1990).

During the 1980s, research into the racial discriminatory practices of housing associations was under-developed in contrast to that for council housing. Despite this, a small number of studies (Niner 1985) demonstrated that similar patterns of discrimination occurred in the housing associations studied. In particular, housing association lettings policies were shown to be discriminatory, both directly and indirectly. BME communities often had less access to association waiting lists because of their lack of knowledge of housing associations:

> 'The sheer number and variety of housing associations.....may in itself have discriminatory consequences.....the indications are that black and Asian people are less likely to be aware of housing associations or may regard them as white institutions' (Morris and Winn 1990).

The areas of operation of housing associations also had discriminatory effects. Those working in inner city areas had large proportions of BME tenants; those working in the suburbs and rural areas less so. Access to associations' housing in the 1980s was primarily through 'referral agencies', local authorities nominating households from their waiting list and direct approaches by applicants. All were shown to have potentially discriminatory effects with BME communities less likely to be able to 'use the system' (Niner 1985). Even when BME applicants had obtained access to housing association waiting lists, discriminatory lettings practices still tended to follow (for example BME applicants tended to wait longer before receiving offers and were subsequently to allocated poorer quality housing) (Niner 1985). The evidence for racial discrimination in housing associations began to mount at a time when Copec's practices were called into question. In the 1980s, Copec's housing service was shaped more by the need to tackle racial discrimination than by most other factors at the time.

This emphasis was sharpened when the CRE served a statutory non-discrimination notice on Copec in 1981. This notice required that Copec put right its policies and practice within six months. It was served after a memorandum about the letting of a particular property showed possible racial discrimination in the way the association was letting its homes. While the CRE was supportive of Copec and its work in the inner city, it recommended that Copec should introduce ethnic monitoring and anti-racism awareness training for staff. Ethnic monitoring revealed that lettings to BME households was about 50 percent. This was a greater proportion than for existing tenants at the time, indicating that Copec was enabling BME communities access to its housing. Variations existed between Copec's housing management offices. In areas of high BME concentration, lettings to BME applicants were proportionately greater (for example, 69

Comedian and 'Dudley lad' Lenny Henry opening OSCAR House in 1989. This was the country's first specialist scheme for sufferers of Sickle Cell Anaemia – mainly people of African and Asian descent.

percent and 50 percent respectively in Birmingham areas of Handsworth and Saltley; 45 percent in Sandwell and 38 percent in Wolverhampton). Lettings to BME applicants were lowest in Copec's Special Projects department (at 20 percent).

Table (9) – Copec's Lettings By Ethnic Group In The 1980s

Period	African/ Caribbea	Asian	Other Minority Ethnic (1)	European (2)
1981/82	39	7	4	50
1982/83	38	8	5	49
1983/85	38	10	6	46
1985/86	31	9	3	57
1986/87	29	10	3	58
1987/88	32	11	4	53

Notes
1 –   Mostly Chinese and Vietnamese.
2 –   At this time included Irish households.

While ethnic monitoring revealed that Copec's performance in housing BME applicants was generally good and considerably better than the BME communities' representation in local populations, some of the qualitative aspects required attention. Monitoring in 1981/82 revealed that 'black tenants were more likely to occupy a flat than their white neighbours' (Empson 1983). It was discovered that this effect was caused by the predominance of flats in Handsworth where the largest proportion of Copec's lettings to BME applicants was registered. Over the next decade, Copec responded by providing more houses in the area, particularly newbuild homes to tackle this problem.

Monitoring throughout the 1980s also found that Asian applicants were under-represented in Copec's lettings, even in areas of high Asian concentration. In Saltley for example, only 13 percent of lettings were made to Asian households in 1986/87. Copec reviewed the reasons for this in consultation with the local Asian community and found that many Asian people did not know about Copec. Coupled to this, their need for larger homes on average was not being met by Copec's housing development programme. This liaison generated larger number of applications from Asian people so that lettings to them doubled over the next year in Saltley to 26 percent. In the longer term, Copec addressed its shortage of large homes by 'deconverting' flats back into houses and providing larger newbuild houses in the area.

Shaping of Copec's service began with the findings from its ethnic monitoring and the responses which were developed to them. Its housing development programme not only shifted towards providing more large homes in areas of high BME concentration, but it also developed policies and practices to ensure equality of opportunity. Like many housing associations at the time Copec developed a fair housing policy and equal opportunities programme. However, Copec also began to develop housing and services designed to tackle racial discrimination in housing and employment. Copec introduced an employment and training scheme for BME people, including graduates, wishing to pursue a career in housing, at its own expense. Housing management trainee Souad Akbur said about the scheme:

> 'When I saw Copec's training scheme advertised it seemed just what I was looking for. Although I have only been on the scheme for a short period I have found the time interesting and am optimistic about my future' (Tenants Newsletter 1988).

It also implemented compulsory racism awareness training (Copec Policy documents and Annual Reports 1980s). Specific schemes were developed for ethnic minority needs (for example, the needs of Sickle Cell Anaemia suffers and those of elderly Asians). Copec worked closely with a range of BME organisations to provide better access to its housing and to obtain advice on how to develop its housing service.

More than bricks and mortar

Copec, and later Focus, continued work started in the very early days of the association to provide other services besides housing. At this time, Shape (see below) was also developing an approach to community regeneration and urban renewal which was to mark it out as one of the most innovative housing associations of the period. Copec worked in partnership with community agencies to tackle poverty, provide employment, improve community safety, meet social needs and provide housing advice and support. More detail is provided below.

- **Anti-poverty approaches**: Copec was a founder member of the Wolverhampton Housing and Exceptional Needs Group (WHEN), which promoted a unified front with community agencies to tackle poverty in the town. WHEN developed a range of services for Wolverhampton's inner area communities including a furniture renovation project, a community skip scheme to remove rubbish and advising on up-take of welfare benefits. In Birmingham, Inner City Partnership funding from the Department of Environment was used to provide a range of projects to combat poverty in inner city areas (Annual Reports 1980-1985).

- **Providing employment and training**: In April 1986, Copec joined with local organisations in Handsworth to create Inner City Contracts Ltd (ICC) to help provide jobs in inner areas of Birmingham, and to ensure that employment opportunities were taken-up by local people, especially those from ethnic minorities. ICC was launched as a response to some of the problems which had precipitated the riots in Handsworth in 1985. The report by Julius Silverman's's committee (1985) into the Handsworth disturbances had commented:

> 'The possibility of employment being attracted to Handsworth is diminished. Everyone is now worse off, not least the rioters whose prospects of employment have moved still further away'.

ICC was formed by Copec and other local associations – Shape, Friendship, and Bournville Village Trust – alongside Handsworth community agencies, most notably the African-Caribbean employment agency – ACAFESS. ICC was launched, with attendance from local press and television media and with backing of a £3,000 grant from the Prince of Wales Royal Jubilee Trust. The objective of ICC was to bid for local building and renovation work and use the resources of the founding organisations to ensure that the tenders won could provide employment for local people. Besides 'bread and butter' work in Handsworth and the surrounding areas, two notable successes for ICC were the £600,000 council contract to improve houses in Saltley and shortlife work for Copec and other associations in partnership with East Birmingham Community Jobs, a company evolved from the Community Programme funded by the Manpower Services Commission. This work enabled local people to find both employment and training in building skills – an early example of an intermediate labour market being developed (Copec annual reports, tenants newsletters 1985-1991). However, ultimately, ICC was wound-up. Copec Chief Executive David Mumford, echoing the difficulties Shape had with stimulating job creation, explains the background:

'Job creation was an emerging issue at this time and there many jobs in inner city areas which needed doing. Our approach was to do this as part of Copec. It didn't work and we pulled back. It took our eye off the main ball.....we were spending more time running these peripheral activities than the main housing business. Although there were good economic arguments, the problem was management time and commitment. In hindsight we were big enough to try it but we couldn't keep it going, but at least we tried' (Interview 1999).

- **Community safety**: Copec took part in a range of neighbourhood improvement initiatives in stress areas in Birmingham, Wolverhampton and Sandwell, providing security measures such as burglar alarms, window locks and better perimeter fencing around properties. One particularly successful scheme in the mid to late 1980s was with the Birmingham Area Improvement Team (BAIT). BAIT grew into Inner City Securities (ICS) in 1990 – a group made up by local housing associations and city council representatives. A £500,000 grant was raised by ICS to undertake security work, primarily in the Westminster Rd area of Handsworth, with a significant amount of the security work undertaken by Inner City Contracts Ltd, a community agency working closely with ethnic minority building contractors. John Morris, deputy housing director of Copec at the time and Chair of ICS commented:

'Surveyors contacted all those living in the area and then carried out an in-depth assessment of potential for improvements. We arranged for the National Association for the Care and Resettlement of Offenders (NACRO) to organise a survey of those homes which have been improved. Three quarters were more than satisfied with the work' (Tenants Newsletter 1990).

- **Community facilities**: Copec joined forces with Midland Area Housing Association in 1990 to invest £56,000 in two play areas in Handsworth and Aston using an Inner City Partnership grant. The vehicle formed to deliver this work was CHOISE Ltd, a company jointly owned by Copec and Midland Area. In Sandwell, Copec undertook a series of neighbourhood surveys in the late 1980s in conjunction with the North Smethwick Housing Development Trust (NSHDT) and an embryonic ethnic minority housing association – SADAHHA – to find out the views of the predominantly Bangladeshi community about the housing and community facilities they required in an area marked for clearance by the local authority. The survey was designed in-house by Copec with interviews undertaken by North Smethwick people. The views expressed by the community were used to develop a community action plan which resulted in new housing provided by Copec and eventually a resource and living centre for the Asian community (Annual Reports 1980s).

- **Giving housing advice:** Birmingham Housing Aid Service continued to provide housing advice, support and advocacy during the late 1980s and into the 1990s. Its case-load gradually increased in the late 1980s from 978 households helped each year to 1,331 over the 1985 to 1990 period. The proportion of those seeking advice who were homeless or facing homelessness also increased from 24 percent to 43 percent over the same period. As BHAS faced the 1990s, it began to expand its services and to target particular services on defined groups. In 1992, BHAS launched its Private Landlord Initiative which consisted of a package of help and information to encourage landlords to make their properties available to homeless single people on benefit (BHAS Reports 1980s).

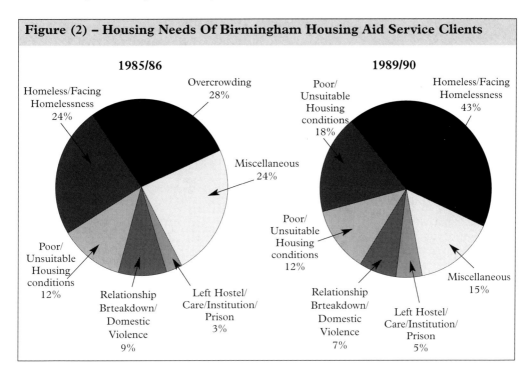

Figure (2) – Housing Needs Of Birmingham Housing Aid Service Clients

1985/86

- Homeless/Facing Homelessness 24%
- Overcrowding 28%
- Miscellaneous 24%
- Poor/Unsuitable Housing conditions 12%
- Relationship Brteakdown/Domestic Violence 9%
- Left Hostel/Care/Institution/Prison 3%

1989/90

- Poor/Unsuitable Housing conditions 18%
- Homeless/Facing Homelessness 43%
- Poor/Unsuitable Housing conditions 12%
- Miscellaneous 15%
- Relationship Brteakdown/Domestic Violence 7%
- Left Hostel/Care/Institution/Prison 5%

Shape's sure approach to community renewal

From small beginnings in the late 1960s (see chapter 4) Shape came to exert a considerable influence within the social housing world of the 1980s and early 1990s. This influence cannot be charted by conventional indicators such as housing stock holdings alone, although Shape had increased its rented homes to over 600 by 1993. From its beginnings, Shape placed equal importance on its influence on the quality of life for tenants and other local people by operating employment, training and community initiatives. To carry out these initiatives Shape sometimes established satellite companies. Some of these initiatives, many of which have now been incorporated into Focus or taken over by other housing and community organisations, are described here (Interviews with Rick Groves 1999 and Chris Wadhams 2000).

- **Added value**: Shape was one of the first associations to recognise that it was able to develop an 'added value' approach to its housing work. Shape believed that value could be added to communities by investment above and beyond the provision of rented homes. In particular, it proposed that a value added approach could provide job and training opportunities for inner city residents; strengthen the local economy; preserve and build community identity. Shape proposed that inner city, community-based housing associations could be the key catalysts for people-centred renewal rather than the more traditional housing-led renewal of the 1960s and 1970s. A primary reason for this, Shape argued, was that community based associations had areas of activity which corresponded well with inner city areas where neighbourhood renewal was necessary. New organisational frameworks were not required as housing associations already had this capacity if it was harnessed correctly. A second reason given was that associations were there 'for good' in that they had the long term investment in their housing, their services and neighbourhood offices to protect. In addition, associations had access to capital and revenue income streams (ie grant and rent) not available to traditional community organisations and were able to lever-in significant resources into their neighbourhoods. Lastly, Shape argued that not only were associations already in touch with local residents and their requirements but they had also become more entrepreneurial thanks to changes in housing policy (Wadhams 1990).

Members of Shape's Ambassador's Programme for skilled unemployed people. Left to right are project coordinator Peter Sullivan, and trainees Maurice Francis, Chris Smith and Frank Inniss.

The launch of People For Action in the early 1990s by Shape and South London Family Housing Association. The tree signified the intended 'growth' of the organisation. Shape's Chief Executive Chris Wadhams is seen holding the tree. At the back is Steve Bendle, Chief Executive of Family at the time. PFA went on to become a major organisation supporting housing associations in their 'housing plus' activities.

- **People-led renewal**:   Shape began to implement its vision by sponsoring government employment and training programmes such as the Community Action Programme, the Community Enterprise Programme, Employment Training and Training for Work. These programmes were most often centred upon the Sparkbrook area of Birmingham. As Shape Chief Executive Chris Wadhams explained:

'With Friendship we 'unilaterally' set up the Sparkbrook Neighbourhood Improvement Area in 1985. This was not a statutory Renewal Area declared by the city council but a means for the two associations to try to improve Sparkbrook through our own efforts. We focussed our housing investment on support for those in greatest need. We also lobbied the DoE for Special Programme urban regeneration funds' (Interview 2000).

Shape began to develop a framework for satellite companies to enable increased and targeted implementation of its non-housing work. In 1987, Shape formed a new company – Shape Urban Renewal Enterprises (SURE) Ltd – to engage more actively with the local community. SURE developed in the next three years and by the early 1990s owned a building company, a fully-equipped garage, a garden centre, a plastering workshop, a metal shop and an architects practice, called SURE architects. The BICBUS register was compiled in the early 1990s to record local businesses which were committed to equal opportunities. This was an attempt to implement 'contract compliance' in housing association purchasing and contracting arrangements. Shape also refurbished its main office in Digbeth to incorporate a conference and training facility and small managed workspaces for local, embryo businesses (Interviews with Rick Groves and Chris Wadhams in 1999 and 2000).

- **Links to Europe**: Shape became involved in a number of training programmes funded via the European Social Fund in the early 1990s. The association was a founder member of the European Social Action Network which enabled trainees from Birmingham to work on a project in Brittany. The Ambassadors' Project was initiated by Shape under the European Union's Horizon scheme to train up to 25 people at a time in one or more construction trades and to start their own businesses. Another scheme, called the Colours Of Europe Scheme was established to train young unemployed people to design and paint murals (the Shape mural can still be seen on the side of the Snow Hill hostel). Links to Europe were furthered when Shape became involved in the French Foyer Federation, which was an organisation promoting housing projects for young people, offering on-site training and liaison with local employers. Shape began planning its own Foyer project earlier than most other foyers developed in England – in 1992, it was eventually built by Focus in 1998 (Platts 1995).

- **People For Action**: Shape's community businesses provided employment and training to the people of Sparkbrook. They were, in the main, marginally profitable, with any profits being used by Shape and it sister organisations to enable this type of activity to be expanded. Shape believed that it was developing a favourable climate in its key areas where community businesses could prosper (ie a 'sheltered market'). Pleased with its early success the association established a new organisation in 1990 with South London Family Housing Association called People For Action (PFA). Originally funded by the Wates Foundation and the Department of the Environment, PFA was an innovative approach to neighbourhood regeneration, which today is a large independent organisation supported by more than 80 housing associations nationally (Shape records, Interview with Chris Wadhams in 2000).

People For Action: Key Functions In the Early 1990s

- assist with physical and environmental improvements;
- implement vocational training schemes;
- support existing local businesses;
- assist with business start-ups in its areas;
- develop community businesses;
- improve security and assist with reductions in crime;
- offer technical support to existing or embryo community groups.

Source: Shape brochure 1993

One, two, three ..... developing group structures

Funding for housing associations to take part in new initiatives, such as homes for sale, was introduced by the Housing Act 1980 (see earlier in this chapter). Both Copec and Hestia began to develop more complex structures in this period. This was because it was not clear at the time whether such activities were compatible under the charitable objects of these associations. Shared ownership activities in particular at the time tended to be carried out by non-charitable subsidiaries. And so Copec began to develop a group structure to incorporate three subsidiaries set up to work on new initiatives. Hestia also set up a home ownership subsidiary, Hestia Homes at this time. In May 1981 Copec Two was formed followed by Copec Three in September 1983 and Copec Services in March 1984. Two related, but less successful developments at the time, were Inner City Contracts and the Heart of England Unit Trust.

- **Copec Two** provided low cost homes for first time buyers and tenants of other housing associations and local authorities. Registered with the Housing Corporation as a non-charitable housing association and under the Industrial and Provident Societies Act 1965, Copec Two refurbished existing homes for outright sale, mainly in the inner areas of Birmingham, Wolverhampton, Sandwell and Dudley. It also built new homes available on a part-rent/part-sale basis (shared ownership) where buyers could purchase between 25 per cent and 75 per cent of the market value. Shared owners could 'staircase' upwards or downwards, buying an increasing share of their homes until they were outright owners, or relinquishing part of the value and

Shows typical Improvement for Sale homes of the 1980s, developed by Copec Two, the home ownership subsidiary of Copec.

increasing the rented element as their circumstances changed. Funding was by the Housing Corporation and through mortgages raised from building societies, Copec Two offered a complete home-buyers service, including help with mortgages, removals, conveyancing and internal amenities such as carpets and decoration. Between 1982 and 1989, Copec Two was developing around 70 to 90 homes each year on average, taking advantage of the booming housing market as the economy emerged from recession in the mid to late 1980s.

- **Copec Three** provided low-cost homes funded without public subsidy for sale to first time buyers and tenants of housing associations and local authorities. Copec Three was not required to register with the Housing Corporation but was an Industrial and Provident Society, able to make profits which were used for new building projects and to 'covenant' back to the charitable Copec parent. These profits subsidised rented housing projects for traditional client groups. Copec Three was an innovative housing association in trying to develop new forms of funding arrangements for housing in the West Midlands. In 1985, it issued a prospectus for the 'Heart of England Unit Trust' to encourage pension funds to invest directly in the housing market. Unfortunately, the Trust did not proceed as responses to the prospectus did not meet the target fund of £2 million.

- **Copec Services** was formed as a company limited by guarantee to provide a gardening, window cleaning, communal areas cleaning and landscaping service to gardens and properties. Service were usually provided for flatted housing schemes and supported housing. By the end of the 1980s, Copec Services was undertaking servicing work on 400 Copec properties with a year-on-year sales turnover of its services of around 30% over the 1984 to 1989 period. Costs of service provision were covered by a service charge, eligible for housing benefit, within tenants' gross rent payments. Servicing visits to Copec schemes were usually fortnightly. As well as undertaking servicing work at Copec properties, Copec Services worked on behalf of other housing associations, such as Hestia, Servite and Birmingham Jewish, and for the private sector. Copec Services worked on behalf of a hotel chain to provide landscaped gardens and provided the groundworks for London-based property developer Tilbury Homes at a 100 homes site at Clee Hill, Shropshire. While never making more than a small annual profit, Copec Services provided valuable services to many tenants who could not undertake such work themselves or who lacked the income to arrange services themselves.

Profits from Copec Two and Copec Three were redistributed within the Copec Group through a special reserve. After consideration of their own internal investment requirements, profits of about £120,000 each year were transferred to the special reserve. By 1989, an accumulated reserve stood at £531,000. The major elements of this reserve were profits made on outright sale of properties by Copec Three and those made by Copec Two 'staircase' sales (these occurred when shared owners bought extra or the remaining shares in their properties' equity) (Copec Policy documents, Annual Reports 1980s). Copec Two and Copec Three became Focus Two and Focus Three respectively after the 1991 merger. Copec Services became Focus Services but traded only a further two years before being wound-up because of poor cost-effectiveness.

Sheltering under the Focus 'umbrella'

By the mid-1980s, Copec had grown to be one of the top twenty largest housing associations in the country through previous mergers, new development and diversification of activities. It had moved a long way from providing refurbished housing for rent to the deserving poor in the 1920s and 1930s. But the financial climate, embodied in the Housing Act 1988, meant that the challenge for housing associations was to raise private finance to enable continued housing provision. Larger housing associations, with their greater asset bases, were more likely to obtain the lion's share of public funding since they could raise private finance at more attractive rates of interest. This was crucial to accessing public grants (Cope 1999).

Newland Court, Coventry. One of the last Hestia schemes for older people built in the 1980s before merger with Copec and St. Chad to form Focus in 1991.

Focus was formed in 1989 as an 'umbrella' organisation to assist four West Midlands associations meet the challenges of the Housing Act 1988, especially in terms of raising private finance. The four associations were Copec, Hestia, Midland Area and St. Chad which provided the new association with an enlarged asset base, on which to raise larger tranches of private finance at lower rates of interest than was possible by the individual associations. The four associations issued a prospectus for potential partners, regulators and investors. Shape had entered discussions about becoming part of Focus in the negotiations' early days but decided not to take this initiative further. As John Duncan, Copec's Chairman, said in 1989:

'A 65th birthday party usually marks a retirement, but for Copec it merely paves the way for new ideas and initiatives designed to meet the demands of the next decade and beyond. By joining with Hestia and Midland Area Improvement Housing Associations, and St. Chad Housing Society, Copec has formed Focus Housing Association to pool the resources of all four members. The advantages of such an arrangement are many and varied. The members will be able to secure enhanced financial resources through public funding and private loans. They will also be able to call on each other's expertise to improve services they provide, and to widen the range of housing options available to those of limited means'.

The joint stock holding of the four associations was more than 9,000 homes in the West Midlands conurbation and in Staffordshire, Shropshire and Warwickshire. For the next two years, the Focus Group of housing associations worked together. While member housing associations retained operational independence, they made joint bids to the Housing Corporation for funding and raised private finance together. However, it soon became evident that three of the Group's associations wished to pursue discussion about forming a unitary association. Midland Area decided that it did not wish to pursue this option and withdrew from the group. Focus became a single housing association in 1991 (see chapter 8 for more on the merger).

The Focus Prospectus: Key Objectives In 1990

- give an improved comprehensive service for existing and potential customers;
- secure access on a group basis to enhanced financial resources and the better management of those resources to meet challenges and risks;
- develop human resources in terms of technical and managerial skills;
- become the leading provider of social housing in the West Midlands;
- maximise opportunities for securing real economies of scale.

Sourxe: Focus Prospectus 1990

Holy Cross Court. A scheme developed in 1992 for people over 60 years old in Coventry. Such schemes represented the wider geographical areas covered by Copec when it became Focus after merger with Hestia and St. Chad in 1991.

Responding to the housing market

The Housing Act 1988 effectively created a new 'housing market', sometimes called a quasi-market, to 're-privatise the housing association sector' (Randolph 1993). Raising private finance, competing for public subsidy and responding to a plethora of government market-driven initiatives were all aspects of the post-1988 regime. Copec, and Focus from 1991, had to deal with the quasi-market if it wished to remain a major player in the housing association sector.

Copec began to raise private finance for housing in 1987 under the Housing Corporation's Challenge Funding initiative. Over the next seven years, Copec, and then Focus, raised around £70 million from a variety of private financial institutions including, the Housing Finance Corporation (THFC) and Nationwide Building Society. The 1980s saw Copec's financial strength grow appreciably. The association became a large social business operating in the West Midlands. Growth in financial strength can be shown in the value of the association's fixed assets (ie mainly the housing stock in ownership). Between 1980 and 1993, the association's asset base grew by an average of 68 percent per year to stand at £252 million in 1993. The association came out of deficit financing in the late 1980s, particularly after the 1988 Act enabled associations to retain surpluses as reserves against which to borrow private finance. From 1989 as Copec, the association's annual reserves grew from £63,000 to £4.6 million as Focus in 1993. Rental income accelerated considerably. The Focus rent roll in 1993 was close to £16 million compared to the Copec rent roll in 1989 of just under £6 million.

Fysh Street in Shrewsbury. These properties were listed buildings which Focus refurbished using Living over the Shops (LOTS) funding from the Housing Corporation in the early 1990s.

Between 1991 to 1993, Focus not only expanded more into rural areas, building on the legacy of St. Chad, but started to develop outside the West Midlands for the first time. Rented housing was developed in West Wiltshire in partnership with West Wiltshire Housing Society, which had been established by Focus as a local authority stock transfer vehicle. Focus sought stock transfers in West Wiltshire, in Hinckley and Bosworth, the East Midlands, and Worcester at this time. Focus also expanded into Milton Keynes, where both rented housing and housing for sale by Focus Two were developed. This expansion required considerable resources. Not only in senior staff time, but also is use of reserves to compete with associations already firmly established in the targeted areas. In addition, the association continued to follow new funding initiatives, such as Do-It-Yourself-Shared-Ownership and Living Over Shops (LOTs) (Annual Reports 1990s).

Table (10) – Focus Housing Stock By Type And Location At End Of 1993

Local Authority	Self-Contained Homes	Supported Housing	Homes For Older People	Total Homes Managed	Total Lettings
Traditional Core Areas					
Birmingham	5356	285	90	5731	1083
Wolverhampton	1004	142	103	1249	326
Sandwell	769	69	–	838	220
Dudley	287	–	–	287	111
Coventry	704	7	78	789	125
Walsall	44	–	–	44	54
Non-Traditional Areas					
Lichfield	267	21	33	321	66
Tamworth	143	–	–	143	47
Warwick	9	–	–	9	3
East Staffordshire	10	25	–	35	2
South Staffordshire	61	–	–	61	5
Bromsgrove	66	–	–	66	22
Shrewsbury And Atcham	4	–	–	4	4
Stoke-on-Trent	11	–	–	11	11
Solihull	–	4	–	4	4
The Wrekin	5	–	–	5	–
Wychavon	6	8	–	14	6
Outside West Midlands					
Milton Keynes	70	–	–	70	11
West Wiltshire	15	–	–	15	16
West Oxfordshire	2	–	–	2	2
Total	8833	561	304	9698	2118

Perhaps a useful illustration of how housing associations were driven by government-backed market considerations in this period was the case of the Housing Market Package (HMP). As Garside (2000) has commented about how associations were used at the time:

> 'Central government was increasingly using them to 'tweak' policy in other sectors.....to reduce the glut of private dwellings through a purchasing package in 1992/93'.

In his Autumn Statement of 1992, Conservative Chancellor Norman Lamont announced this new, one-off fund for housing associations to buy empty and repossessed homes and let them to homeless families or others in housing need. The HMP was part of the Government's approach to tackling the slump in the owner-occupied market, which had seen record repossessions by building societies and the emergence of 'negative equity' as a major concern in may areas of the country (Cope 1999). Some £580 million was made available to just 27 of the country's 2,300 housing associations to undertake this work. Focus was one of only a handful of West Midlands housing associations to receive HMP funding of £14 million. Adding £11 million of private finance, Focus launched 'Operation Advent', to mark the time of year when the HMP funding was made available, to acquire 578 properties across the region – more than 28 percent greater than its original target of 450. One snag with the HMP was that associations had to identify and buy properties by the end of March 1993. Focus established two purchasing teams which acquired a range of properties. Some were brand new homes acquired from building companies, often with small and previously unoccupied housing developments bought 'off-the-shelf'. Most were older, private homes repossessed by building societies in inner city areas or repossessed RTB council houses. Focus liaised with its local authority partners for the purchase of council properties. Focus also used the HMP to try to increase the number of large homes, with three or more bedrooms, in its housing stock (Annual Report 1994). Tony Bowron, Focus' Operations Director commented at the time:

> 'The scale of the task with which we were originally faced was immense, but we put together two top-level teams and have been working all hours to make it a success. We were very careful to ensure that the homes we bought met the needs of local people and worked closely with local authorities to make sure that this new initiative forms part of their strategies to meet housing needs in general'.

The first homes bought under the HMP were let in February 1993 following comprehensive surveying work by Focus' maintenance staff, identification of necessary improvement work and reconditioning or minor repairs where required. Focus' and other associations' work on the HMP received praise from the Housing Corporation when West Midlands Director, Philip Champness said:

> 'Housing associations in the region have done exceptionally well with the HMP. They have shown that they can respond quickly and effectively to the programme to purchase vacant houses. An added bonus has been the meeting of housing needs which are a priority for local authorities. I congratulate Focus on their achievements' (Tenants Newsletter 1993).

However, undertaking a programme on such a scale over such a period of time, much of it in areas where Focus did not already have a presence, made this difficult to achieve. While this programme had provided another opportunity to demonstrate the ability to deliver government objectives, it also contributed to a loss of community focus and sense of overall purpose for housing management. The very speed of the programme also exposed Focus to greater risks of fraud as the National Audit Office investigation (2000) indicates:

> 'Focus was a major recipient of the Housing Market Package funding, receiving £15.5 million with which it bought 577 empty houses and flats, mainly from builders and building societies, although 57 were bought through dealers. The corruption and overpayments at Focus affected only a small proportion of these sums'.

Phoenix Rise – Focus' first refurbishment of a former local authority tower block in Wolverhampton in 1993.

Moving towards social investment

We have seen that Copec, Hestia and Shape developed group structures with subsidiaries that provided a wide range of housing and services to tenants and people in their communities. Diversification, and the resulting growth in the scope of activities, were the order of the day. Following the merger of Copec, Hestia and St. Chad to form Focus, the association was even more   growth-centred and provided low-cost home ownership through successor associations to Copec Two and Three – Focus Two and Three. Hestia Homes was disbanded after the merger. The growth strategy included expansion outside of the West Midlands for the first time.

In the late 1980s and early 1990s, Shape was developing an innovative approach to community renewal. Focus had extensive links with Shape from the 1980s and cooperated on a range of initiatives aimed at renewal of depressed communities (for example, Focus liaised with Shape on its European links, including the visit to the French Foyer Federation). As 1993 turned into 1994, however, the link between Focus and Shape was to become permanent as Shape found itself financially over-extended and sought, at the insistence of the Housing Corporation, a merger partner (see chapter 8).

By the end of this period it was becoming apparent that growth for its own sake was beginning to cause problems for the organisation's identity and ethos. Questions such as development for what and for whom were beginning to be raised by the management committee. The next chapter takes the story forward into the mid 1990s when Focus undertook a radical re-appraisal of its role and direction, and sought to re-connect both with changing government agendas and with its own organisational roots.

6

Social investment: the modern era 1994-2000

The 1994 to 2000 period saw a further fundamental transformation in Focus. Following the retirement of David Mumford, Chief Executive of Copec and Focus since 1970, a new Chief Executive, Richard Clark, was appointed. Richard Clark's background was marked by a long commitment to urban renewal in the most disadvantaged communities. As a former Housing Corporation Regional Director and local authority manager, Richard Clark brought perspectives of both regulator and the public sector to his new role. Changes in direction, outlined in this chapter and set in a broader context in chapter 7, show a return to inner city roots and retraction of operations from the outlying areas into which Focus had moved in its push for growth in the early 1990s. The chapter describes Focus' evolution into a Social Investment Agency, linked to its merger with Shape Housing Association, and the launch of a new type of group structure under the charitable parent organisation – 'Prime Focus'.

Pine Court, Wednesbury. The final stage of the scheme was opened in 1999 by Gwen Stafford Good, Major of Wolverhampton. Pine Court was operational from 1990. It was a Registered Care Home, but deregistration by Focus, completed in 1998, enabled the scheme to offer a new management philosophy and extra services, such as self-development services in the scheme's activity centre. The scheme now offers individually tailored, flexible care and support packages to residents, who have increased rights following the deregistration process. The process of deregistration, believed to be a national 'first' for a housing scheme for older people, was carried out in close partnership with Wolverhampton MBC's Social Services Department.

- **Housing associations as principal new providers** – housing policy in the 1994-2000 period, under which both Conservatives and Labour governments placed increasing competitive pressures on housing associations as the main providers of new social housing, to become more efficient and move into regeneration activities.

- **Focus at the crossroads** – the association's organisational thinking changed, geographical expansionism was dropped and Focus re-committed to the inner city.

- **Back to the future: old lessons relearned** – Focus rediscovered its past as an urban renewal agency but modernised its approach to cope with new realities, including setting up a unit to manage community regeneration activities.

- **Social enterprise: managing in the late 1990s** – Focus forged new ways to deal with its position as a large social enterprise.

- **People-centred renewal** – the concept of the Social Investment Agency began to be implemented in practice with tenants and communities placed at the centre of Focus' strategy.

- **The 'supertanker turns': Prime Focus** – new organisations were created and old ones were recast into a new group structure with a new name.

Housing associations as principal new providers

The 1990s were a decade of major change for housing associations. In the early part of the decade housing associations became the principal providers of new social housing while local authority house building almost ceased. This left associations to meet new housing needs while local authorities were left to 'patch-up' or transfer their dwindling stock of council housing to secure funds for re-investment (Cope 1999). Between 1990 and 1994, around £2 billion annually of public investment had been made available to housing associations producing more than 120,000 homes (Housing Corporation 1996). Cuts in public grant, as part of a wider restraint of public expenditure to housing associations in 1995 to 1998, meant that housing development was undertaken with an increasingly large private financial component (Malpass 2000). As investment declined, housing associations had to compete with each other for public grant at lower levels, with most associations unable to develop at all (Cope 1999). The increasingly commercial climate in which government asked housing associations to operate also placed an emphasis on value for money and cost-effectiveness as has been described by Garside (2000):

> 'It has been said that......the character of housing associations was transformed from the 'charitable' to the 'commercial'. Primarily this was because the government fundamentally altered the funding regime, introduced fixed and steadily reducing grant levels and reliance on private borrowing. Associations, therefore, became subject to the discipline of the money markets. They responded by resorting to competition between one another, deals with local authorities over nomination agreements and compromises over building standards'.

A dramatic decline in housing refurbishment followed, due to the relatively high cost compared to building new housing. Investment in inner city areas subsequently declined, with a shift to building in suburban and rural locations (Cope 1999). Focus followed this shift. By 1994, newly built housing accounted for about two thirds of Focus' housing development programme and most was located outside of inner city areas. Some housing associations and their trade body, the National Federation of Housing Associations, were increasingly concerned about the quality of new homes, the rents charged for them and the large numbers of tenants forced into the poverty trap (Cope 1999). Focus' rents almost doubled from £25 to £43 over the 1988 to 1993 period. Housing investment for both associations and local authorities was moving away from 'bricks and mortar' to subsidising higher rents. Malpass (2000) comments about this trend:

'Significant change......was the shift away from general subsidies for local authorities and capital grants away from housing associations into means-tested housing benefit, which had grown to £11 billion in 1995/96'.

The Bismillah scheme, completed in 1996, was originally a Shape project. The Bismillah is located on the edge of Birmingham's Jewellery Quarter, adjacent to the key areas where Copec reconditioned its first housing in 1926. It was a former silver factory located within the Newtown and South Aston City Challenge area. The project involved rehabilitation of the existing Bismillah building, which provided 90 flats, with 60 newbuild flats built at the rear of the building around a large courtyard. The project, with total scheme costs of £5 million, provided 150 flats with a high level of security (eg closed circuit television, door entry systems), a laundry room, on-site housing management presence, concierge staff and a private lounge for residents' use. Eight flats were specifically designed for wheelchair users. The ground floor is let for retail usage and houses Focus' Social Investment Centre.

New roads to regeneration

Despite these problems for housing associations and their tenants, new opportunities emerged with the introduction of a plethora of regeneration policies. These policies, such as City Challenge and the Single Regeneration Budget, aimed to revitalise run-down or inner city areas through a competitive bidding process (Brown 1999). This provided renewed opportunities for housing associations like Focus to meet community needs. Partly in response to these new initiatives, and to the findings of a series of research reports (David Page 1993, 1994) the Housing Corporation formally introduced the concept of 'Housing Plus' into its funding and bidding strategy. Housing Plus was not new to housing associations such as Focus and Shape (indeed, both were pioneers – see chapters 2,3 and 5), but the Housing Corporation saw the initiative as cementing associations' work in disadvantaged communities through the provision of community facilities and support for vulnerable tenants (Clapham et al 1998). As the Housing Corporation (1997) stated:

> 'Significant evidence continues to emerge that the task of managing social housing is now different from the past. Not only do tenants need a wider range of services to support their tenancies but tenancy management can no longer be divorced from the needs of the wider community......in such circumstances, a revised approach to social housing becomes essential. A Housing Plus approach is an important element of the management and development of social housing into the 21st century'.

The Housing Plus approach was particularly applicable to Focus' tenants. Tenants were characterised by high levels of economic and social deprivation (and still are). Only 15 percent were in full or part-time work; more than 85 percent were eligible for housing benefit; their average net weekly income was just £85; around one third were lone parent families; 45 percent were from an ethnic minority; and 1 in 10 tenant households had a person with a disability or long-term illness.

Examples of 'social investment' work. The first shows Aston Single Regeneration Budget development ('Breaking the Cycle'). The second shows a multi-cultural effort to improve the environment in Small Heath.

New Labour, new opportunities?

1997 saw the election of a Labour government for the first time in 18 years. The new government was keen to develop policies to combat social exclusion in areas of greatest disadvantage.   But it also retained many of the spending plans of the previous Conservative government for the first two years of its office. While it introduced a range of new policies for housing and regeneration (DETR 1998), the government also sought to curtail rent rises and housing benefit growth. Increases in housing investment, in the form of capital receipts accumulated by local authorities from the sale of council houses since 1980, went mainly to local authorities. Investment in housing associations saw little increase (Malpass 2000). Yet the Labour government continued to build on some of the most positive aspects of the regeneration policies of the previous government. It retained but modified some regeneration programmes (such as the Single Regeneration Budget) and introduced its own (for example the New Deal for Communities).   Some new funding was made available, but as Mullins and Riseborough (2000b) found in their study of housing association responses to the new policy agenda, the key activity for housing associations in the post election period was to demonstrate their relevance to the new government's project:

> 'The election of a new government presented a window of opportunity to convince ministers and civil servants that they had a useful role to play in the new policy agenda..They had also begun to demonstrate their role by engagement in the earliest pilot stages of emerging programmes such as welfare to work – demonstrating that 'what mattered was what worked'.

Focus at the crossroads

While Focus had responded positively to government housing agendas since the watershed of 1988, it was grappling with a certain organisational 'split personality' in 1994. Its traditional work had been in the inner city and catering for special needs groups. The poverty and disadvantage of its tenants and their communities had always been primary concerns. But in recent times the association had placed expansionism at the top of its organisational agenda. This was increasingly causing distress for Focus' management committee. It was concerned that housing was being increasingly provided in suburban and rural locations to the detriment of existing tenants in cities and towns (Committee Seminar 1994).

Rents on new build properties in these new locations were high and growing. Alongside this, Focus' tenants in the inner city were living in older, deteriorating housing, most of which had been built before 1919 (although it may have been rehabilitated more than once).   Both tenant satisfaction and stock condition surveys were showing that tenants in older properties were less satisfied with their homes, which were now overdue for modernisation, as this quote from a Wolverhampton tenant at the time shows:

> 'For the past five years I have experienced great difficulty keeping my home warm during Winter. I think this is because of the very high ceilings and there being only two gas fires in the house (Tenants Newsletter 1994).

While tenants' satisfaction with their homes overall had increased during the 1990s, some were still dissatisfied. As well as dissatisfaction with older homes, some tenants were also dissatisfied with the space standards and amenities of many new build properties, as a tenant from Handsworth commented in 1994:

> 'I wish you could provide more houses with 3 or 4 bedrooms, make the bedrooms bigger and put in fitted wardrobes. Better heating, coloured bathroom suites and improved gardens would also help. Generally all Copec's houses look the same from the outside – we need a greater degree of choice' (Annual Report 1995).

The final phase of Focus' Black Country Region's newbuild scheme at Exeter Road, Smethwick. The scheme was developed in partnership with Sandwell Council and Nehemiah and John Grooms Housing Associations.

Stock-taking

By 1994, Focus had grown to be the largest housing association in the West Midlands. At this time it was one of England's largest 15. With more than 10,000 rented homes, Focus was developing across the West Midlands, mainly in the conurbation, but increasingly in the rural areas of the region. This was partly due to the 1990 merger with St. Chad Housing Society which provided Focus with 270 properties and subsequent opportunities to expand beyond Focus' urban base. Housing projects were developed across Shropshire and Staffordshire, close to St. Chad's main areas of activity in Lichfield and Tamworth. Focus also developed housing up until 1994 in West Wiltshire, Milton Keynes, Oxfordshire and Buckinghamshire. Growth in both the number of homes developed and the areas into which Focus expanded were defining characteristics of the early 1990s (see chapters 5 and 7). Even so, the legacy of previous housing development from 1925 onwards meant that the majority (92%) of properties remained in the conurbation. Most were located in the inner areas of Birmingham, Wolverhampton, Sandwell, Coventry and Dudley. Focus' Coventry stock holding came from the merger between Copec and Hestia. Mergers with Shape and Harambee in 1994 and 1995 added to the stock of inner city housing and the number of supported housing schemes (see chapter 8 for more detail).

With the arrival of Richard Clark in 1994, the expansionist strategy was abandoned and a principle of 'responsible growth' was introduced in its place. Focus withdrew from its 'outposts' in West Wiltshire and, through agreements with Knightstone Housing Association and the West Wiltshire Housing Society disposed of the management of its stock there. Plans to expand outside the West Midlands were put on hold, despite offers of stock transfer from local authorities in the South-West, and Focus set about a business planning exercise to 're-shape the organisation'. A series of business planning exercises were carried out over the 1994 to 1999 period, culminating in the development of the 'Social Investment Agency' concept and the foundation of 'Prime Focus' (Business Plans 1994-1999). As Mullins and Riseborough (2000a) report in a study of 'What Housing Associations are Becoming', it was quite common in the late 1990s for housing associations to review their business strategy in the light of both a changing environment and their core social values:

> 'It is possible to identify linkages between values and (business) strategies.....it is clear that some decisions were rejected because they were not consistent with values.....leaders were conscious of their roles as leaders of values based organisations, and their decisions were, therefore, likely to be influenced by factors that could not be justified entirely on a business case basis'.

The Focus 'Responsible Growth' Principle – Key Elements

- Targeted housing development, at a much lower level than in previous decades, as part of a wider strategy of neighbourhood and estate renewal;
- Paying more attention to the existing housing stock, predominantly in areas of low demand, to improve the quality of housing and its desirability;
- Expanding its repertoire of development activities into market renting, the provision of home options and services to owner-occupiers and flexible tenure.

Focus was not willing to proceed in the ways of the early 1990s, when growth was the driving force. As public spending on housing associations declined and the proportion of public grant for housing development fell, Focus was increasingly mortgaging its asset base and using reserves to compete (Cope 1999). This was putting pressure on rents and the delivery of services to tenants. In 1994, Focus' loan portfolio was about £90 million and grew to £140 million in 2000 as the table below shows, despite a reduced rate of growth in new housing. Much of the increased borrowing was to fund the Home Improvement Programme (see below).

Table (11) – Focus Private Loans (£ Millions) By Lender At March 2000

The Housing Corporation	10.34	Haven Bond	16.00
Nationwide Building Society	21.25	Allied Irish Bank	5.00
Halifax Building Society	0.54	Britannia Building Society	1.94
HALO	9.99	Co-operative Bank	4.97
West Bromwich Building Society	1.54	Housing Corporation	4.72
The Housing Finance Corporation	16.00	Staffordshire Care	1.89
National Westminster Bank	17.04		
Abbey National Building Society	30.00	Total	141.22

Chief Executive Richard Clark 'accepting' a £20 million cheque from Abbey National Building Society in 1996. These funds from the private sector were used in Focus' development programme and to support the association's Home Improvement Programme.

Focus' management committee decided to discontinue developing large tracts of new housing without first reviewing the direction the association should follow for the next five years. A major change at the top took place in 1996 when John Duncan retired as Chairman. He had been Chairman of Birmingham Housing Trust, Copec and Focus for more than thirty years. John Duncan was succeeded as Chairman by Dr Peter Knight, Vice Chancellor of the University of Central England, who was a committee member of longstanding, who marked his election by commenting:

> 'The policy of development expansion cannot continue unabated. Focus has acknowledged that we need to put greater emphasis on the services we provide, in particular the repair and maintenance of our existing homes. While Focus will maintain an important development function, it recognises that housing is actually about people, not bricks and mortar, and it is on the people who are our tenants that we should concentrate our efforts' (Annual Report 1997).

At the same time Focus was seeing growing rates of vacancies in its traditional areas alongside other housing associations operating there. Housing in inner city areas was particularly under pressure with vacancies in areas such as Birmingham districts of Handsworth and Sparkbrook; All Saints in Wolverhampton; and Smethwick in Sandwell climbing as potential tenants were housed in other sectors (especially the private rented sector) (Gulliver 1999, Nevin 2000). Consequently, Focus' approach to housing development and renovation in the late 1990s had to respond to these changed realities. Moreover, Focus realised at this time that responsible growth had to be related in some way to ensuring that a locality would be improved by its intervention. In previous decades, social landlords had tended to focus on growth and lose sight of the impact on localities or tenants.

Key Themes Of Focus' Business Planning (1994-1999)

- The type and location of housing work to be prioritised:
- The balance between organisational growth and the needs of existing tenants;
- The probability of new housing policies to be enacted and their likely direction;
- How the association was to be governed and managed;
- The emergence of community regeneration as a core activity;
- And the financial strengths which the association could call upon to underpin its chosen strategic direction.

Source: Business Plan 1997

Despite Focus' decision to couch its housing development within a responsible growth principle, the association retained considerable assets to carry out its work. This contrasts with its earlier history when more limited impacts could be made on the problems of disadvantaged communities. By 1999, Focus managed £0.5 billion of assets in its housing stock, an increase of 59 percent from 1994. This was due mainly to mergers with Shape in 1994 and Harambee in 1997. Development of new housing projects, such as the Focus Foyer, the Ladywood estate in Birmingham and smaller new build and refurbishment schemes across the West Midlands also played their part. During the 1994 to 1999 period income from rents, service charges and other miscellaneous sources grew by 47 percent to stand at almost £40 million. At the same time, reserves increased by 117% to just under £25 million (Annual Accounts 1994 1999).

Table (12) – Focus Housing Association – Financial Performance 1994 To 2000 And Forecast Up Until 2004 (£ Millions)				
Year	Total Income	Assets (Stock)	Annual Surplus	Reserves
1993/94	26,920	290,616	3,665	11,396
1994/95	25,803	384,385	3,189	14,585
1995/96	32,792	413,156	3,538	18,123
1996/97	36,490	423,412	3,090	21,213
1997/98	37,281	447,782	1,244	22,457
1998/99	39,273	466,466	1,030	23,487
1999/00	39,626	462,064	1,282	24,769
2000/01	39,219	476,281	502	25,271
2001/02	40,701	488,890	921	26,192
2002/03	42,169	501,167	1,020	27,212
2003/04	43,708	513,422	1,096	28,308

Focus supported the Aston Reinvestment Trust (ART) in the late 1990s. ART was a 'community bank' formed to mirror banking experiments in the USA. Focus and Birmingham Settlement, another ART supporter, developed a close link with Loyola University, Chicago, where the South Shore Bank provided a model for ART. Seen here is Focus' Chief Executive Richard Clark investing in ART to the tune of £10,000. Accepting the cheque on ART's behalf is Sir Adrian Cadbury. This is an example of Focus' 'reciprocal philanthropy' developed in the late 1990s. It also demonstrates Focus' ongoing relationship with the Birmingham Settlement and the Cadbury family, which goes back to the 1920s.

Back to the future: old lessons relearned

During the late 1990s, Focus' work reflected several concepts, some of which it rediscovered from its past. First, regenerating and helping to build positive identities of localities. Second, adding hope and responding to community needs. Third, adding dignity and independence to peoples' lives. This is best illustrated by the range of schemes provided by Focus at this time. Major examples were the Bismillah project in Birmingham's Jewellery Quarter gateway; the regeneration of a former local authority estate in Gilby Road, Ladywood; and involvement in Estate Action on the Galton Village estate in Sandwell. These were large schemes for Focus, involving up to 200 properties, developed in partnership with local authorities, communities and tenants. They sought to regenerate deprived local authority estates and mixed-use communities as well as provide much-needed housing (Annual Reports 1994-99).

New lessons learned: adapting to the changed environment

Like many housing associations, Focus was posed with real dilemmas and challenges as a result of government policy, the poverty of tenants and the economic pressure on its financial position resulting from using private finance to develop new housing. The nub of these challenges concerned the role Focus should play in meeting the needs of its communities and the balance to be struck between providing new housing and investing in its ageing housing stock. The changed economic, social and demographic environment which faced Focus in 1994 meant that it had to make policy choices about its future. As Garside (2000) has concluded about the position of the voluntary housing movement in the late 1990s:

> 'Competition had replaced shared purposes, and increasingly disparate views had been expressed about the way forward. There was a particular divide between the largest, well-resourced organisations.....and the small to medium size organisations who felt vulnerable in the increasingly competitive environment. The 'commercial philanthropists' of the late 20th century seemed poised to dominate the voluntary sector while traditional segments, unless they can transform themselves, are likely to be forced from the field'.

However, this appears an unnecessarily simplistic assessment of the behaviour of housing associations (which became known as Registered Social Landlords after the Housing Act 1996) (Malpass 2000). The concept of social entrepreneurship helps to capture the decision making environment faced by social businesses including the larger housing associations. Such businesses operate with a 'double bottom line' in which social purposes and values must be balanced with the need to at least break even across overall activities. One association in a survey by Mullins and Riseborough (2000a) put it this way:

> 'The social purpose determines the type of activities you are involved in, business efficiency is the way in which you ensure that you do your best for service users'.

Focus was determined to operate in a social entrepreneurial manner and therefore rejected options which would produce a housing association based on PLC lines, where the size of surplus generated and maximisation of turnover were predominant factors. It also decided against becoming a specialist provider for a section of the population such as older people. Instead, Focus decided to move towards an approach which emphasised its role as a locally-accountable organisation, that was responsive to customers and had strong links with the communities it served. The central platform on which its future strategy was to be built was to evolve into a 'Social Investment Agency'.

Like many housing associations Focus adopted strategic planning techniques to ensure that it could make progress in the more commercial housing environment (Mullins and Riseborough 2000a). Focus began its review by proposing that its organisational 'vision' should be applicable to the 21st century and that this should be translated into a mission statement and range of supporting policies which reflected this vision. Central to the vision was the need to concentrate on providing a high quality service to tenants, partners and other stakeholders with particular emphasis on cost-effectiveness and value for money. Focus' future direction also emphasised the need for an improved service to tenants and communities. Part of the approach was to move services closer to tenants and communities by decentralising housing management, repairs and core financial services. Decentralisation was supported by the formation of local management committees and tenants groups. Moving services closer to communities was part of Focus' response to its existing customers in contrast to the growth strategy of the previous ten years. The Focus Business Plan of 1994-97 sums up the reasoning:

> 'The recent dramatic growth in Focus' development programme, given the increasing subsidy it has needed, has brought into sharp relief the issue of loyalty to existing tenants, many of whom live in homes over 100 years old'.

By 1997, Focus was ready to start work as a new kind of organisation. Calling itself a 'Social Investment Agency', Focus aimed to:

> 'Provide social goods and services, usually in partnership with others, to communities which experience significant and multiple disadvantage and lack of opportunity and investment'.

> 'Put social investment at the centre of our work, with all development and housing activities used to lever investment into our prioritised communities in the West Midlands. The aim will be to provide wholesale community regeneration through the provision of housing, community and environmental projects, employment creation, developing training opportunities, credit initiatives and increased customer control' (Business Plans 1994-1999).

Focus was widely seen as a pioneer within the voluntary housing sector when it went public at the CIH conference in 1997 as working towards becoming a 'Social Investment Agency'. Part of the success of this launch was that it enabled Focus to show it had predicted, rather than reacted to, the emerging 'social exclusion' agenda of the Labour government. The concept of social investment subsequently became a key theme underlying many of the new government's policies. The 'social investment state' was elaborated as a central element of Labour's 'Third Way' agenda by Anthony Giddens (1998). Thus, within a few years, Focus was seen as the embodiment of the new government's approach to policy and politics (Mullins and Riseborough 2000b).

A stepping stone to the development of the social investment agency concept was to establish an internal specialist Community Regeneration Unit in 1995. By the time the Social Investment Agency was being planned, Focus had already made a positive impact on regeneration in the region. The lessons learnt through this work were that dealing with poverty, physical regeneration and community development required a structured rather than a piecemeal approach.

The Community Regeneration Unit

The CRU was set up to address the wider issues of poverty, unemployment and poor environment. It was also responsible for overseeing tenant participation and the work of the Tenants Forum. The CRU was one of the first agencies of its type to be established by a housing association. Many other associations have since introduced specialist teams to organise community regeneration activities (for example Hyde Plus). Focus' CRU was established in the Autumn of 1995 and had two managers, Susan Spencer and Louise Kilbride, in its 4 years existence. The CRU's functions were decentralised in 1999, with staff being relocated to Focus' regional offices. The decision was made to do this because each regional team increasingly required closer collaboration with the CRU's specialist staff as Focus became more and more involved in dispersed regeneration projects. This process was part of the transition to the Social Investment Agency with community regeneration becoming part of the core work of each region of the association rather than a specialist 'add-on'. However, between 1995 and 1999, the CRU made many successful contributions to Focus' community regeneration activities, including:

- **Single Regeneration Budget (SRB) programmes:** both as partners (Black Patch in Sandwell) and as the lead agency (Aston Birmingham). In Black Patch, Focus and the Business Network set-up a training programme for single parents and a food co-operative. The Aston SRB was the first housing association-led SRB programme in England, with Focus, the Birmingham Settlement and a range of other community partners attempting to 'break the circle' of deprivation by supporting local businesses and developing support for Asian women.

- **Economic development:** Focus supported a spin-off from the Birmingham Settlement – the Aston Reinvestment Trust – to act as a community bank in north Birmingham. Focus provided £10,000 to ART alongside a major donation from Sir Adrian Cadbury, the latest example of the 75 year old relationship with the Cadbury family and Focus.

- **Development of a community-based housing association:** at Birmingham's Castle Vale Housing Action Trust. The community housing association was registered with the Housing Corporation in 1996. A large number of tenants were involved. Castle Vale's properties were transferred to the new association and four tenants had places on the management committee.

- **Employment and training:** the CRU developed local labour initiatives providing employment and training on Focus' home improvement schemes. Initiatives also included securing funds for child care and travel allowances for tenants involved in employment and training schemes and establishing a skills register to help tenants find work.

- **Establishment of tenants associations:** in All Saints Wolverhampton, the CRU assisted a residents and tenants group to get up-and-running to link into the local authority's plans to bid for SRB funding. Focus provided a vacant house for the group to use as an office base.

- **Running tenant training programmes:** aimed at prospective tenant management groups, training was provided in meeting and chairmanship skills, and covered the administrative arrangements for establishing tenant groups to manage social housing.

Focus' Tower Street development in Dudley. This scheme was built right in the centre of Dudley as part of the council's strategy to regenerate the town centre. Dudley Castle can be seen in the background. Tower Street, opened by Solicitor General Ross Cranston MP in 1999, includes houses and flats for local people.

Changes in Focus' approach were seen as helping it to develop a strategic role in social and economic regeneration programmes in the inner areas of the West Midlands' cities and towns. Richard Clark summarised the purpose of the change:

> 'We want to build an association that is acceptable to the community, make it a legitimate part of the regeneration agenda and big enough to make a material difference. We want to turn advantages of scale to the benefit of the community. I believe that we are on the threshold of a quantum leap'.

The Social Investment Agency: Key Principles (1997)

- Achieve responsible and strategic growth, meeting priority needs and playing a leading role in regeneration activities;

- Give priority to existing tenants in the use of resources, placing tenants' needs at the centre of working practices;

- Provide high standard, customer-centred and cost-effective housing and services;

- Be accountable to tenants, shareholders and stakeholders, operating in an open and responsive way;

- Maximise housing and care opportunities for a broad range of people in need;

- Pursue social housing objectives in an ethical manner, adopting best business practice.

It was recognised that the new 'Social Investment Agency' would have broader aims and objectives than a traditional association and Focus later approached the Housing Corporation and the Charity Commission to register the new agency. An in-depth consultation exercise was carried out with shareholders, tenants and other stakeholders. Initially, Focus undertook discussions with lenders to gain their support and to assure them that their loans for housing development were not jeopardised by the new objectives for Focus. It then consulted the Housing Corporation, which had new powers under the Housing Act 1996, and took advice from the Charity Commission. A series of presentations were made to tenants groups and communications were made to a range of agencies that had a direct or indirect stake in the organisation, including local authorities and community organisations. A resolution was finally passed at the Focus Annual General Meeting in September 1997. Ninety-eight per cent of shareholders, including the majority of tenants, supported the motion that Focus should evolve into the new agency (Annual Report 1998).

Social enterprise: managing in the late 1990s

During the late 1990s, Focus was becoming increasingly aware what being a 'social entrepreneurial organisation' meant (Mullins and Riseborough 2000a). From 1997 to 2000, the Labour government introduced a range of policies, designed to make housing associations more efficient as well as more responsive to tenants and communities. In its first two years the government repealed legislation covering Compulsory Competitive Tendering (CCT) and introduced the concept of 'Best Value' (BV). This was part of the government's agenda for developing public services through a process of continuous improvement, consultation with customers and external comparison to provide competitive services. The new BV framework was compulsory for local authorities but a voluntary approach was followed by the Housing Corporation culminating in a key document (Housing Corporation 1999).

Focus was changing its business culture in ways consistent with this agenda. It introduced performance management systems in all areas of the organisation. Individual staff members, now numbering 650, were included in a variety of ways, with perhaps the most important being annual appraisal pegged to organisational objectives. Staff conferences were held annually from 1994 onwards. Performance management within Focus was refined over the next three years to ensure a consistent approach to service delivery and to meet the requirements of Best Value. To further enhance service delivery, several initiatives were implemented, such as improving the skills and performance of staff through the establishment of a dedicated training and development section in September 1998. Further developments included:

- adoption of the European Quality Standard (EFQM);

- affiliation to the Investors In People quality approach;

- development of an internal Business Excellence Model (Business Plan 1999).

Focus' staff conference 2000. Black Country Regional Staff Pam Dhillon, Samin Cox and Suman Varma.

Focus Chairman Peter Knight accepting the Investors In People award from councillor Andy Howell, Deputy Leader of Birmingham City Council in May 2000. The award was one of many which signify the more people-centred approach to management in Focus at this time. Previous moves in this direction had been marked by an award for the best tenancy agreement and accreditation to BS5750 for the Focus repairs service.

Bringing services closer to communities

Focus also divided its housing management services on a regional basis, located around Birmingham, the Black Country and Coventry and the surrounding shire areas. Further moves to regionalise Focus' operations were made in 1998 and 1999. Regional structures were created with the Community Regeneration Unit being devolved to the Focus regions. Each region had specialist social investment and tenant participation staff. New offices were opened or refurbished in this period (for example, Handsworth and Coventry), and Focus moved into a new Head Office at Daimler House in Birmingham. Bringing services closer to communities was under-pinned by the implementation of a new Information Technology system. A 'Call Centre' was also experimented with in Birmingham.

Management of housing with care and support was also regionalised. The three regions had specialist financial staff to ensure closer collaboration with front-line staff. Regions operated as semi-independent housing and regeneration agencies, liaising with the local authorities in their areas, linking-up with community agencies and being responsible for involvement of tenants and their neighbourhoods. Chairman Peter Knight summed-up the approach:

'Each region has total ownership and responsibility for service delivery, with their constituent teams sharing their skills and expertise' (Focus Annual Report 1999).

People-centred renewal

The social investment agenda began to merge with that of Best Value over the next two years. Tackling social inclusion through community development was based on improving consultation. Focus increased opportunities for local people to participate in the planning, delivery and evaluation of services provided in their communities. The development of an anti-poverty strategy sought to improve the quality of life of communities and people on welfare benefits and to provide incentives for those who were seeking work.

An example of Focus' £4 million per year Home Improvement Programme. The HIP is a refurbishment programme funded totally out of Focus' own resources. Between 1995 and 1999, more than 1,000 homes were improved with better heating and insulation provided plus replacement of worn-out elements.

Economic regeneration was placed alongside this strategy with Focus facilitating access to pre-vocational training guidance, work experience, employment and follow-through support. Economic regeneration was also tackled through stimulating local business activities (for example, through local procurement policies, provision of support for existing businesses, encouragement of local enterprise and direct investment in the Focus housing stock). Focus began to improve the quality of the physical environment through its Home Improvement Programme and became involved in environmental improvements and development of community safety initiatives. This initiative was broadly welcomed by tenants:

> 'Many of us on our estate have already benefitted from things like improved draught-proofing but I'm glad to see that the scheme's being extended. Some of us here have central heating but others don't and that's sometimes a bone of contention. But its nice to see that Focus is making an effort through its home improvement programme' (Secretary of Handsworth Wood residents association, Annual Report 1995).

Focus Home Improvement Programme 1995-2000

The forerunner of the Home Improvement Programme (HIP) was the Warm Homes initiative in 1993. The aim of the HIP was to improve around 300 of Focus' oldest homes each year, by providing new heating and insulation, new plastic windows and improvements to internal elements, such as kitchens and bathrooms. The HIP averaged about £10,000 per home between 1995 and 1999. Funding was through a mixture of Focus' own reserves, private finance and increased rents. Rents did not increase significantly and increases were phased over three years. The HIP initially concentrated on both occupied and vacant homes, but later moved to provide current tenants with the most of the improvements.

Year	HIP Expenditure (£m)	No. Improved Homes
1995/96	3.9	153
1996/97	5.4	303
1997/98	5.1	246
1998/99	4.8	78
1999/00	3.0	230

This was one of the largest internally-funded home improvement programmes by a housing association outside London in 1996 and 1997. In 1998/99 the HIP produced fewer improved homes because of concentration on a major refurbishment project at Tillyard Croft. The HIP in future years will be based on Focus' new asset management strategy, and will concentrate on a large number of homes and component replacement.

The new approach received comprehensive support from tenants and communities. In the association's tenants' survey in 1997 (Brocklehurst), questions were asked which covered wider subjects than traditional tenants surveys. The results for these questions, from a sample of 1,300 Focus tenants, showed that 92 percent wanted Focus to help with improving their neighbourhoods and 91 percent wanted the association to implement community safety measures. Close to 86 percent of tenants welcomed Focus helping with employment and training. A similar percentage wanted Focus to improve community facilities. Below is shown what Focus has done in these key community development areas. Focus' main social investment activities in this period were:

- **Neighbourhood and estate regeneration**: Focus' commitment to working locally in the most deprived communities was apparent from the Index of Local Deprivation (ILD) which demonstrated that more than half of Focus' housing stock was located in the ten most disadvantaged wards in the West Midlands. Social investment teams working out of the three Focus regions via neighbourhood offices and supported housing projects were key to a number of initiatives involving social investment within these disadvantaged areas. Neighbourhood regeneration activities included involvement in the Handsworth Area Regeneration Trust (HART) with the formation of a community-based organisation to coordinate inner city service delivery; provision of a one-stop shop in the Foleshill SRB project in Coventry; development of a Home Options Agency to oversee regeneration of non-Focus properties in the inner city; and wholesale physical regeneration on local authority estates at Ladywood, the Holmes in Small Heath and Castle Vale in Birmingham; at Blakenhall, Pine Court and Galton Village in the Black Country and in Torrington and Willenhall in Coventry (Annual Reports 1997-1999).

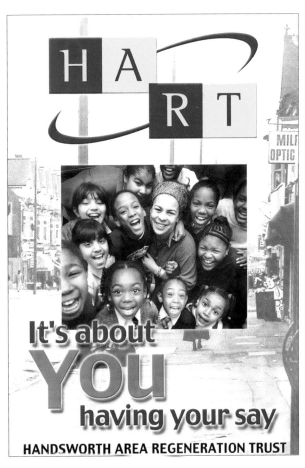

Handsworth Area Regeneration Trust (HART). Focus is a member of a seventeen-strong partnership of public, voluntary and community agencies which came together in the late 1990s to work with local people in regenerating the Handsworth area of Birmingham. HART is currently running £3 million programme funded by the government's Single Regeneration Budget, for which Focus is the accountable body. In partnership with the City Council HART is currently bidding for more funds under the next phase of the SRB.

- **Housing, employment and training**: Perhaps the best illustration of how Focus put its social investment approach into practice was the development of a purpose-built Foyer at Snow Hill in Birmingham. The £4 million development, first envisaged by Shape, provided support for 18 to 25 year olds to improve their social, economic and housing situations. Foyers aim to break the 'no home, no job' cycle of deprivation and have the support of a number of Cabinet Ministers; most notably the Chancellor Gordon Brown and Secretary of State for Education and Employment, David Blunkett, who said about the Focus approach:

'They are already providing excellent examples of how local partnerships can draw together expertise and commitment in order to give a real chance to those marginalised from society for too long'.

The Focus Foyer at Snow Hill, Birmingham. The first purpose-built Foyer in the West Midlands. Providing 80 study bedrooms for 16 to 25 year olds, and access to education, employment and training opportunities, the award-winning Foyer was built using a 'funding cocktail'. Chief funders were Birmingham City Council, British Telecom, English Partnerships, European Social Fund, National Lotteries Charities Board, the Housing Corporation, Newtown and South Aston City Challenge, Newtown/Ladywood Task Force and Focus' reserves.

- **Housing and health**: In the late 1990s health promotion became a broad government objective. Focus became involved in planning for a National Lottery funded Healthy Living Centre Birmingham's Newtown area. The Centre will offer health care from many of Focus' supported housing schemes. Plans for the Healthy Living Centre included seven GPs, a community-based mental health team, ambulance service, a nutrition project, on-site gym and health information projects. Snow Hill is a 150 unit hostel with support for homeless men with on-site access to primary health care and the provision of a detoxification unit.

- **Advising citizens**: The Birmingham Housing Aid Service (BHAS) developed its services throughout the 1990s, to include, for example, a Department of Environment-sponsored Homefinder Project, which assisted young homeless people to find homes and provided resettlement services. But by 1995 it became clear that housing advice services required some rationalisation in Birmingham. Focus approached Shelter and proposed a merger between BHAS and Shelter's advice service in the city. BHAS became independent of Focus after 22 years. However, Focus grant-aided the new advice service over the next 3 years and continued with its involvement on the steering committee. BHAS moved out of Focus' offices in Paradise Circus and took up residence in Corporation Street as part of Shelter's national network of advice agencies. In this way, the partnership between Focus and Shelter, stretching back to the mid-1960s, was renewed at this time.

Focus staff raise funds for Shelter in the 'Get Your Kit On' campaign.

- **Care and support:** Between 1994 and 2000, Focus, following the merger with Shape in 1994 (see chapter 8), became one of the largest providers of supported housing in the English housing association sector with more than 1,351 bedspaces in management (a growth rate of 140 percent since 1993) . Of these bedspaces, Focus managed 909 in-house. Focus provided housing with care and support to 15 designated 'special needs' groups. Its provision for homeless people was one of the largest in the country's voluntary housing sector (at 583 bedspaces). Focus was increasingly working with special needs groups including those suffering from sickle cell anaemia, people who were HIV positive, people with substance dependencies and refugees. Managing agencies included MIND (the mental health charity), NACRO (the ex-offenders resettlement agency) and OSCAR (the sickle cell anaemia sufferers charity.) Focus also developed a growing role in the late 1990s in the delivery of care in the community by providing:

  - outreach support for people with mental health problems to be able to stay in their homes (Focus won a contract from Birmingham Social Services to deliver such support in North Birmingham);

  - delivery of care and support services for people coming out of long-stay hospital care to be resettled back into the community;

  - provision of an aids and adaptations programme in a range of 'mainstream' homes for people with physical disabilities and for the frail elderly to remove or postpone their requirements for residential care (Annual Reports 1993-1999).

World Mental Health Day celebrated by a release of balloons at Albert Pritchard School in Wednesbury on 10th October 1999.

The 'supertanker' turns: Prime Focus

In 2000 Focus formed a new group structure to cement the future of the Social Investment Agency and finally 'turned the supertanker around' (see chapter 7 for the origins of this powerful image of Focus' change of direction). This was seen by Focus' management committee as providing a fresh image, approach and legal structure; a classic example of an organisation rebranding itself in order to deliver its core mission in changing times (Mullins and Riseborough 2000a). The group structure provided a new organisational vehicle to bring together housing and non-housing work to achieve social investment objectives. Chief Executive Richard Clark commented about the new group structure in the Business Plan (1999):

> 'The election of a new government in 1997 has seen a change in the thrust of housing policy to a strategy based upon tackling social exclusion ......In correctly forecasting this shift, Focus is launching a new social investment structure which will provide a pioneering model linking together housing, regeneration, personal support, research and practice to provide an innovatory and flexible structure capable of establishing Focus as a market leader within this field'.

The New Group Structure 2000	
Prime Focus:	The strategic hub of all group activities. The parent of the group, it looks after the overall direction and policy development. Its key objective is to develop a strategy which encompasses a broad range of social action and ensures that the component parts of the group support this strategy.
Focus Housing:	Focus Housing is the biggest entity within the group with 650 staff and around 50 sites in the West Midlands. It manages more than 12,000 social rented homes as well as 1,200 supported housing bedspaces. It also delivers the social investment agenda of the group.
Black Star:	Black Star is a community-based organisation that reflects the diverse needs of the black and minority ethnic communities in North Birmingham. It manages 450 social rented homes and two supported housing schemes.
Focus Home Options:	Focus Home Options manages and develops shared ownership and market rented homes. It currently has 900 homes. It also provides facilities management services to other organisations. It is working on regeneration projects to improve the quality of private housing.
Focus Pathways:	Focus Pathways is the training agency for the group. It delivers both nationally and internationally-funded training programmes, with its core business being the delivery of training contracts to unemployed people, helping them to gain skills that lead to work.
Prime Focus Finance:	Prime Focus Finance is a specialist agency within the group set up to borrow on behalf of Focus housing and Black Star. Due to the volume that it will be borrowing, the marginal cost of funds will be lower than at any time in Focus' history. It also creates opportunities to reduce management costs.

A new parent company was seen as key to Focus being able to work in non-housing areas, such as health, employment, education and community development, and to continue its community regeneration and neighbourhood renewal activities through housing and related activities. The charitable parent was called 'Prime Focus', a Registered Social Landlord with the Housing Corporation, but had wider powers through registration with the Charity Commissioners and under new Articles and Memorandum of Association. The creation of the new group structure in July 2000 resulted in a name and image change for the third time in Focus' history. This was done to indicate the shift in emphasis that took place in Focus from 1994. The change in structure enabled the new group to organise its existing activities into autonomous social businesses beneath the Prime Focus parent. This approach was chosen to enable other housing associations and social purpose organisations to join the group and thereby achieve further socially responsible growth. As the Prime Focus 'launch document' commented:

> 'Our remit still firmly embraces our core business of providing homes for people, but enables us to offer many related services as well. In becoming a social investment agency we are able to engage in many areas of activity that support our primary work of providing housing to those who need it. Our new structure will support our efforts to benefit our tenants, staff and all the partners that work with us now and in the future'.

Chief Executive Richard Clark launching Prime Focus in July 2000. Prime Focus is a new charity and parent organisation of the Social Investment Agency. Other members of the Group include Focus Housing Association, Black Star Housing Association, Focus Home Options, Focus Pathways and Prime Focus Finance.

Another century dawns

By 2000 Focus had developed into a major social housing enterprise from a small housing society at its foundation in 1925. Part I of the Focus story has shown how this came about by outlining some of the main reasons for Focus' growth and changes in its approach and style. However, it is important to reflect on the processes underlying these changes. Part II does this by reviewing the main transformations from a broader vantage point; looks at the role of mergers in Focus' development; traces how it was governed over the 75 years and describes its accountability to tenants. Part II also highlights one of Focus' historical hallmarks – its continuing commitment to people in need and its campaigning approach on their behalf.

PART II

O'Keefe Close, named after Birmingham councillor John O'Keefe, opened in 1989, by the Right Honourable Roy Hattersley MP. Seen here with Copec tenants, members of the O'Keefe family and Sir Richard Knowles, Leader of Birmingham City Council at the time. The scheme provided 25 newbuild homes in Sparkbrook.

7

From Copec to Prime Focus: transformations

'Much of the continued dynamism of voluntary housing lies in the repeated ways that new, energetic organisations have been able to re-define the movement, and in the flexibility of existing organisations, which have transformed themselves, often more than once' (Malpass 1999).

Transformations have figured prominently in Focus' history. A series of name changes from the Birmingham Copec House Improvement Society in the 1920s, to the Birmingham Copec Housing Trust in the 1960s, then Copec Housing Trust in the 1970s, and into Focus in the 1990s and finally into Prime Focus in 2000, only hint at some of the underlying transformations. The Focus story has been one of organisational transformations to meet new needs and requirements. Transformations have often been in response to national and local housing policies. Yet, for most of its 75 year history the core mission has remained largely constant: to work with disadvantaged communities in inner city areas to provide and improve housing conditions. Through careful planning and with an eye on the world outside, Focus has been able to influence policy and to develop new ways of delivering its core mission. As Chapter 8 will illustrate, Focus was revitalised in each of the last three decades of the twentieth century through merger with newer housing associations. These associations were formed in different times to Copec and sometimes embodied different values and purposes. The influence of these partner associations can be seen in many aspects of the organisation's transformation. Three examples illustrate this:

- In the 1960s the impact of Birmingham Housing Trust (BHT) was apparent in the way in which the merged organisation refocused on voluntary sector purposes of housing those who no-one else would at the same time as taking a more aggressive approach to securing development opportunities and expanding the housing stock.

- Similarly in the 1990s the merger with Shape helped Focus to develop an organisational purpose for the new millennium based around social investment.

- Also in the 1990s the need to develop a viable future for the former Harambee stock led Focus into new networks of partnership with the black and minority ethnic sector, learning lessons along the way about the importance of equality and trust in partnership working.

These mergers were among the most significant influences transforming Focus into what it is today but this chapter explores other dimensions of change. In doing so it revisits the 75 year history described in Part I, providing an interpretation of these events in the light of contemporary thinking about the changing role of voluntary organisations in the twentieth century.

An early example of Copec's 'slum-patching' at Talfourd Street, Small Heath.

Social origins and transformations

This chapter illustrates the transformation of Focus from its origins in Christian social concern into a modern social entrepreneurial organisation through key examples of changes in direction. Our review of Focus' transformations considers both the ways in which the world outside was changing and the strategic decisions made by those in control of the organisation (an overview can be seen in the table in the appendix):

- Perhaps the most significant external factors to consider are the role of the state, and its policies towards the involvement of voluntary organisations providing housing. This includes the types of legal form that voluntary organisations may adopt, and the ways in which organisations are funded and regulated. In England the gradual inclusion of housing as a part of the social democratic welfare state between the First World War and the late 1970s had important implications for the role played by organisations like Copec. Changes since the 'Thatcher revolution' began to 'roll back the state' in the 1980s transformed the role for voluntary organisations such as housing associations. Other key external factors are values and beliefs operating in wider society, and the ways in which citizens may organise themselves to care directly for those in need or campaign on behalf of such needs.

- Turning to strategic decisions by those in control of the organisation; the most important factor to recognise is that there are always choices to be made. There may be choices between taking opportunities provided by the latest funding programme or holding to longer term values and purposes. Other strategic choices may be between working in a particular geographical area or seeking to expand elsewhere. For most organisations the ultimate strategic choice is whether to continue to operate as an independent organisation (for example, after the initial objectives have been met or when funding or staffing constraints make it difficult to continue to pursue these objectives alone). All of these choices have been faced by organisations involved in the history of Focus.

Five key examples of transformations in the Focus' history are discussed in this chapter:

- **The call to Christians to become slum landlords**- social origins of Copec in early twentieth century philanthropy.

- **Dropping distribution**- the move towards a non-profit charitable model in the 1930s and 40s.

- **Campaigning for change** – developing a new relationship with the welfare state in the 1960s and 70s.

- **Going for growth** – responding to the new liberal agenda in the 1980s and early 90s.

- **Turning around the 'supertanker'** Becoming a social enterprise for the new millennium.

C.O.P.E.C.

Helping to Solve the Slum Problem.

ONE of the greatest problems the present time is the question which face all political parties at of reconditioning the poorer areas of our great cities.

The providing of new houses for what may be described as the better class of the working population in no way deals with the far greater problem of how adequately to house those large numbers of working-class people in our cities, who, for economic reasons, are utterly unable to pay the rents required for Municipal dwellings, or for business reasons are unable to live any distance away from the centre of the city.

The Copec Society, which was founded as a result of the Conference on Christian Politics, Economics and Citizenship held in Birmingham in 1924, is organised on business lines and has been registered under the Industrial & Provident Societies Act with £1 shares and 4 per cent. Loan Stock. The Society has given a clear-cut illustration of what may be done in this all-important matter. In the very heart of the poorest part of our great City of Birmingham the Copec

PROFESSOR TILLYARD, C.B.E.
Chairman of the Birmingham Copec House
Improvement Society, Ltd.

Professor Frank Tillyard, Copec's first Chairman, calls on Christians to become 'slum landlords' in 1926.

The call to Christians to become slum landlords – the social origins of Copec

Professor Tillyard's pamphlet was published in 1926 to accompany an appeal to churches and individuals to support the new society by purchasing shares and loan stocks. Its title and the associated appeal capture the essence of Copec and set it in its times. Housing associations have taken different forms at different times reflecting the circumstances of the time and how people perceived the 'housing problem'. The immediate origins of new housing associations have usually been local; often involving churches, local elites and local authorities. However, what happened locally was frequently affected by national networks and social movements. National influences have also tended to determine the legal and funding models, and housing management approaches and reactions to models developed in earlier periods. The influence of the type of state; the extent of poverty and the adequacy of welfare provision made directly by the state in defining how voluntary organisations operate are all considerations.

By the 1920s, when Copec was established, a new style of limited profit organisation was being developed, which was different from the model dwellings companies and large endowed trusts of the 19th century, although they shared some characteristics. In particular, raising capital from investors at less than the market rate of return (up to 6%), and essentially 'top-down' in character. They were also often established by people from various religious denominations and from local social elites. Usually termed Housing Societies, a distinctive feature was a determination to focus on improving slum housing

A visit by Prime Minister Stanley Baldwin. His wife and Copec tenants are shown here. Copec was a 'op-down' philanthropic housing society with links to influential networks of supporters.

that had been bypassed by both nineteenth century philanthropy and the emerging welfare state (there were upwards of 50 such societies nationally by the early 1930s) (Garside 2000). Many of these organisations survived to the present day. Examples include St Pancras and William Sutton which are amongst the largest modern housing associations.

Copec was one such 'top-down' Christian-inspired housing society set up in 1925 following the Christian Conference On Politics, Economics and Citizenship (COPEC) in 1924. COPEC was a multi-denominational conference, and led to the establishment of housing societies in Altrincham, Bangor, and Manchester as well as Birmingham (Garside 2000). Copec was set up by a continuation committee drawing strength from involvement of a wide range of denominations. The Bishop of Birmingham Hamilton Baynes, was a committee member from 1925 to 1932. As Frank Tillyard commented:

> 'Copec is a joint effort of the Christian community in the widest sense of the term. As the direct offspring of the Copec Conference, it was started with a representative committee, but it had not at first a direct link with either Unitarians or the Roman Catholics. In both cases this has been remedied. Attempts have been made to bring the various local churches into direct contact with the work of the Society by getting them to find money required for the acquisition and improvement of properties' (Congregational Quarterly 1932).

There were especially close links with the Society of Friends (the Quakers) who were well represented among business leaders in early twentieth century Birmingham. One such connection was through the Cadbury family and the Bournville Village Trust (BVT), an employer sponsored housing organisation, they had set-up in 1895. BVT's architectural department provided services to Copec until its merger with Birmingham Housing Trust in 1970. Members of BVT sat on Copec's management committee for the next twenty years (including Frank Barlow, BVT's general manager). A number of joint schemes were pursued with BVT, who also supplied land for Copec's special needs schemes including Brook House and Wolseley House.

Copec also developed strong links with the Birmingham Settlement, founded in the Summer Lane area of Birmingham in 1899 (a major part of the world-wide Settlement Movement) (Glasby 1999).   Both Copec's Chairman, Professor Frank Tillyard, and the Honorary Secretary, Miss Florence Barrow, were closely connected to the Birmingham Settlement. Frank Tillyard, a Professor of Law at the University of Birmingham, was a lecturer at the Settlement's social studies classes and a leading figure in the Poor Man's Lawyer Movement. Mrs Tillyard was a member of the Settlement's committee from 1904 to 1909 (Glasby 1999). Florence Barrow was a resident at the Settlement and had been responsible for running a number of classes for local people with disabilities. The Barrow family as a whole were involved in the Birmingham Settlement for many years. Mrs Barrow, Florence's mother, was Honorary Secretary to the Settlement in its early days (Glasby 1999). Another important family were the Sturges. Joseph Sturge, made a posthumous donation to Copec in 1937 to assist in reconditioning of 47-55 Hospital St, off Summer Lane. His daughter was a Copec committee member and in 1931 his granddaughter became a Copec housing trainee (Fenter 1960). In addition, local councillors had two to three places on the committee of management throughout the 1920s and 1930s.

This network of the 'great and the good' demonstrates the nature of the early Copec. Its management committee was effectively 'tuned-in' to the local power structures in church and city council. Copec was managed by a committee of twelve, all of whom were drawn from wealthy and influential families in Birmingham at the time. Committee members were known as Directors and became virtually self-sustaining throughout the 1925 to 1969 period. By 1949, four members of the original twelve were still serving on the committee, with Florence Barrow having been Honorary Secretary for twenty-five years. Committee members sought re-election on a rolling basis, but in practice only stood down when personal circumstances dictated.

Two other external influences worth recording are that of the emergence of state housing and of a housing management profession. The scope of Copec's activity was influenced from the start by its complementary relationship with the newly emerging public housing sector, while remaining largely independent of state funding. At this time, the city council was concentrating its efforts on providing municipal housing on the outskirts of Birmingham. Copec focused its efforts on the city's central areas. The 1920s saw Copec buy and recondition more than 200 slum houses. Although the majority of houses bought in this period were of a low standard, Copec also bought houses which were structurally sound in order to balance investment risks.

As a Public Utility Society (PUS) Copec would have been eligible to access funding from the same source as local authorities under the Housing Act 1924 (Malpass 2000). However, there was no public funding for refurbishment work which the management committee chose as Copec's core business. Copec chose to remain largely financially independent of the state during this period. The majority of income came from issuing shares and loan stock. Copec was also successful in attracting donations from charitable trusts and from public appeals. Copec benefitted from 'gifts in kind' ((for example, an office was loaned to Copec by its treasurer, Mr Hickinbotham, and office equipment was supplied by a local company). As Fenter (1960) acknowledged:

> 'the financial contributions of many public-spirited people were essential to the foundation Copec, but it could not have functioned without the generous help received in numerous other ways from a large number of people'.

As shown in chapters 2 and 3, Copec's management approach was developed from methods advocated by Octavia Hill. Unlike the local authority, Copec did not initially select its tenants. Reconditioned homes were usually let to sitting tenants of the previous private landlord. Houses bought with vacant possession were let to families referred by the city council. Initially, rent collection and other housing management work was undertaken by members of the Copec committee, especially women members. As full-time manager, Margaret Fenter, was appointed in 1927 and put into operation an efficient and caring, if a somewhat paternalistic approach to dealing with tenants (see chapter 2).

Thus Copec was a product of its time. It was influenced by a national movement in which the 'front line housing societies' (Garside, 2000) of the 20s and 30s were transforming the models of nineteenth century philanthropy to target unmet needs. It used professional housing management methods deriving from the same period. Its scope was affected by the emergence of the state's housing role. Yet above all its development was firmly rooted within local elite and religious networks of 1920s Birmingham. These networks were of crucial importance for an organisation relying almost exclusively on individual contributions for its funding.

A Copec Annual General Meeting. The association had become a charity before the war to more accurately reflect its philanthropic aims and to ensure that it reduced its tax burden. This enabled Copec to maximise is limited funds for its housing and social care activities.

Dropping distribution

One of the main features of housing associations today is that they operate on a 'not for profit' basis. Strictly speaking this means that while surpluses may be accumulated they cannot be distributed to shareholders and board members. As we have seen this was not the basis on which Copec was established. While there was very little transformation in the general organisational model described above until after the Second World War, the principle of distributing dividends to shareholders was a significant area of change. This was a gradual process, reflected in early committee discussions on setting the rate of return, and later rehearsed in the annual report before a decision to convert to charitable status in 1939. Even then Copec continued to issue small amounts of loan stock at lower returns than previously (2.5 percent in contrast to the previous 3 and 4 percent), but encouraged stock holders to forgo interest or to gift or redeem their holdings (see chapter 2).

As a PUS, an early legal form covering most housing societies but not the older endowed trust such as Guinness, Copec was empowered to issue shares and loan stock and to pay dividends of up to 6 percent. Copec used both shares and loan stock; these were not tradeable on the open market but did involve distribution to holders. Unlike the £1 shares issued by Industrial and Provident Societies today, those issued by Copec in the 1920s and 30s carried dividend payments. Copec's management committee had considered it unwise to pay dividends until the end of 1927, but each year between 1927 and 1939 a 3% dividend was paid on all shares. Loan stocks were issued to accumulate additional funds for buying and reconditioning properties. Stock holders were entitled to payment of dividends from the subsequent rental income. A fascinating debate took place in Copec's early years as to how these factors should be balanced. Frank Tillyard (Congregational Quarterly 1932) gives an insight into these discussions:

> 'In Birmingham there was much controversy as to the interest rate to be offered on the loan stock. Some were for a business-like 5 percent. Others were for a philanthropic 2.5 percent. The committee made a shrewd guess that they were not likely to be able to work to a 5 percent basis so that on that footing what was overpaid to business lenders would have to be subtracted from the shareholders' dividends. On the other hand, the committee hoped to make more than 2.5 percent, in which case the shareholders would profit at the expense of the philanthropic lenders. We finally settled on a 4 per cent loan stock, and since the end of the first year (1925/26), Copec has been able to pay a 3 percent dividend on the share capital and carry a reasonable sum to a depreciation reserve'.

This discussion indicated unease about the principle of profit distribution that was to resurface in the late 1930s. In 1936 loan stock holders were invited to convert from 4% to 3% interest on the understanding that the savings in interest payments would be used for repairs and modernisation, which were difficult to fund from rent income. By 1938, the society's capital included £13,979 in paid up shares and £48,300 in loan stock; £35,155 of the latter had been converted to the 3% rate. By the late 1930s, Copec was undertaking a major review of its legal standing. This was precipitated by a debate about the public perception of an organisation making money out of slum housing. The 1938 Annual Report indicates that the issue was coming to a head:

> 'It has been increasingly felt that it is becoming more and more difficult to describe the work of Copec as a commercial venture, since the adequate housing of the lowest paid workers is a work of social importance from which it is not possible or desirable to expect more than a very modest return on capital'.

Table (13) – Profits Made By Copec (1925/26 To 1930/31)

Years	Gross Rents	Net Income	Surplus After 4% On Loan Stock	Income Required To Pay 3% On Shares
1925/26	£494	£218	£115	No Dividend
1926/27	£1,453	£738	£477	£145
1927/28	£2,835	£1,153	£638	£224
1928/29	£3,330	£1,402	£553	£247
1929/30	£4,395	£1,763	£773	£272
1930/31	£4,759	£1,849	£704	£299

And so the possibility of converting Copec into an organisation with charitable status was investigated. The proposal was agreed at the 1938 Annual General Meeting and subsequently approved by the Charity Commissioners and the Inland Revenue. No further dividends were paid on shares but Copec continued to pay interest on loan stock. Copec converted from a PUS to an Industrial and Provident Society with charitable rules in 1939, thereby also gaining tax advantages. While it continued to issue loan stock in the

1940s, it encouraged stock holders to offer their holdings for charitable projects or to redeem their holdings. As late as 1952 the interests of stock holders were still an important consideration for Copec. Compensation payments were received from the city council following acquisition of some of Copec's properties. It was also necessary to consult loan stock holders on how this income and the associated 'assets' should be dealt with.

Copec had gradually shifted its funding basis from providing a limited return on investment to shareholders and stock holders towards a charity model in which income came either from gifts or from trading activities, in the form of rental income (see Chapter 2). For example, funds for newbuild schemes for special needs in the 1930s, such as Sturge House, came almost entirely from charitable donations and legacies. Meanwhile, Copec had begun to dip its toe in the water of state funding. First, receiving public subsidy from Birmingham City Council for rehousing associated with demolition and clearance under the Housing Act 1930. It later received fees from the city council for managing properties designated for clearancce and some public funding under the War Damages Acts. However, Copec was only able to expand slowly during this period and it was many years before significant public funding was received. However, it was many years before significant public funding was raised.

Copec had been set up using a legal model available at the time as a result of external influences. Working with this model had convinced its management committee that it was not entirely appropriate to the purposes or indeed the image of Copec, and when the opportunity arose a change was made. It is important, however, not to discount the impact of external changes too, (the formation of the National Federation of Housing Societies in 1935 promoted alternative models). As Miss Fenter (1960) put it:

> 'Much useful information has been obtained and exchanges of views arranged as to the work of other societies in addition to which the Federation acts as the mouthpiece of housing societies in negotiation with the government'.

Nevertheless, the decision to convert to charitable status was made relatively early compared to other housing societies (see chapter 3).

Campaigning for change

The next transformation in Copec's role took even longer to mature than had dropping distribution. This involved the organisation re-inventing itself to engage in new ways with the post-war welfare state. The expansion of the welfare state into activities that had previously been Copec's core business posed challenges, to which it took time to respond. It was only really after the merger with BHT (described in chapter 7), and the allocation of new roles to voluntary housing organisations by the state, culminating in the 1974 Housing Act, that this transformation was complete.

The period between the Second World War and the mid 1960s was relatively quiet for Copec, an era in which its initial mission had largely been achieved and longstanding committee members and staff, including Miss Fenter the first paid staff member, had left the organisation. The very success of Copec's campaign for improvements to the inner areas had seen a reduction in its own stock (114 homes were demolished between 1945 and 1950). Instead it was allocated a temporary 'bit part' in managing acquired properties on behalf of Birmingham City Council which now assumed the leading role in redeveloping the inner areas (see chapter 3). The old 'settlement' in which Copec had worked in the inner areas with existing properties, albeit with resources totally inadequate for the task, while the city council built new homes in the suburbs was now over. While Copec had long recognised the need for action on a scale that only the municipal authority could provide, there was a sense of loss of purpose associated with what can now be seen as a notable campaign victory (see chapter 10).

In the 1950s Copec had begun to look for new complementary roles including provision for single women, and older people (see chapter 3). This activity developed more fully in the 1960s. Similarly, BHT was concerned from its formation in 1965 with the needs of those who were not catered for by the expanding municipal sector. It brought this concern to its merger with Copec in 1970.

Finding a new role was associated on the one hand with the emergence of new social movements and the re-invigoration of the voluntary sector and with it voluntary housing and a more overt campaigning approach in the 1960s. On the other hand the full realisation of this new role was dependent on a transformation in the frameworks of the welfare state itself leading to significant funding for voluntary housing in the 1970s.

Des Wilson launching the Shelter campaign in 1966.

Reinvigoration of voluntary housing in the 1960s

The 1960s is commonly seen as a time of dramatic social change in which new attitudes began to challenge the conformity of the 1950s. This was an era in which poverty was rediscovered and campaigns established to achieve social change. In the housing world this was symbolised by the birth of Shelter in 1966 and the documentary 'Cathy Come Home' by the BBC. Both demonstrated to the public and policy-makers alike that the problems faced by homeless people and those living in substandard housing were not eradicated. Shelter was bound-up with the housing association movement from the start. The five voluntary organisations involved in Shelter's foundation included the Housing Societies Charitable Trust, the charitable arm of the NFHS. Shelter in turn sponsored the formation of a range of new housing associations in the country's major cities and towns.

Four new housing associations were formed in the West Midlands as part of this movement, Birmingham Housing Trust (BHT) in 1965, Wolverhampton Housing Association (WHA) in 1967 and Hestia and Shape Housing Associations in the early 1970s. BHT was a direct product of voluntary groups involved in the foundation of Shelter campaign. WHA, Hestia and Shape were also established partly as a local response to the Shelter campaign, although only WHA had direct links to a local Shelter Group. Hestia was less connected to Shelter. Rather, its management committee of largely property professionals, anticipated public funding for housing associations in 1974. Shape was a community-based association with primary concerns for housing those least able to help themselves and the provision of training opportunities. Copec and BHT were the two recipients of Shelter grants in Birmingham.

A visit by Prime Minister Harold Wilson to a BHT scheme before the General Election in 1970.

The four associations were all managed by voluntary committees drawn from the original campaigning and founding groups, supplemented by others drawn from the church, academic institutions, the business community and voluntary organisations.   These networks were of different 'social standing' to the Copec network of the 1920s and 1930s described earlier. Greater emphasis was placed on links with the community, charitable funding bodies and local authorities.   Only BHT had a full-time employee from its inception. All had close ties with their respective local authorities, with some having local councillors on their committees. WHA was promoted by a Conservative council to provide an alternative to municipal provision in Wolverhampton to be involved in area improvement policies brought in by the Housing Act 1969. BHT's link with Birmingham City Council was through David Mumford who was a senior councillor. It used links with the Leader of the Council and the Town Clerk to raise funds. At this time, BHT was more of a campaigning organisation than the other two and used its impressive list of patrons (see chapter 10). BHT also led the local Shelter fundraising campaign. Copec was used to running campaigns about poor housing conditions in Birmingham and developed 'arms length' links with the Shelter campaign. Despite this, it established a sub-committee in 1968 to 'shadow' Shelter's activities and develop common ground on campaigning with the new charity.

> 'Copec congratulates the organisers both on the amount of money raised so far and the way in which it has drawn the public attention to the needs of so many families without proper accommodation. Copec is glad to be associated with the Shelter movement' (Copec Annual Report 1968).

The campaign went much wider than simply supporting organisations like BHT and Copec. It extended to seeking changes to the welfare state to provide a right of access to housing for homeless people. It also sought to move housing associations on from depending primarily on charitable fund raising to being involved in state funded programmes to rehabilitate poor housing and to house homeless people. These aims were to be achieved over the next decade.

Transforming the role of state funding for the non-profit sector

While public funding had been available since 1919, it was not until the 1960s that housing societies were employed on a significant scale as instruments of central government housing policy. It was a Conservative administration that decided to use non-profit organisations to provide for better off, mobile workers who needed to rent until they could afford to buy. Most of the homes produced under this approach were eventually sold for owner-occupation. However, it did produce a new wave of housing associations, many of which are active today. Like many existing housing associations, Copec was not significantly involved in this regime, but was later to benefit from the precedent established by the 1961, 1964 and 1967 Housing Acts for involving housing associations more directly in delivering state policies.

The Housing Act 1974, brought housing associations into closer collaboration with the public sector by introducing financial support and associated regulation. This generous public subsidy system covered both capital grants for housebuilding and renovation and revenue requirements. It led to most housing associations becoming dependent upon the Exchequer for their subsequent growth and deficit funding of their running costs. As Malpass (1999) has commented:

'It has been recognised that since the mid-1970s, as housing associations moved towards a closer relationship with government and to a more central role in housing policy, the price of increased financial support was a certain loss of independence. It is clear...that the government, via its agent the Housing Corporation, possessed powerful tools with which to shape, regulate and steer both individual associations and the sector as a whole'.

Table (14) – Copec's Financial Circumstances 1965-1970 (£)

Year	Share Capital	Loan Capital	Capital Reserve	Revenue Reserve	Sundry Funds	Gross Rents
1965	9,633	46,904	8,517	76,679	65,380	17,919
1966	9,673	46,654	8,517	82,737	66,526	19,307
1967	9,677	46,654	8,577	88,348	75,061	20,740
1968	9,678	46,454	8,577	92,816	79,029	24,076
1969	9,678	46,404	8,577	97,634	82,377	26,331
1970	9,678	46,404	8,577	115,889	82,377	28,002

The housing associations which now make up Focus took advantage of the 1974 provisions by registering with the Housing Corporation. Copec saw the legislation as a key opportunity. As Chairman John Duncan remarked:

'The Act has provided a stable foundation upon which the Trust has been able to expand its scope and work......considerable time has been given to recruiting members of the committee and staff (now numbering 40), and also in developing new committee and management structures to handle our widening activity. We are regarding this time of development as the most significant stage in the Trust's life since Copec and BHT merged in 1970. The Trust now has the opportunity to respond to the housing needs on a wider front than previously' (Copec Annual Report 1975).

This period of transformation began and ended with the success of campaigns in which Copec and BHT had been directly involved to influence the shape of the welfare state. The long-standing aim of the early Copec had been to secure significant improvements in the 'back-to-back' housing which made up much of Birmingham's inner areas. Whether or not Copec was amongst the most influential pressure groups at this time is debatable. Copec's management committee certainly thought that its campaign had some effects on the approach of Birmingham City Council:

'In no small measure Copec helped to prepare the way for the tremendous effort made by the city council after the last war to deal with Birmingham's central areas and, whether or not credit is given for this, Copec has had the satisfaction of knowing that many of the measures it recommended have been adopted'.

'Though Copec could not make extravagant claims to have influenced the policy of the city council, on one occasion the Lord Mayor said that Copec's work had been a means of stimulating members of the city council in matters of housing' (Fenter 1960).

In the postwar period, however, local authorities were able to bring much greater resources to bear on slum clearance and rebuilding. A long period of search for a new role followed, culminating in involvement in the Shelter campaigns of the 1960s. Copec, BHT and WHA were involved in local campaigns which were to result in public funding for housing associations as well as eventual legislation to provide local authorities with a duty to assist homeless people. As David Mumford was later to comment:

'The 1974 Act did not change what we were trying to do, but it enabled us to do it more quickly. For the first time we were solidly backed. If we could put up good enough ideas for schemes the funding was there' (Interview 1999).

The expansion achieved by Copec in the decade in which public funding was introduced was out of all proportion to what had been achieved in the previous 50 years of largely voluntary effort. Between 1970 and 1980 the number of homes owned increased by a factor of 10 to 3,500, stock value increased by nearly 20 times to £25 million and the number of staff employed increased more than fivefold to 95.

Following merger with WHA in 1976, Copec Housing Trust was formed and developed a structure to manage 2,000 homes and to develop 300 new homes each year. Management was decentralised and branch offices opened in Wolverhampton and Sandwell, with offices opening later in Saltley, Moseley and Handsworth. A Special Projects department was set up to co-ordinate housing with support to groups referred to at the time as 'battered wives' and 'the disabled'. A housing advice service was set up in partnership with Birmingham city council. As described in Chapter 5, a group structure was developed with subsidiaries for shared ownership, low cost ownership without public subsidy and services to communal areas and gardens. Hestia took a similar approach to these opportunities growing to manage 2,000 homes by the time of merger in 1991 and setting-up a profit-making home ownership subsidiary – Hestia Homes.

Copec's growth strategy and diversification in the 1980s saw it forming subsidiaries to provide low cost home ownership options to first time buyers. Secretary of State for Employment, Kenneth Clarke, is shown here meeting Copec managers.

Going for growth

Transformation in the scale of Copec's activities set the scene for the next period in which growth took over as the main raison d'etre of the association. Between 1985 and 1995 the organisation grew to own nearly 10,000 homes with a capital value of £385 million and increased its staff to over 600. This was achieved not only through taking advantage of the public funding programme to develop new homes for rent, but also through expanding into home ownership programmes and other activities and (as we have seen in chapter 5). Mergers with other housing associations were also vital to growth (see chapter 8). It is possible to rationalise this growth strategy by comparing it to the aims earlier periods.   As David Mumford put it

> 'We had a tunnel vision, there were 40,000 on the city's housing list and now there was money to expand. I wanted to do things in a big way' (Interview 1999).

However, it is also possible to see the increasing expansion in the 1980s and early 1990s as a symbol of the new competitive mood in the housing association sector. This mood may be associated with the election in 1979 of a new Conservative government with a radical reform programme for the welfare state. For housing this meant the end of half a century of growth of the municipal sector and its gradual replacement by the non-profit sector. Two pieces of legislation were of particular importance in setting a new (neo-liberal) agenda and redefining the relationships between housing associations, local authorities and the state; the 1980 and 1988 Housing Acts:

- The 1980 Housing Act stimulated a process of dramatic decline in local authority housing through introducing the 'Right to Buy' for council tenants. This eventually led to over 2 million properties being sold. Housing associations were also affected by this provision since it extended to non-charitable associations. Several converted to charitable status to avoid the provisions of the Right To Buy. While Copec, Hestia, St Chad and Shape were already charitable housing associations, the subsidiaries enabled by the Act were treated somewhat differently, and while some were registered as charitable or non-charitable Industrial and Provident Societies, others such the SURE, an agency linked to Shape, were non-registered companies limited by guarantee.

- The 1988 Housing Act had a more dramatic impact on housing associations through their 're-privatisation'. Randolph (1993) comments:

> 'The Conservative government intended the Housing Act 1988 to stimulate a major shift in the orientation of housing associations. The objective was to move them firmly away from the quasi-public housing sector which associations had become as a result of the Housing Act 1974 and back towards the private, or more precisely, the 'independent' rental sector'.

The effects of the 1988 Housing Act on the development of Focus was profound. Within a year of the Act's introduction, Copec, Hestia and St Chad, along with Midland Area had formed the Focus group as a vehicle for joint bidding for development funding and raising private finance. By 1991, all but Midland Area had merged to form Focus. Shape joined the group later in 1994. Turning to the more general impacts of housing framework

Copec's management committee in the late 1980s. Back row, from left to right are Derrick Fysh, Jim Hewitson, Bert Massey, Chris Patterson, Mike Potter, Professor Ken Spencer, and the Reverend Rob Morris. Front row, from left to right, are Hazel Wright (Secretary), the Venerable John Duncan (Chairman), David Corney (Treasurer) and Connie Evason.

associated with the Conservative government of the 1980s and early 1990s, three examples illustrate the ways in which Copec/Focus embraced the new competitive ethos to 'go for growth'. Geographical expansion, the Housing Market Package and home ownership activities can be seen below:

Geographical expansion

The growth in the number of homes managed in the 1980s and 1990s was achieved partly as a result of increasing the number of geographical areas in which Copec/Focus was operating and thereby securing a greater share of the overall funding programme for housing associations. By 1993, Focus was working in 25 local authority areas compared to just 4 in the 1970s. David Mumford comments on the strategy in this period: 'we saw our core area as the Midlands- from Stoke to the M4!' This expansionism was viewed with suspicion by some other local housing associations and often by local authorities. While expansionism was being encouraged by the Housing Corporation. This caused some problems for David Mumford in his dual role as Copec Chief Executive and Housing Corporation Board Member:

> 'We were never the favourite. The Housing Corporation was worried that we were getting too much of the cake. I found out that the Midlands office had set a maximum limit of 10% of the programme to go to us. I took this up with the Board. There was no such policy' (Interview 1999).

However, there is also evidence that Copec's willingness and ability to work as an effective 'agent of the state' was appreciated by the Housing Corporation's programme staff. In 1989 when Copec received its largest allocation to date of £13 million (14% of the entire

The 'Dimbles', Lichfield. An example of geographical expansion in the early 1990s.

West Midlands programme), Housing Corporation Chief Executive David Edmonds commented that 'this large allocation of housing funds reflects the high esteem in which Copec is regarded by the Housing Corporation'. (Tenants Newsletter 1989). The West Midlands Housing Corporation regional office was later to actively support the merger between Copec, Hestia and St. Chad.

Duncan Edwards Close in Dudley. Another example of newbuild schemes at the time, developed in partnership with local authorities and increasingly more geographically diverse.

The Housing Market Package

Perhaps the most striking example of expansionism came in the very last year of growth of the Housing Corporation's programme in 1992, when the Chancellor Norman Lamont's Autumn Statement provided a one-off £580 million grant for housing associations to buy empty homes. The policy was designed to react to the prolonged slump in the housing market by removing 25,000 former owner-occupied homes from the market. Twenty-seven housing associations nationally were identified to spend this grant in record time to buy these homes, most of which had been repossessed by building societies. Focus bought 578 homes using £14 million HMP funding matched with £11 million private finance. This rampant expansionism had its price, with Focus' commitment to core areas brought into question and its control procedures breached by some instances of fraud in the acquisitions process (see chapter 5).

In the Housing Market Package, Focus bought many repossessed homes, some of which needed extensive refurbishment work.

Home ownership

The third example of a willingness to go for growth with only limited reference to the social purposes and values of the organisation was extensive involvement in low cost home ownership activities through Copec Two and Copec Three. While facilitating home ownership is a legitimate objective for housing associations, it was never seen as an organisational priority by Copec. The justification was an opportunistic one. These activities were simply undertaken because there was funding available, as a result of the top slicing of the Housing Corporation programme nationally for home ownership initiatives. David Mumford recalled that 'my view was if they're going to do it, we're going to be there' (Interview 1999). In the case of Copec Three, which undertook home ownership development without public grant, the aspiration was to generate surpluses that would subsidise the core purposes of the charitable Copec.

The Burns family at Rookery Lane, Coventry – a home ownership scheme.

During the 1980s and early 1990s Focus had become one of the most successful 'contractors of the state' in the housing association sector. By demonstrating the ability to deliver, the association was able to play a role in housing provision in the Midlands that would have been beyond the wildest dreams of Copec's founders. However, when the association came to take stock of its direction in advance of the 1997 General Election there was a sense that some of Copec's early social concern had been lost. A further transformation was necessary to restate Focus' core values and update these values in the light of changing times.

'New Deal' trainee at Hillfields Estate, Coventry. Focus has pulled together a partnership to help regenerate this local authority estate. The partnership covers, training employment, construction and the WATCH (Working Actively to Change Hillfields) group. £1 million is also being invested in the Victoria Street development on the estate.

Turning around the 'supertanker'

In a corporate planning process commencing in 1995, Focus determined to go back to its roots in terms of organisational direction. It decided to place the regeneration of communities at the centre of its organisational strategy, to tackle poverty and deprivation in the communities where it worked and to offer a regeneration service to partner agencies in new areas. This approach was influenced by the incorporation of Shape, and its extensive experience of community regeneration into the group. Central to the vision for the 21st century was the need to concentrate on providing a high quality service to tenants, partners and other stakeholders with particular emphasis on cost-effectiveness and value for money. As part of this approach, Focus recognised that concentration on its core business was essential. This meant a renewed emphasis on inner city work where the majority of its tenants and partner agencies were located. Focus disposed the of the management of its housing in the south-west through agreements with local housing associations (Knightstone and West Wiltshire).

By 1997, Focus had developed its organisational thinking to the extent where it decided to dramatically change the nature of the work it was undertaking and become a new type of organisation – a Social Investment Agency (see chapter 6). Social investment may be defined as an investment made principally for social purposes where the financial return is a secondary concern. The social investment agenda developed within Focus over the next two years. Increasing social inclusion through community development was a key principle, with Focus providing opportunities for local people to participate in services. An anti-poverty strategy aimed to improve the quality of life of communities and those on welfare benefits and provide incentives for those seeking work. Economic

Birmingham Regional Director John Morris briefs an audience of guests from local authorities and the voluntary sector on the aims of the Social Investment Agency. His was one of a series of Focus 'regional forums' in Birmingham, Coventry and the Black Country.

regeneration initiatives facilitated access to pre-vocational training guidance, work experience and employment. Local businesses were stimulated by Focus buying from local suppliers. Investment in Focus' homes through its Home Improvement Programme also enabled more money to circulate in local communities. Community health was targeted with the health needs of tenants and other residents promoted through better use of existing resources and levering in new resources. Lastly, Focus began to improve the quality of the physical environment through its Home Improvement Programme.

The launch of the Social Investment Agency – Prime Focus in July 2000. From left to right are the Reverend Peter Mortlock (Focus Coventry and Shire Chairman), John Edwards (acting Chief Executive of Advantage West Midlands), Richard Clark, (Focus' Chief Executive), Dr. Peter Knight (Focus' Chairman) and David Butler (Chief Executive of the Chartered Institute of Housing).

When the Labour Government came to power in 1997, Focus set about trying to influence the policy agenda and to demonstrate the relevance of its stance to emerging policy priorities. New policies emerged that have provided major opportunities to develop the social investment agency concept. Initiatives include the New Deal for Work, the New Deal for Communities and the work of the Social Exclusion Unit. Focus engaged directly with each of these initiatives as they began to filter through into concrete projects. In 2000 the social investment agency was being developed with the full implementation of a new Focus group structure fulfilling the strategy which began in 1994. The new group is called 'Prime Focus' (see chapter 6 for more detail). Summing up this final transformation to date, Chief Executive Richard Clark commented:

'Many people have compared what we are trying to do to changing the course of a supertanker- and I'd say we're half way there. In the last twelve months we've pulled the organisation around from being 'bricks and mortar' led to face in the right direction, towards social investment. Now the task is to move in that direction' (Annual Report 1998).

8

Forming Focus:
the role of mergers

The story of Focus is one of seven housing associations. Although it can trace its history back to 1925, when Copec was established, Focus today is also the product of more recent developments within the housing association sector. This includes amalgamations with six other associations formed in the 1960s, 1970s and 1980s. Thus while Focus can claim to be an old housing association with roots in the Church inspired philanthropic housing initiatives of the 1920s, it also has more modern roots in the social movements and public policy developments which led to the formation of Birmingham Housing Trust (BHT) and Wolverhampton Housing Association (WHA) in the 1960s; Hestia, St Chad, Shape and Harambee Housing Associations in the 1970s. Today, while a significant number of Focus' committee members are linked to the Christian Church, others are from a range of faiths and convictions, as might be expected in today's pluralist community. Perhaps the primary way in which Focus has developed into the organisation it is today has been achieved through mergers and takeovers of other housing associations. While not all developments within the evolution from Copec to Focus can be identified

One of Copec's early refurbishment schemes – Mosse Houses in Tower Street, Summer Lane. The refurbishment included retention of the shops on the ground floor. The scheme was named after Canon W. G. Mosse by his parishioners at St. Anne's Church Moseley who raised funds to buy and refurbish the properties. The scheme was opened by Bishop Hamilton Barnes in 1930.

with mergers solely, the acquisition of stock, skills and commitment of committee members and staff have played key roles in making Focus what it is today. Growth and expansion of activities have been the key drivers of these developments, although each example reflects slightly different purposes as this chapter will illustrate.

Reading national trends

In many ways, Focus in growing through mergers and in moving towards a new group structure has reflected national trends in the wider housing association sector. As figure 4 below indicates the sector has been losing about 1 percent of associations each year since the 1970s. This activity has been fairly steady but there were two main peaks:

Figure 3. Housing Association Transfers of Engagements 1976/7 to 1999/2000

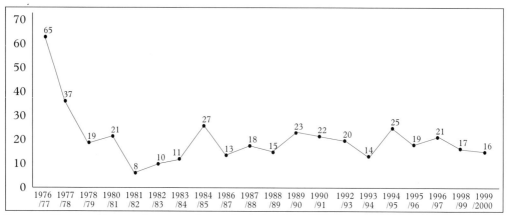

Source: Housing Corporation manual records analysed by CURS.
Note: Dates to March 1992 refer to date of application of completed ToEs, from April 1992
          dates refer to date of deletion from the register

- After the Housing Act 1974 when smaller associations such as WHA were encouraged to join larger associations to take full advantage of opportunities to develop with public subsidy.   This was one of the most intensive periods of expansion and development of the sector resulting from the introduction of public subsidy and registration of eligible bodies with the Housing Corporation. Helen Cope (1999) comments that this Act marked 'the end of an era of reliance upon largely voluntary effort and charitable donations'.

- After the Housing Act 1988 when arrangements such as the Focus 'umbrella' (a strategic alliance of four housing associations) were used to enable associations to achieve the scale necessary to access private finance at competitive rates. Cope (1999) writes that 'smaller associations have felt especially threatened by the impact of private finance'. The eventual decision of Copec, Hestia and St. Chad to merge also reflected national trends. During this period large associations such as Circle 33, London and Quadrant and Metropolitan were also consolidating stock holdings through Transfers of Engagements.

Figure 5 indicates that Focus' recent move to establish a group structure to accommodate both housing and social investment activities has also been in line with key trends in the sector. There was a significant growth in the registration of group structures by the Housing Corporation after 1996. These groups were formed for a number of reasons including:

- tax efficiency (to transfer surpluses to charitable organisations not liable for corporation tax);
- to accommodate diversification such as social investment;
- to provide central services to enable new subsidiaries such as stock transfer organisations to get benefits of scale while maintaining a degree of independence.

Figure 4. Housing Corporation Consents for Transfers of Engagements and Group Structures 1993/4 to 1999/2000

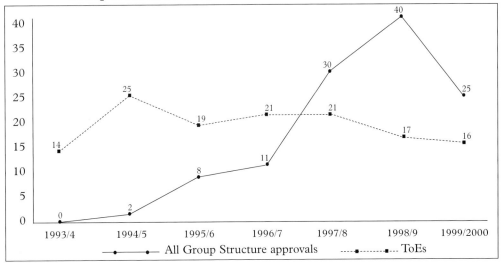

Source: Housing Corporation Registry Data.
Note: Group Structures include consents for parent/subsidiary rule changes, new subsidiaries for existing RSLs and new Group structures with non-asset holding parents.

Mergers and group structures: key factors

Focus' experience of mergers and group structures over a thirty year period has reflected a variety of external pressures and internal motivations. These are discussed below and may be summarised as follows:

- **Old meets new: the Copec and BHT merger of 1970** – brokered and supported by Shelter, which had worked with both associations, but wanted a single strong association partner in Birmingham as a recipient of Shelter grants;

- **Moving out of Birmingham: the Copec and WHA merger of 1976** – supported by the Housing Corporation to enable Wolverhampton to take full advantage of the new public funding for housing associations introduced by the Housing Act 1974;

- **Benefits from being bigger: establishing Focus as an 'umbrella' organisation** – to coordinate the operations of Copec, Hestia, Midland Area and St Chad Housing Associations in 1989 to raise private finance to enable mixed funded development and competitive bidding after the Housing Act 1988;

- **A new unitary housing association: the merger of Copec, Hestia and St. Chad** – minus Midland Area, into a unitary association – Focus – with merged subsidiaries as a response to growing commercial pressures on smaller housing associations such as St. Chad in the early in 1990s;

- **The take-over by Focus of Shape Housing association** – as a response to the financial problems of Shape in overstretching its operations as it sought to retain its community renewal commitments while developing large experimental, housing projects;

- **Maintaining BME community control of local housing: Harambee and Black Star** – Focus takes over Harambee because of financial and management problems, followed by a relaunch of the association as Black Star with the support of three other BME associations – HAMAC, United Churches and Nehemiah;

- **A merger too far?: the abortive merger talks with Mercian Housing Association** – as part of the development of a group structure in which to place the 'social investment agency' concept;

- **Group structures** – developing a group as the final step in developing a charitable legal status for the 'Social Investment Agency' – as the 'Prime Focus' group.

Housing conditions in the 1960s. Birmingham Housing Trust was formed to tackle such conditions in the city.

Old meets new – the Copec and Birmingham Housing Trust merger

By 1970 Copec had already been in existence for nearly half a century. It had succeeded in many of its early objectives, particularly in securing municipal commitment to clearing and improving inner area slums, including ironically many of its own properties. It had achieved excellent standards of housing management through a professional staff and the Octavia Hill system. It was also financially secure, with '£50-60,000 sitting in a bank account' (David Mumford Interview 1999). It had begun to develop new priorities, for example, housing for single women. But there was a need for change summed up by its long time housing manager, Janet Rushbrooke who said that 'by the late 1960s the time was right for a change – we needed a shot in the arm'. As Malpass (2000) has confirmed:

> 'It must not be forgotten that existing organisations continued to grow and change, to a greater or lesser extent. Some of the dynamism of the new associations rubbed off on the older ones, leading to conscious attempts to modernise themselves and their dwellings'.

The Copec and BHT merger exemplifies this situation. The shot in the arm for Copec was to be provided by a 'brash newcomer', BHT, chaired by Birmingham University Chaplain, the Reverend John Duncan, and directed by Birmingham city councillor, David Mumford. BHT had only been in existence for five years, and had quite limited financial resources. As David Mumford put it:

> 'There was never quite enough money, but by borrowing, buying homes and hoping inflation would increase the asset base we were able to expand quite rapidly' (Interview 1999).

However, BHT was in tune with the times and had excellent connections with the city council, who funded the association's start up and lent money to buy properties, and with the national 'movers and shakers' such as Bruce Kenrick, founder of Shelter and Notting Hill Housing Trust, both of whom made funding available to BHT.

Negotiating the merger

Like many voluntary sector mergers, the idea was promoted by an external funding body, in this case the national homelessness campaign charity Shelter. Shelter was already funding both housing associations, but brokered the merger because they wanted to fund a single and larger association in Birmingham. This is illustrated by a quote from Shelter at the time:

> 'We wish to express our strong hope that the merger goes through. Larger housing associations have proved to be more acceptable to local authorities and the Ministry of Housing. There can be no doubt that a great wealth of experience now exists within and between Copec and BHT. As a merged body they are well placed to take up the opportunities represented by the Housing Act 1969 and the improved interpretations that the Ministry are expected to promulgate...... Shelter affirms that it will be ready to aid your merged associations as to the shortfall in finance' (Copec/BHT merger contract 1970).

THE BIRMINGHAM COPEC HOUSE IMPROVEMENT SOCIETY LIMITED

To: THE MEMBERS OF THE SOCIETY.

YORK HOUSE,
38 GREAT CHARLES STREET,
BIRMINGHAM 3.

28th October, 1970.

DEAR SIR OR MADAM,

MERGER WITH THE BIRMINGHAM HOUSING TRUST

Our letter of March 7th advised you of discussions between Copec and The Birmingham Housing Trust ("BHT") regarding a possible merger. After careful examination both Committees have agreed to recommend to members that we proceed. We accordingly enclose the following documents:—

(A)   A joint Memorandum of proposals from the Chairmen of Copec and BHT.

(B)   A copy for your information of a letter and Notice of Meeting which is being sent to all the Copec Loan Stockholders.

(C)   A Notice of a Special General Meeting of Members to be held at 5.30 p.m. on November 12th at Dr. Johnson House, Birmingham 4, setting out the Resolutions to be put to the Meeting.

(D)   A white proxy card for the Special General Meeting.

Briefly the effects of the proposed Resolutions are:—

1.   Copec assumes the undertaking and responsibilities of BHT.
2.   Copec issues shares to BHT members, one for one.
3.   Copec changes its name to Birmingham Copec Housing Trust.

The effect of these first three Resolutions is to merge the two organisations into one body ("the Trust") combining the resources, knowledge and experience of Copec and BHT. Resolutions 4 and 5 define the Council of the Trust and revise the Copec Rules to suit the Trust. The amendments, as far as possible, follow the model rules of the National Federation of Housing Societies. It should be especially noted that the first part of Resolution 5 alters the Rules to permit Copec to give security to its loan stockholders by creating one or more charges on its assets. Please see paragraph headed "Birmingham Copec Housing Trust" on page 3 of the Joint Memorandum.

Resolution 6 appoints the first Council. Resolution 7 approves the mortgage deed by which Copec will charge certain properties in favour of the loan stockholders.

Your Committee recommends the proposals to you and trusts that you will attend the special meeting on November 12th and vote in favour. The members of the BHT Committee have been invited to attend the meeting.

Dr. Johnson House is reached through the entrance to the Friends' Meeting House in Bull Street, next to Lewis's. Coffee and sandwiches will be served after the meeting.

Will you please let us know whether or not you will be coming to the Meeting by completing and returning to us the form at the foot of this letter. If you are unable to attend we hope that you will complete and return the enclosed proxy card.

We believe that the merger will forward the purpose for which Copec exists and will enable us to enlarge and speed up work for housing. Members who wish to support this work further may do so by interesting other people in the new organisation. Anyone can become a member by taking up one share. Financial contributions and gifts of loan stock either immediate or by will are very welcome.

Yours faithfully,

SARAH E. SYKES,
PHILIP R. SOUTHALL,
Joint Hon. Secretaries.

The Copec and Birmingham Housing Trust Merger document for the Special General Meeting in 1970.

Merger negotiations were undertaken principally by Mr. Christopher Taylor, Copec Chairman since the early 1940s, and the Reverend John Duncan, the Chairman of BHT since its inception in 1965. Alongside the two chairmen, the negotiating teams included prominent committee members and the two respective managers of Copec and BHT – Janet Rushbrooke and David Mumford. David Mumford was the prime mover in arguing for a merger:

> 'I had empire building tendencies from the beginning! – a duty to expand to meet the needs of the homeless' (Interview 1999).

All involved in the negotiations were motivated by the need to develop a new type of housing association which brought together the best traditions of the senior and longstanding partner, Copec, with the new dynamism of BHT and its better links to Shelter and the city council. John Duncan, who became the first Chairman of the merged housing association summarised the mood of the negotiations:

> 'Those involved in the negotiations were determined to see that the new trust should be just that – a new trust formed by a joining of equals, rather than a takeover by either one or the other. In consequence, it should not be surprising that the new organisation has a somewhat different ambience to either of the original associations' (Annual Report 1971).

David Mumford commented: 'When the Copec committee said 'yes', I thought that it was a brave decision – I have never understood why they did it!'

Building a new organisation –
a gradual path to integration

Birmingham Copec Housing Trust (BCHT) came into being in November 1970 when Copec accepted the assets and liabilities of BHT. This was the result of over nine months of negotiations between Copec and BHT with the view of forming a new housing association which would effectively be able to meet the needs of those in Birmingham who fell outside the housing programmes of the local authority.

In many ways this was a 'reverse takeover'. At the time of the merger, the new organisation owned property with a value of £1.5 million with 532 tenancies in management (358 from Copec and 174 from BHT, but BHT also had close to 200 properties in development) (Copec/BHT Merger Document 1970). The Copec name was retained as a means of marking the new association's historical links with the housing societies of the 1920s. With a full-time staff of 18 people, the 'new' Copec was managed by a 'Council' of three key officers, including Chairman John Duncan, Secretary Peter Loose and Treasurer Robert Reardon – all three being former committee members of BHT. Thus despite bringing a minority of the physical and financial assets to the new organisation, BHT through its dynamism was able to walk away with effective control of an organisation several times its original size. Perhaps in recognition of this, it was decided to take a gradual path to securing the full benefits of integration, allowing Copec to be managed in a traditional style for a while longer.

Following the merger, both committee members and staff explored and developed the structure and role of the new organisation. However, integration of the two housing associations continued to be affected by the differing philosophies of the two original associations. For the first 18 months, Janet Rushbrooke and David Mumford operated as de facto joint managers of Copec, with each initially keeping their own departments, their management styles and approaches to housing development. The Copec philosophy was a product of its time and its origins, being Quaker, often philanthropic and paternalistic, 'for the deserving'. BHT saw itself as working with those client groups no-one else would consider (such as women experiencing domestic violence). This produced a clash of styles which continued until the two housing associations began to feel more comfortable with each other. John Duncan diplomatically summarised the two styles when he said:

> 'Janet Rushbrooke brought to the new organisation wisdom and long experience of managing property in the Octavia Hill tradition; David Mumford brings his flair for public relations, forward planning and relationships with those vital partners in our work, Shelter, the city council and government departments' (Annual Report 1973).

The 'Council', Copec's primary policy-making body, was supplemented by a full management committee of sixteen people – eleven from BHT and five from the original Copec. The housing management committee was chaired by Frank Barlow, a Copec committee member from the 1950s and general manager of the Bournville Village Trust. The first meeting of the new management committee passed a resolution indicating the new philosophy which Copec wished to put into practice in the coming years:

Copec committee members attending an Annual General Meeting after merger with Wolverhampton Housing Association in 1976. With John Duncan are Connie and Muriel Evason and guest speaker.

- Copec exists to identify and serve those in housing need of various kinds;

- In the first instance, continuing and holding under review the types of work and quality of management previously undertaken by the constituent trusts;

- Undertaking further work in new fields and investment in property with amenities appropriate to particular groups of people in need;

- Copec's work will be linked, where suitable, with the possibility of establishing improvement areas in consultation and cooperation with the city council, voluntary bodies and other voluntary housing associations.

This resolution was clearly a 'holding' resolution in that it enabled the two organisations to become more familiar with each other in the early years while allowing more integrated approaches to management, housing development and new ways of meeting housing needs to be explored. While the former Copec and BHT semi-independent methods of working continued throughout 1971 and 1972, the way was cleared for a fully integrated approach when Janet Rushbrooke retired after twenty-five years service at Christmas 1972. The former Copec Chairman, Christopher Taylor, who did not become a council member or sub-committee chairman in the new organisation, also retired in 1973. David Mumford then became Copec's sole general manager and the process of post-merger integration was complete.

Moving out of Birmingham – the Copec and Wolverhampton Housing Association merger

The next merger in 1976 was very different. It is a good example using merger rather than organic growth to extend the geographical coverage of an organisation. Director David Mumford summed this motivation up when he said that 'it was better for Copec to expand by working with local people. 'We didn't know Wolverhampton – they did'. Thus the benefits to Copec were not confined to the 100 or so properties transferred, but also extended to the network of relationships that Wolverhampton Housing Association (WHA) had established and the opportunities this brought to access public subsidy and to work in newly declared Housing Action Areas (HAAs) in Wolverhampton.

We may also look at the merger from WHA's point of view. The association had been successful in building voluntary support from individuals and from bodies such as the Wolverhampton Council of Churches and the local Probation Service. It employed staff and had acquired and converted over 100 properties in the nine years after its formation in response to the Shelter campaigns of the late 1960s. It had a good record of charitable fund raising as well as local authority and bank mortgages and successfully registered with the Housing Corporation in 1974 to receive new public funding. However, it was still not seen as sufficiently experienced to manage the scale of investment envisaged in the HAAs. The local authority had 'come round to the potential housing associations could

Refurbished properties at the time in Wolverhampton.

bring to urban renewal' but did not see WHA as capable of performing this role (Interview with David Gregory 2000).   As retired bank manager Bert Massey, WHA Chairman at the time of the merger explained:

> 'WHA, the local authority and the Housing Corporation met at the town hall. The conclusion was that WHA was too small to do HAA work. Copec was suggested as a potential partner' (Interview 1999).

By becoming a local committee of a larger association (under Bert Massey's Chairmanship), members were able to extend their work to become involved in the major housing investment planned for Wolverhampton.

Doing the deal

On this occasion the merger was brokered by the Housing Corporation who approached Copec to begin discussions about collaborating with WHA.   Copec had grown significantly since the merger with BHT and had 1,300 homes in management with close to 400 in the development pipeline by the time of the Wolverhampton negotiations. Following 6 months of discussions between the two associations in late 1975 and early 1976, the decision was made that WHA would be subsumed into Copec. The merger was completed in August 1976.

The merger created WHA as a branch office to Copec, which dropped the 'Birmingham' from its name and became Copec Housing Trust for the first time, signalling moves outside of the Birmingham area (plans were already afoot to develop 65 homes in Sandwell as part of the Beeches Rd HAA, thus filling in some of the space between the two territories). Copec retained the staff of WHA although there were some subsequent changes in senior management and a new Wolverhampton area committee was established, made up of the existing management committee of WHA, and responsible to the Copec Council. Three members of the old WHA committee (David Gregory, Jim Hewitson and Bert Massey) were also invited onto the management committee, which had at this time replaced the former 'Council' (Bert Massey became Chairman of the Wolverhampton area committee and remained so until 1997). This approach enabled committee members of WHA to play an active role in the future development of Copec and for Copec to retain the local knowledge of committed people. In this sense, the merger may have been a more equal partnership than the earlier 'reverse takeover' of Copec by BHT.

Grade II listed buildings in Birmingham's George Street West. This was one of the last major refurbishment schemes carried out by Copec before merger with Hestia and St. Chad in 1991. Local MP Clare Short, later Secretary of State for International Development in 1997, plants a tree to mark this development.

Benefits from being bigger – the Focus 'Umbrella'

Beginnings: a strategic alliance

The Housing Act 1988 was a major stimulus for housing associations to seek economies of scale through larger organisations and groupings. There were two main reasons for this. First, the introduction of mixed funding as the norm for new developments meant that associations needed to raise private finance themselves. The expertise required to do this favoured the creation of larger organisations which could afford specialist posts and external advice. Also, groupings with other housing associations provided opportunities to use the housing stock as equity to raise larger amounts of funding and to negotiate private finance at keener rates. Second, the greater competition associated with the 1988 Act regime encouraged associations to seek more general scale economies in their operations, for example by spreading central overhead costs across a larger number of properties and activities.

Focus was formed in 1989 as an 'umbrella' organisation to assist four West Midlands housing associations to meet these challenges, especially in raising private finance. The four associations were Copec, Hestia, Midland Area and St. Chad who together had joint stock holdings of more than 9,000 homes in the West Midlands conurbation and in Staffordshire, Shropshire and Warwickshire. This joint asset base, enabled the four associations to raise larger tranches of private finance than they could have on their own, and at lower rates of interest. Initially Focus was seen as a form of partnership or 'strategic alliance' in which partners retained a large degree of autonomy, including exit from the partnership. It issued a prospectus for potential partners, regulators and funders

The Chairmen of Focus' four member housing associations in 1989 after signing an agreement to work together under the 'Focus Umbrella' organisation. From left to right the are Cliff Edwards (Midland Area), the Venerable John Duncan (Copec), the Reverend Peter Mortlock (St. Chad) and Dick King (Hestia).

which elicited responses from Shape and St. Basils (a Birmingham charity for single homeless people). Shape formally applied to join the existing Focus grouping in September 1989 as a 'late comer' but its unwillingness to lose its unique identity as a community agency was a stumbling block. As a letter from Shape Chief Executive Chris Wadhams indicated:

> 'We accept that our participation in Focus would be on a 'take it or leave it' basis. Notwithstanding this, we would like to feel that our participation would be subject to a number of 'understandings'.....recognition of Shape's somewhat wider brief.....freedom for Shape to negotiate initiatives for non-housing activities.....an accceptance of our other 'partnerships' – Sparkbrook NIA, BICBUS and Inner City Contracts'.

Focus Key Objectives 1989

- Providing an improved and comprehensive service for existing and potential customers;
- Securing access on a group basis to enhanced financial resources and the better management of those resources to meet challenges and risks;
- Developing the group's human resources in terms of technical and managerial skills;
- Creating the leading provider of social housing in the West Midlands;
- Maximising opportunities for securing real economies of scale.

St. Basils, now a Registered Social Landlord, but not in 1989, had ambitions to become a housing association. It shared committee members with Focus (most notably Chairman John Duncan) and Focus had transferred a homeless persons scheme to St. Basils' management in 1988. St. Basils saw Focus as a way to achieve its ambitions, as a letter from Director Les Milner at the time shows:

> 'It was encouraging to know that Focus may respond positively to a move by St. Basils to be part of your organisation whether we are registered or not and to realise that through such a partnership registration may be enhanced as a possibility'.

However, neither Shape nor St. Basils took their applications forward, partly because their aims could not be met by the Focus partnership at the time, and because Focus moved to become a fully merged housing association very quickly; not something that the other two housing organisations wanted at this time.

A new unitary housing association

For the next two years, the Focus Group worked together while retaining operational independence, bidding jointly for Housing Corporation funding and raising private finance. However, there are indications from correspondence at the time that the Housing Corporation could not see the benefits of this 'umbrella' arrangement in contrast to a fully merged association. A letter from the Housing Corporation's West Midlands office in 1990 demonstrates the way things were moving:

> 'We hope that Focus will be able to demonstrate that it has been able to provide 'one stop shopping' to combine the resources of all the participating associations and to provide a better choice for applicants and tenants'.

Previous St. Chad Chief Executive Barbara Whitfield, celebrating the opening of Arbourtree Court in Wombourne, Staffordshire in 1997. She was Director of Focus's Coventry and Shire Regional Committee at the time.

As is often the case with strategic alliances, for some members success in one area of collaboration can lead to increasing collaboration and eventually to the decision to cease operating as independent organisations.   All four associations had participated in working parties on joint issues relating to development, housing management and support services. It became increasingly clear that three of the associations wanted to go further than work in partnership and to pursue discussion about forming a unitary association.   Midland Area decided that it did not wish to pursue this option, as its management committee did not want to lose its independence, and withdrew from the group. After further negotiations, the remaining three associations were wound up and their assets were transferred to Copec which then changed its name to Focus. The motivations for proceeding to partnership and thence to full merger varied between the associations:

- For Copec this was another natural step in remaining a key player. The Chief Executive of Copec at the time, David Mumford, commented that they did not want to get left behind their peer group, which he saw as the large housing associations in London and the north. They wanted to 'stay in the same league', in housing development terms. Focus' goal was to manage more than 10,000 homes, placing it in the large housing associations group at the time.

- In the case of Hestia, although the housing association had built up a rented housing stock of 2,000 since its formation in 1970 by a group of Birmingham businessmen, its home ownership arm, Hestia Homes, had run into financial difficulty at the end of the late-1980s property boom. The subsequent slump in the housing market caused considerable financial difficulties for the charitable parent association. It was partly this need that made Hestia turn to Copec for financial and management assistance leading to the initial strategic alliance. Hestia's management committee had 3 places on the Focus committee and transferred committee members to a new area committee in Coventry.

- St. Chad had quite different origins to Hestia, having developed from Methodist Church roots in Lichfield in the early 1970s. It had expanded more slowly than Hestia and had retained a geographical identity with more than half of its 200 stock in Lichfield, and the remainder in Staffordshire and Warwickshire. In advance of the 1988 Housing Act the association had commissioned a review of its structure and finances and been advised that it would need to double its stock to cover the costs of employing qualified financial staff. However, St. Chad's management committee were not keen to lose their identity by merging with another Staffordshire association and two years of talks with the most likely candidates had come to nought. Into this limbo stepped Copec. This time the merger broker was Copec's housing director, Kevin Bentley, who had been invited onto the St Chad's committee. Barbara Whitfield, St. Chad's Chief Executive at this time remembers:

'We   had a number of abortive partnership discussions with similar and small associations locally, but Kevin suggested that we open discussions with an inner city association like Copec. Although we had not thought of this before, it seemed to make sense as Copec's priority was not to develop in our sort of areas and the   arrangement might be mutually beneficial' (Interview 1999).

Rather than seeing Copec as an 'outside predator', the personal connection and difference in scale seems to have led to the view that it was less of a threat to identity than a merger with a smaller local association. The former St. Chad Chairman the Reverend Peter Mortlock said: 'the merger was based on a great deal of trust, touched by realism' (Interview 1999). St. Chad's management committee then became Focus' town and country committee, overseeing activities in Staffordshire and other rural areas. As with the Copec/WHA merger, the association managed to retain local knowledge and commitment.

Play area at Lozells, Birmingham. Both Focus and Shape were involved in providing community facilities.

The take-over of Shape by Focus

The next merger, with Shape Housing Association in 1994, superficially provides a clear example of a takeover of a housing association in financial difficulties brokered by the Housing Corporation as industry regulator. However, beneath the surface the unique philosophy and willingness to innovate that drove Shape, and which some might argue led to its financial difficulties, may be seen in retrospect to have had a significant impact in reviving Focus' social mission.

Shape had been formed in the late 1970s to meet the needs of the inner city, at first through short life housing programmes. and other programmes for single people such as the acquisition and refurbishment of the Snow Hill hostel. From its early days, Shape developed wide networks of support for community renewal activities, accessed European funding and co-founded People for Action (PFA) to promote innovative approaches to neighbourhood regeneration (following the merger with Focus, PFA became an independent organisation, which is now a major advocate for the community investment activities by housing associations). As non-housing activity expanded, Shape developed a structure to accommodate linked organisations such as Shape Urban Renewal Enterprises Limited (SURE) which developed a construction company, a fully-equipped garage, a garden centre, a metal shop and a linked architectural practice.

Focus Housing Office at Bradford Street, Digbeth. This was the former office of Focus merger partner Shape Housing Association in the early 1990s.

However, the ambitious and innovative approach eventually led to an urgent need for Shape to find a better resourced partner. Shape Chairman Rick Groves, an academic at the Centre for Urban and Regional Studies, summarises Shape's trajectory leading to the Bismillah project that was to be their undoing:

'Shape grew quickly in its early days because it was fulfilling a function of housing and supporting the very poorest groups – those most socially excluded through the changes in the economy in the 1980s. The key aim was to house mainly homeless men and provide some training or working component. Shape later became what I term an eclectic organisation – developing ideas and initiatives from a wide range of sources and deriving its impetus from a growing body of research. The 'Bismillah' project was a huge undertaking for a small association such as Shape, it involved converting a former silver factory in Birmingham's Jewellery Quarter' (Interview 1999).

Shape's plan for Bismillah was to provide 180 flats for single people in the working part of the city through construction of newbuild flats behind the facade of the listed Silver factory. It began to appear to the Housing Corporation that Shape could no longer maintain its financial commitment generally and to this scheme in particular

Focus was asked to begin merger negotiations with the Shape management committee. Following three months of talks, Shape agreed to become part of the Focus group, bringing to the merger 400 rented homes, 280 hostel bedspaces, the Bismillah scheme and the proposed development of the Foyer project which had won a design award. Focus merged with the Shape group in November 1994.

While in many ways this was a takeover of Shape by Focus, there were some echoes of the earlier BHT/Copec merger where the smaller partner had a greater impact on the future organisation than one might expect from the balance sheet alone. Shape brought into Focus its considerable experience and track-record of non-housing activities, particularly its neighbourhood regeneration work, development of employment and training initiatives and its experienced staff and committee. The Shape philosophy prefigured the approach to social investment activities that characterised Focus in the late 1990s and its organisational structure had some similarities with today's 'Prime Focus' group.

Focus Chairman John Duncan and Shape Chairman Rick Groves celebrate the coming together of 'two parts of the jigsaw' when merger discussions were completed in 1994.

Maintaining minority ethnic community control of local housing: Harambee and Black Star

Another merger with an apparently similar agenda of rescuing a beleaguered housing association in support of the Housing Corporation was that with Harambee. This housing association was black and minority ethnic (BME), operating out of Handsworth with 400 rented homes and supported housing schemes for African-Caribbean people with mental health problems. Harambee had been in management difficulties for some time and was about to be wound-up by the Housing Corporation when Focus mounted a rescue operation at a late stage. The merger process took a little over three months but at the end of this period the assets and housing stock of Harambee were taken over by Focus.

This time the distinctive sub-plot was to ensure that Harambee's housing remained in the management and control of minority ethnic communities in Handsworth. To this end, Focus had facilitated discussions between existing minority ethnic housing associations in Birmingham – United Churches, Handsworth Single Homeless (later HAMAC) and Nehemiah – and these three put forward committee members to establish a new minority ethnic-led association – Black Star. Focus retained ownership of the Harambee stock but leased it back to the new association and transferred some of its own stock to improve the rental income of Black Star. Focus also acquired housing from North British Housing Association which had previously leased this stock to Harambee.

After the merger, Focus provided a range of support services to Black Star, including financial assistance and management. However, in 1999 the Housing Corporation expressed further concern at the financial position of the new association, and there were additional management problems with a major scheme for people with mental health problems. As Focus was still the owner of the housing stock, and the lease of the stock to Black Star was due to run out in January 2000, the onus fell on Focus to assist Black Star to overcome its problems. As Birmingham Regional Director of Focus, John Morris, said:

> 'Although we were determined to assist Black Star to succeed, the concerns of our regulator had to be taken into account. We looked at a range of options with the committee of Black Star and decided that the association should continue, but have the shelter of becoming formally part of the Focus Group' (Interview 2000).

While far from successful, the formation of Black Star in partnership with other BME associations provided one model of support for the continued development of a BME housing association in financial difficulties. It clearly indicates the difficulties encountered in using business models such as mergers, which imply control, in a context where the need for equality of partnership and sensitivity to community needs are the hallmarks of success. Despite this, as a member of the Prime Focus group, Black Star has new opportunities to enlarge its activities in Handsworth through involvement in the newly formed Handsworth Area Regeneration Trust (HART is a regeneration agency established by Focus and other local housing associations). As with all unequal mergers, only time will tell whether such benefits to Black Star will outweigh the limited autonomy that inevitably faces a smaller partner.

The relaunch of Black Star Housing Association in its new offices in Handsworth following the demise of Harambee Housing Association. Black Star is now part of the Prime Focus Group.

Photography courtesy of John Harris

Children at 'Black Patch' Smethwick. Focus helped the association to develop its 'housing plus' and community regeneration agenda. 'Black Patch' was a small estate developed using Sandwell Council's Single Regeneration Budget allocation. Lone parents were provided with business training, of which a high percentage found work after training was completed. A food cooperative was also developed.

A merger too far?: the case of Mercian

Focus and Mercian began discussions about developing a group structure in early 1998. Focus had been developing its ideas about a new group structure with a view to creating a substantial charitable parent body to oversee its housing and regeneration activities in pursuit of its 'social investment agency' status and work. Mercian was considering its long-term future and was interested in Focus' social investment approach as a potential model for its future. Exploratory talks were held between the associations' committees and staff, with working parties reviewing a range of options for future partnership arrangements within a group structure. Two key concerns were that there would be benefits from economies of scale, especially in terms of management costs; and, benefits to tenants through improved service delivery.

Although agreement was reached on the broad issues of partnership, 'the devil was in the detail'. In particular, the opportunity for refinancing both associations' loan portfolios, developed over ten years of raising private finance, could not deliver the benefits envisaged (such as reductions in interest repayments on loans and therefore management costs). Re-negotiating Mercian's loans, as part of the proposed merged association's large loan portfolio, would have brought significant benefits to Mercian and its tenants, in terms of lower interest payments and lower rent rises. However, Mercian's loan covenants would have imposed substantial early redemption penalties, effectively wiping out any advantage from lower interest rates. Comparisons between the housing and tenants of the two housing associations also revealed major differences. Mercian was a considerably smaller association than Focus, managing mostly newbuild homes, much of which was outside inner city areas. Mercian also had considerably lower management costs, rent arrears and property vacancies than Focus. Part of the reason was that Focus housed a more disadvantaged tenants in older, less popular properties in the inner city. It was not possible for increased benefits to Mercian's tenants to be demonstrated on this basis, despite the opportunities for regeneration and social investment work which the partnership promised. Exploratory talks were subsequently abandoned. As Richard Clark, Focus' Chief Executive said about this outcome:

> 'We were never going ahead unless we could bring genuine benefits to tenants. I am naturally disappointed, but we believe we have made the right decision' (Tenants Newsletter 1998).

Perhaps the most unusual feature of the merger discussions was that they were so well publicised. Research on merger proposals in the housing association sector indicates that a high proportion of talks are abortive, and that most never get into the public arena Mullins (2000b). The inability to deliver demonstrable benefits to tenants was also a significant feature. Guidance on Constitutional and Structural Partnerships issued by the Housing Corporation in Autumn 1998 requires associations to identify a business case for mergers, to ensure that tenants are informed and that their position is made no worse as a result of the merger. This was not possible in the case of Focus and Mercian.

Table (15) – Key Drivers Of Focus Mergers (1970 To 2000)

Merging Association	Key Drivers Of Mergers	Resulting Association
1970 Copec House Improvement Society and Birmingham Housing Trust	Shelter. Need to blend traditional skills of Focus and new approaches of BHT. New larger association desired.	1970 Birmingham Copec Housing Trust
1976 Birmingham Copec Housing Trust and the Wolverhampton Housing Association	WHA not able to develop in HAAs; lack of asset base and experience. Housing Corporation brokered.	1976 Copec Housing Trust
1990 Copec Housing Trust, Hestia Housing Association and St. Chad Housing Society	Need to meet challenges of Housing Act 1988, Hestia had financial problems. St Chad wanted to continue to grow.	1991 Focus Housing Group
1994 Focus Housing Group and the Shape Housing Group	Shape financially overstretched, large schemes exposed poor revenue stream and cross-subsidy with 'Housing Plus'.	1994 Focus Housing Group
1995 Focus Housing Group and Harambee Housing Association	Harambee finances poor. Management problems with mental health scheme.	1995 Focus Housing Group and Black Star Housing Association
1998 Focus Housing Group and Mercian Housing Association	Mercian wishing to become involved in social investment activities. No merger due to differing tenant/stock profiles (could not meet Housing Corporation merger criteria).	1998 Focus Housing Group and Mercian Housing Association
2000 Focus Housing Group and Black Star Housing Association	Re-emerging financial problems for Black Star. Taken into Focus Housing Group. Housing Corporation advocacy of option.	2000 Prime Focus with Focus and Focus Two, and Black Star amongst subsidiaries.

Group structures

An early example of a group structure in the housing sector was provided by Copec in the early 1980s. Because it was unclear at the time whether charitable associations such as Copec were empowered to undertake low cost home ownership activities it became common practice to establish non-charitable bodies to undertake this work. Copec set up such a subsidiary in 1981. Gradually the group became more complex as new activities were added and new subsidiaries established to undertake diverse activities. By 1984 there were three new subsidiaries; Copec Two, Copec Three, Copec Services and plans for a fourth – the Heart of England Unit Trust which never materialized (see chapter 5 for details of the role of each of these subsidiaries).

In many ways the Copec group structure was ahead of its time. The management case for the Group Structure was based on accommodating diverse activities. As Copec had grown and each of its main business streams differed and required different management and business skills, there were advantages in delegating responsibility for each main stream to 'a champion who believed in it'. This served the need to undertake non-core activities in ring-fenced subsidiaries and offered the prospect of producing surpluses from these activities which could be covenanted back to the charitable parent as part of a special reserve. In the event about £120,000 a year was generated in this way and by 1989 the special reserve account stood at £531,000. However, diversification was not without its pitfalls.

New group structure for the Social Investment Agency

In housing organisations 'what goes around comes around' and the development of Focus into a social investment agency in the late 1990s brought new pressures to establish a group structure to accommodate diverse activities. Phased withdrawal of corporation tax relief from non-charitable housing associations, and the need to covenant surpluses to a charitable arm were also factors. Add to that Focus' ambitions to create a new form of social enterprise and the case for structural reform was irresistible. In 2000 Focus developed a new group structure which emphasised its ethos to provide 'more than bricks and mortar'. Incorporating some of the innovative agenda developed by Copec and Shape, Focus became a subsidiary of a new parent organisation – Prime Focus (see chapters 6 and 7). This parent is a registered charity, with Focus, Black Star and Focus Home Options (previously Focus Two) alongside a training agency and a finance services arm as wholly owned subsidiaries.

Prime Focus is the 'Social Investment Agency' with subsidiaries providing housing and related services, homes with care and support, urban regeneration services and community development. It is experimenting with methods of tackling poverty in the inner city areas of the West Midlands and developing models of housing and regeneration to provide solutions. Access to a wider funding base, including charitable sources, the European Community and non-mainstream housing finance (for example the New Deal for Communities initiative) were equally important objectives.

This chapter has demonstrated how a series of mergers have led to this modern interpretation of Focus' mission. The different drivers and functions of these mergers are recapped in Table 15. But this is only half the story of how Focus came to this pass. Chapter 7 has provided the other half by reviewing the organisational transformations and changes in philosophy which have underpinned the changes leading to Prime Focus' current organisational form.

9

Governance and accountability

Views on what is good governance in housing associations have been subject to enormous changes over the period that Focus and its forerunners have been in existence. For example, the idea of accountability based on being held to account would not have appeared relevant to philanthropic organisations, driven by their sense of moral and civic duty. In the late 19th Century and the early years of the 20th Century, independence and freedom from government were seen as key virtues by many of the voluntary housing organisations of the day (Cope 1999). Most housing associations did not until very recent times set out to be formally accountable to those they were founded to serve – their tenants or to their communities.

As housing associations expanded in the 1960s and 1970s, and as they began to receive public funds on a significant scale, there were calls for greater accountability. New regulatory frameworks, particularly the Housing Corporation's (housing associations' chief regulator today) were overlaid on systems of governance ruled by statutory instruments, deeds of trust and even in some cases, such as Guinness Trust, their own

The housing conditions which Copec was formed to help tackle in Gee Street Hockley in 1926.

Acts of Parliament (Cope 1999). Later, the introduction of a mixture of private and public funding brought even stronger pressures to be accountable to external bodies, especially private financial institutions. To a large extent, then, modern housing associations have taken on new forms of governance to deal with changing regulatory systems while retaining many archaic forms, prescribed by a bygone age. These forms of governance do not always sit well in the current environment.

This chapter looks at some of the issues surrounding governance and accountability within Focus and its predecessor associations. It assesses the ways in which Focus has developed its governance system and how it has tried in more recent years to become more accountable to its tenants.

- **Self-perpetuating oligarchies?** – questions to what extent housing associations were and are accountable voluntary bodies.

- **Tenants in the lead?** – traces the rise of tenant involvement in housing association management after 1980, contrasting recent models of tenant empowerment with the earlier adherence by Copec to the Octavia Hill model of housing management.

- **Stakeholder networks** – describes 'stakeholding' drawing on two examples of Focus' relationship with stakeholders: first with networks used to secure funds, second with networks developed to provide greater community accountability.

Self-perpetuating oligarchies?

Although some housing associations have developed reasonable levels of accountability to their memberships, these memberships have often been very narrowly drawn. Hence they have been open to accusations that they are managed by 'self-perpetuating oligarchies' of self-selecting individuals who remain on management committees for as long as they see fit (Alder and Handy 1985). As Malpass (2000) has commented:

> 'In the majority of housing societies that lacked massive charitable endowment the shareholders were the main source of investment funds and so boards elected by shareholders at annual general meetings could genuinely claim to represent major financial stakeholders.....in most cases boards consisted of people who were themselves significant shareholders' (Malpass 2000).

The notion of what is called 'stakeholding' (Hutton 1995) today (making decisions transparent to shareholders, tenants and communities) would have been alien to these housing organisations given the nature of their work and the prevailing economic and social philosophies. How competent or accountable the governing bodies of voluntary housing organisations were in earlier times was viewed as a matter for them alone (Cope 1999).

From its foundation in 1925, Copec, as a Public Utility Society and Industrial and Provident Society, had specific governance responsibilities based around the Housing and Town Planning Act 1909 and the Industrial and Provident Societies Act 1883. However, these responsibilities were predominantly concerned with the relationship between the governing body (ie the management committee) and the shareholding membership. The

Copec management committee consisted of twelve to thirteen people, including the chairman and honorary secretary, and co-optees. Copec's management committee was responsible to its shareholders, who numbered 402 with 13,979 in shares by 1939 (Copec Annual Report 1939). An analysis of the shareholding membership reveals that 72 individuals (18 percent of total shareholders) actually controlled 76 percent of shares, pointing to a less democratic organisation than 'surface' figures would suggest. Nevertheless, as Malpass (2000) has pointed out, the management committees of the day played a role similar to non-executive directors on the boards of private companies today. That is, they represented shareholders' interests on the governing body. Unlike some associations (Malpass 2000), however, Copec's committee members did not take fees for their services (Tillyard 1932).

Copec's management committee in 1927. Chairman Professor Frank Tillyard is at the back on the right. Secretary Florence Barrow is on the left on the front row. The management committee did not include tenants or representatives of local communities at this time.

Usually, Copec's management committee met eleven times per year, initially in offices donated by Frank Hickinbotham, Copec's Honorary Treasurer, of Rabone, Petersen and Co. Three members of the committee stood down at each Annual General Meeting, but were usually willing to be re-elected unless their personal circumstances meant that they no longer could attend committee meetings. Over the 1925 to 1970 period very few changes were apparent in how Copec's governance developed. As Malpass (2000) has confirmed:

'Management committees were, and still are, rather strange hybrid bodies, reflecting the position of housing associations between public and private sectors, deeply rooted in the historical traditions of voluntary housing'.

1935 – tenants were treated with firm kindness but their views were rarely sought at this time.

Sub-committees were established at various times to which issues were devolved from the management committee. Merger with Birmingham Housing Trust in 1970 saw some changes in approach with a small group of 'senior' committee members forming a council (like cabinet government) to oversee Copec's management, although the main management committee still retained power. This can be seen as an administrative change rather than a change in the legal status of Copec's governing body. However, area committees in Birmingham, Wolverhampton and Sandwell were formed at this time to increase accountability to local people. Over the next 15 years, Copec's constitution changed little, even after merger with Wolverhampton Housing Association in 1976.

After 1974, the Housing Corporation placed increasing importance on how housing associations were governed. Attention began to focus on how they were managed, by whom and for what purpose. However, their governance was determined largely by their status as Industrial and Provident Societies under the 1965 Act and their registration with the Housing Corporation under the Housing Act 1974 (Cope 1999). While the 1965 Act applied to all associations registered under it, the legislation had little to say about the precise form of governance (and accountability) that housing associations should pursue. The 1974 Act gave the Housing Corporation supervisory powers over associations, chiefly through the monitoring process (Malpass and Murie 1994). But accountability to tenants and the wider community at this time was also underdeveloped. As Alder and Handy (1997) state:

'Community involvement is achieved in many cases by formal consultation arrangements with local interest groups or by representation on a reciprocal basis on relevant committees. Unfortunately, there are no legal requirements relating to these matters'.

A completed refurbishment in Hospital Street Summer Lane just before the war in 1938.

Responding to debates about governance and accountability

In 1978 the Corporation published a circular 'In The Public Eye', which emphasised that although associations were de facto voluntary and independent bodies, certain standards of accountability were required. In the following year, the NFHA published its first Code of Conduct for housing associations, including recommendations on committee structures, the conduct of members and staff, and development and housing management practices (Cope 1999). This has subsequently been updated (NHF 1999).

In the late 1970s, Copec had less than 100 members, many of whom were of longstanding, going back to the prewar period. The legacy of its long history was that many shareholders were either deceased or inactive. The association also had no formal methods of involving tenants and communities in its formal governance. However, informal arrangements existed, including the use of community agencies to refer new tenants. Copec's 1978 annual report referred to the Corporation's Circular and outlined its commitment to greater accountability. In the report Chairman John Duncan said:

> 'We look forward towards extending and broadening the membership. The management committee is now open to tenants and staff as observers. We have given a fair amount of time to considering comments upon our activities from various quarters – tenants and staff for instance. That has often been valuable and has led to a shift in emphasis in our administration, management and practice. We are working steadily on communication between those concerned with the daily activities of Copec and a wider body of opinion'.

Membership continued to remain largely static, but Copec used the process of co-opting individuals onto its management committee to access a wider range of views. Even so, this was very much a 'by invitation' process. Other initiatives to enhance Copec's accountability were attempted over the next few years. In the mid 1980s, Copec reorganised its committee structure and allocated resources for supporting tenant involvement for the first time. As John Duncan commented:

> 'This year, the Copec Group has been able to establish itself constitutionally, with all members of the Copec 'family' under the Committee of Management of Copec Housing Trust. Consultation with our tenants is an increasing feature of our work as we seek to meet their needs in a more detailed way' (Copec Annual Report 1987).

By the early 1980s, Copec had developed a number of subsidiaries. Key changes to the Copec constitution were made at the management committee meeting in October 1986 to accommodate these subsidiaries. Copec had previously set up satellite organisations, Copec Two, Copec Three and Copec Services, to undertake home ownership work and to provide non-housing services to tenants. These satellites became wholly owned subsidiaries of Copec at this time (see chapters 5 and 7). It was also agreed that to retain proper control of the Copec Group's affairs, the management committee should delegate some of its responsibilities. This resulted in the formation of the charitable housing committee to oversee the rented component of Copec's work (Committee Minutes 1980s).

In the 1990s, housing associations were virtually the sole providers of new social housing. They had grown considerably and had more influence in the communities in which they operated. The scale and breadth of the voluntary housing sector had also

COPEC HOUSING TRUST
TENANT NEWS
No.13   JULY — SEPTEMBER

A letter from the Chairman

An early example of the Copec tenants newsletter in the 1970s – consultation with tenants was still in its infancy at this time.

I am very pleased to have the opportunity to send a greeting to all those who make their homes in properties owned by Copec.

'Tenants News' hasn't appeared for some time. I hope that, in its new form, it will help all of us who are involved in Copec to be in touch with what goes on in what is now a big organisation.

Your home is just one of over 2,000 Copec properties. Copec wants to try and provide for the housing needs of all kinds of people - families large and small, single people, young and old, people with special problems and handicaps.

It is always my hope that Copec will get increasingly good at helping people quickly and sympathetically. The staff of the Trust bear most of the responsibility for that and they are committed to the special kind of service that Copec has the opportunity to offer. They are always looking for ways to be more efficient and that is important when we are hoping to be of service to so many different people in so many different properties. And I'm sure that you would not want Copec to forget those who have no reasonable home, who are hoping to join you as a Copec tenant.

Many of you have been in Copec property for several years now and we are glad to have 'satisfied customers'. But we are not complacent and I hope that you will always feel able to come in to Waterloo Street and discuss any problems or ideas you may have for improving Copec's service. You will always get a hearing from our staff who, within the limits of available time and money, are always keen to solve problems.

By co-operation Copec's tenants, staff and Committees can make Copec something of which Birmingham can be proud.

Good wishes,

John Duncan

CONTENTS

page 2
Copec Committees,
Editorial.

page 3
Introducing :-
Sandwell &
Wolverhampton.

page 4 & 5
Re-organisation of
Copec Mainstream.

page 6
Gardening
Competition,
New Advice Centre,
Emergencies.

page 7
Battered Wives
and the law.

page 8
Advice Centres in
Birmingham.

grown, partly from stock transfer from local authorities and partly through their increased level of funding, from private sources, as a result of the Housing Act 1988 (Malpass 2000). In 1991 Copec, Hestia and St. Chad Housing Associations had merged to form Focus and the new unitary association stepped-up its approach to governance and accountability. Under the Focus management committee, there were three new committees, although these were later extended at the suggestion of the Housing Corporation (Monitoring Visit 1992). Focus Two incorporated Copec Two from the 1980s and Focus Homes was an amalgamation of Copec Three and Hestia Homes home ownership associations. Area committees were later rationalised into three regional committees covering Birmingham, the Black County and Coventry and Shire Counties. Two key Inquiries in the mid 1990s influenced the future development of governance and accountability within associations:

- the Independent Inquiry Into Housing Association Governance chaired by Sir David Hancock; and

- the Committee on Standards in Public Life (the Nolan Committee) (Copec 1999).

The Hancock enquiry recommended a number of changes to the way associations were managed, including the use of the term 'Board' to distinguish the governing body from the senior officers of associations; the recruitment of at least one new board member each year to reduce the development of self-perpetuating oligarchies; and, recommendations about the role of the Chairman, the Board and the Chief Executive. The enquiry recommended a Code of Governance which has since been adopted by most housing associations and been built into the Housing Corporations' Performance Standards (Cope 1999). The Nolan Committee reviewed the governance of housing associations alongside other quangos, such as Training and Enterprise Councils, higher education bodies and grant-maintained schools. While Nolan generally thought that associations were well-regulated and well run, the report made a number of recommendations.

Key Recommendations Of Nolan Committee Relating To Housing Associations

- Housing associations should be encouraged to develop membership schemes as a means of increasing accountability.

- Housing associations should be expected to involve tenants and communities in their activities and reduce restrictions to their management boards.

- The Housing Corporation should publish more information on their regulatory activities (Nolan 1994, Cope 1999).

Source: Cope 1999

Richard Clark was invited to address the Nolan Committee because of his experience as both a regulator with the Housing Corporation and as a Chief Executive with a large association. The key theme in his written evidence was that:

'A more formal approach to Governance amongst associations is vital with freedom of information and an ongoing commitment to accountability to tenants and other stakeholders essential to the future health of the housing association movement' (Evidence to the Nolan Committee).

Focus' governance and accountability were fully tested in late 1995 when an internal investigation of Focus' property services department was triggered by the receipt of three anonymous letters alleging improper conduct of the department's members. Chief executive Richard Clark established an investigation in December, ensuring that all relevant documentation within the department was secured. An investigatory team of senior staff was set up under the supervision of a sub-group of Focus' management committee. The sub-group was chaired by Peter Knight, a senior committee member who became Focus' Chairman in 1996. Focus then contacted the West Midlands police and its main regulator, the Housing Corporation, and informed its auditors. All were briefed extensively about the situation.

The scope of the investigation traced the department's purchase of properties from local dealers, primarily in inner city areas, for the period 1990 to 1995. It also reviewed the procedures for commissioning and completing repairs once properties were acquired. The nub of the investigation was that a small number of Focus' staff in its property services department had been overpaying local property dealers for properties acquired for refurbishment. The implication was that these staff had made financial gains from these fraudulent activities. Two staff were suspended and later convicted of fraud (Focus Internal Report on the Investigation 1996).

Despite the difficulties arising from the fraud investigation, there were many beneficial results for how Focus developed its governance and accountability approach during the late 1990s. First, the involvement of management committee members in closer scrutiny of Focus' operations yielded benefits. This knowledge was supplemented by inviting new people onto the management committee, including people with stronger business and financial skills. Second, all Focus' procedures, particularly those for property services and maintenance, were overhauled, leading to an increased level of quality control of key activities. This led to a greater emphasis on developing quality services and moves to affiliate to external quality accreditation systems, such as the European Quality Award and Investors in People. Third, Focus 'opened-up' its activities to greater scrutiny by tenants and partner agencies in the community. A major drive to recruit more tenant and community shareholders resulted in Focus widening and deepening its accountability. Related benefits were a renewed relationship between Focus and the community. This had long been part of the approach envisaged as Focus pursued its goal of becoming a 'Social Investment Agency' (see chapters 6 and 7).

Governance changes fundamentally

In 1997, the National Housing Federation (NHF) published its Action For Accountability report which widened the debate surrounding accountability and focussed on how associations should be accountable to a wide range of stakeholders, including tenants, local authorities and local communities. Associations were asked to consider mechanisms which could improve their performance in this area (Cope 1999). Tenants of associations which were Industrial and Provident Societies were able to invite tenants to become shareholders and to vote for members of the management committee (Hood 1999).

In response to these developments, Focus reviewed its own accountability arrangements and made a number of changes. The constitution was rewritten to enable tenants to become shareholders. This enabled tenants to constitute 40 percent of the total shareholding membership. It also enshrined tenants' rights to become Focus committee members for the first time. Two places by right were reserved on the management committee, which were taken up by Birmingham tenant Gillian Saunders and Colin Spalding, a tenant in Coventry. Colin Spalding later became a member of the Housing Corporation's 'consumer panel'. Tenant representation on Focus's regional committees was assured. As Gillian Saunders said at the time:

'Eighteen months ago, Focus meant well but it was all on paper. Now it is doing rather than talking. We are now being told what is going on and feel like real partners' (Annual Report 1997).

A skills audit was carried out of existing management committee members and invitations were sent to potential candidates with skills that were needed (for example finance, personnel and health). The shareholding membership was reviewed with the aim of increasing representation amongst tenants and community agencies. Those shareholders who no longer wished to be involved were allowed to give their share back to Focus, mirroring an earlier transformation when shareholders were asked to fundamentally change their relationship with the association (see chapters 3 and 7). Some shareholders had passed on their shares to agents of their estate after death, and many of these shares were redeemed also. The purpose of this review was to develop a more up-to-date shareholders profile, incorporating those agencies and individuals who had a real stake in the modern Focus. The review of the shareholding membership was followed by an updated committee structure with strengthened sub-committees reporting into the management committee on financial matters, remuneration, housing development and policy (Annual Reports 1997-1999).

Results of a survey of associations carried out in the early 1990s provides a yardstick (Malpass 2000) against which Focus could measure itself. The survey revealed that the average number of the association's shareholders to committee members was 5:1. The ratio for Focus in the late 1990s was 17:1. Of 272 shareholders in 2000, 39 percent were tenants and 15 percent were drawn from community groups which worked closely with Focus. As the 1997 Annual Report commented:

> 'Voluntary organisations became shareholders and Focus had a particular success with Black and Minority Ethnic agencies'.

The formation of the Prime Focus Group shows the latest changes to the governance of the association. Focus, and its subsidiaries Focus Two and Focus Three became subsidiaries of a new charitable parent organisation, alongside Black Star Housing Association. The new charitable parent was run by a 'Board of Management' with members drawn from the subsidiary organisations and regional committees. As Malpass (2000) has observed, there was a lot wrong with housing associations but good progress had been made to tackle out-dated practices.

Tenants in the lead?

From the early history of housing associations in the 1920s up until the 1970s there were no specific statutory obligations for management committees to consult their tenants or to be accountable to the wider community. The Copec management committee in the 1920s and 1930s, as was common in voluntary housing organisations of the day, did not see the need to formally consult tenants, although in practice there were close relationships. Commentators have identified why this was so:

> 'The top-down nature of philanthropy.....meant that tenants were absent from the boards of the great majority of voluntary housing organisations' (Malpass 2000).

> 'The notion of accountability to the community or tenants was somewhat alien given the prevailing ethos of laissez-faire and the concept of the deserving and undeserving poor' (Cope 1999).

Copec's approach incorporated aspects of the relationship between private sector landlords and their tenants, and as 'paternalist benefactor'. Octavia Hill methods were strongly supported by Copec's management committee and housing staff. This approach has been well summarised in the following ways:

> 'From the beginning, in managing properties Octavia Hill put into practice a careful attention to the landlords' duties, such as repairs, together with a personal relationship with the tenants and an expectation that in the long run the tenants would behave in a way which was responsible both to their neighbours and to the landlord' (Brion 1995).

> 'The relationship between Copec and its tenants is primarily a business one, but.......our voluntary workers, who either as rent collectors or club leaders, know the circumstances of the tenants, have been able to visit them in times of illness, and by sympathy and friendly interest have helped to keep them from apathy and despair' (Fenter 1960).

Copec's principles, based on those of Hill, included the:

> 'Coordination of all aspects of management, insistence on the mutual responsibility of landlord and tenant: the former for maintenance of properties, the latter for the rent payment and the proper use of the accommodation provided. When choosing tenants, the main considerations were whether the family would fit the house, whether they would be likely to get on with the neighbours, pay the rent with reasonable regularity and have a sufficient standard of cleanliness' (Fenter 1960).

Further statements from Copec at the time demonstrate the 'top-down' character of its approach to accountability. The implications of these statements are that Copec was not only the landlord but the catalyst for tenants to improve their lives generally, outside of the landlord-tenant relationship. No mention is made of tenants' aspirations or any potential desire to take control of their own housing and environment. Copec saw itself as tenants' chief benefactor and guiding influence:

> 'There are always a certain number of people needing help in emergency, particularly at times of illness, and it is our practice to put them in touch with the Citizens Society, to whom we are able to give details of the help required. The manager and her trainees can often suggest a wise course for tenants to adopt in cases of difficulty about pensions or insurance or urger them to join such useful organisations as the Hospitals Contributory Scheme......tenants have often in this way been induced to improve their conditions which, without advice and encouragement, they would suffer to continue' (Annual Report 1933 and 1936).

Improvements in the way tenants were involved in decisions about their housing and neighbourhoods did not surface in Copec until its merger with Birmingham Housing Trust (BHT) in 1970 (see chapter 8). The influence of the new association on the old precipitated some changes in approach. At the time of merger, Copec's 'paternalist benefactor' origins were still very much in evidence as new general manager of the association, David Mumford, recalls:

> 'The Chairman of Copec was an 'old-school' Cadbury. I was the hired help. He always called me 'Mumford!' (Interview 1999).

We are not paternalists

BHT's more inclusive approach to tenant involvement developed during the 1970s, demonstrated by a pamphlet distributed to committee and staff. Called 'We Are Not Paternalists', it was written by Chairman John Duncan to tackle still in-grained attitudes to tenants as 'us and them'. However, meaningful involvement of tenants was largely 'frozen in time' until statutory obligations to consult were imposed on housing associations in the 1980s. A tenants newsletter was produced from 1974 onwards, but it was mainly a means for Copec to impart information. The decentralisation of housing management in Birmingham and the area offices in Wolverhampton and Sandwell enabled closer collaboration between tenants and staff, but this process remained informal. It was a generally held view at the time that inviting tenants onto Copec's committees was not required in order to improve accountability. Arguments of being

Involvement of tenants in redesigning the Holmes Estate in the 1980s. Tenant Participation Manager Susan Spencer is seen talking over plans with Holmes' tenants.

'ultra vires' to the constitution were often used. Some movement to support tenants groups can be seen in early newsletters, although specific resources were not allocated for this purpose at the time. However, grassroots stirrings for greater involvement can be detected amongst some tenants. The 1976 Tenants Newsletter contained extracts from a letter by the Chairman of the Sparkbrook Residents Association:

> 'Copec needs a strong tenants association to protect the interests of tenants, and like other housing associations, Copec ought to be answerable to some democratically elected body for the public money it spends'.

The Housing Act 1980, through Section 43, introduced a statutory requirement on associations to publish their arrangements to consult tenants, but, significantly, only about changes in housing management policy and practice (Alder and Handy 1985). This usually entailed providing certain information to their tenants and consulting them about major changes in housing management policy. Copec relied on sending letters to tenants when it wished to consult them on changes in housing management practice, which usually received a low return rate. However, attitudes to tenant involvement were at last showing rapid change within the association, supported by Housing Directors John Morris and Chris Handy (now Chief Executive of Accord). Copec subsequently published a Tenant Consultation Statement to extend rights of consultation to its tenants. Copec Chairman John Duncan commented:

> 'Consultation with our tenants is an increasing feature of our work as we seek to meet their needs in a more detailed way' (Copec Annual Report 1987).

COPEC TENANTS CONSULTATION STATEMENT (1981)

- **Newsletters:** an information sheet issued about changes with a tear-off strip so that tenant can give their views.

- **Personal letters:** sent to individual tenants or small groups of tenants.

- **Visits:** carried out for individual tenants or small groups of tenants.

- **Tenants Meetings:** arranged to discuss with tenants things of a general nature where an exchange of views is felt to be required.

- **Publication Of Notices:** on matters probably requiring statutory notice in the press, tenants are more likely to be consulted by newsletters.

- **Tenants Associations:** the Trust wishes to encourage the formation of tenants associations – once the views of the Trust's tenants are known, consideration will be given to matters raised and it will then decide to carry out the proposed change.

Supporting and listening to tenants' groups

Copec began to involve tenants more and began to support and develop tenants groups in the late 1980s. The Housing Act 1985 encouraged associations to support tenants groups, as well as establishing specific requirements for them to publish various policies (Cope 1999). Copec then began to invest staff and financial resources in tenant involvement initiatives, which began to 'bear fruit'. A Wolverhampton Tenants Consultation Committee was established in June 1987 and a similar Committee for Birmingham was established in 1988. Assistance was provided by Copec to publicise the existence of these groups, including coverage of costs of tenants' produced newsletters. John Gardner, Chairman of the Wolverhampton group puts tenant involvement at this time into perspective:

> 'The Wolverhampton tenants group has been active for three years, but we are still trying to find the best times and venues for meetings and also looking for new members of the group. Although not as large as we would wish, we feel we have built a strong relationship with the management. However, we feel that a lot more has been done by tenants themselves to improve and maintain some areas of concern' (Tenants Newsletter 1990).

The tenants committees were not formally constituted at first but open to all tenants who wished to attend. Later, elections were held for tenant representatives from specific neighbourhoods. Consultation committee meetings were established and these were held with invited speakers from Copec's management committee and from the senior officers group. Topics discussed in the early years were:

A tenants group meeting in the 1990s.

- how tenants complaints are handled;
- rent arrears and procedures for recovery;
- the services received in area housing offices;
- the efficiency of the repairs service;
- tenants' views on the mainstream housing service.

In 1991, Focus was formed as a single housing association (see chapters 5 and 8). The decision of Copec, Hestia and St. Chad to merge was supported by 86 percent of tenants in a poll. Following the merger, Focus moved further to involve tenants in its work and decision-making. From its early days, the association established a tenants forum, called the 'Focus Fifty', which aimed to bring together a group of tenants, broadly representative of the tenants group as a whole, to provide the management committee with a 'tenants' standing conference' from which it could take soundings. From discussions with the 'Focus Fifty', the association developed a more pro-active tenant consultation policy. The policy stated that Focus wished to expand its approach to tenants participation beyond statutory obligations (Annual Reports 1991-1993).

Focus Actions To Increase Tenant Involvement (1992)

- Ensuring regular consultation with tenants via a wide range of methods, including personal visits and letters, newsletters, handbooks and surveys.
- Take tenants' views into account when considering changes to the housing service and respond to their views.
- Enable tenants to become more involved in the management of their homes, including co-operatives and joint management boards.
- Encourage and enable tenants to influence housing policy and practice.
- Help and encourage the formation of tenants' associations and tenants' groups in each area of operation, by providing financial and administrative support, and training.

In 1992, a Director of the association, David Ranceford-Hadley, was appointed as 'tenants advocate' with specific responsibilities to follow-up complaints. Focus began to supply a wide range of information for tenants, including a new tenants handbook and performance reports. Translations into minority languages were provided and the tenants handbook was recorded on tape for tenants with sight or reading problems.

A specialist Tenant Participation Unit was formed in 1992 under Susan Spencer, previously a manager with Birmingham Cooperative Housing Services (BCHS), and later Chief Executive of the Birmingham Settlement. Focus had formed a major partnership with BCHS in undertaking joint tenant consultation and 'planning for real' exercises on a number of estates (for example Birmingham's Holmes Estate). The Unit was part of the housing management department and aimed to take tenant and community participation to new level, through the development of tenant co-operatives and estate management boards, at which is was moderately successful. The Focus' Tenants Forum, which developed from the 'Focus Fifty' was established in 1993 to bring together a growing number of tenants' groups across the West Midlands. At Focus's AGM in 1993, a year's work of developing stronger tenant and community participation led to the formal adoption of a Tenants Charter. The Charter was a detailed eight page document, written in conjunction with tenants groups.

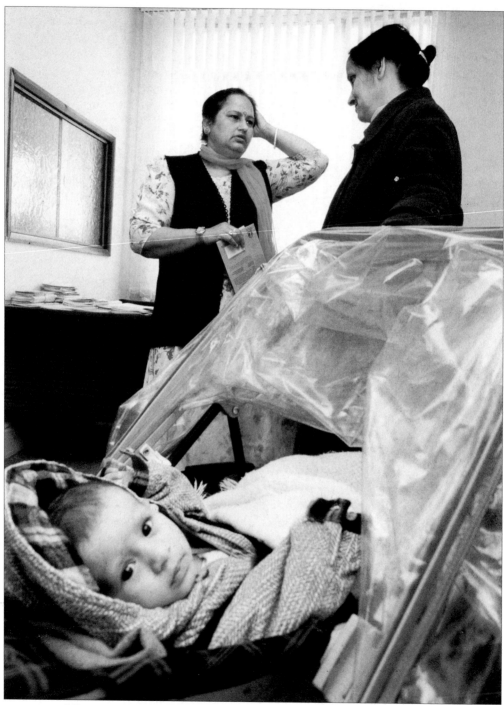

A Focus property used as an office by a local tenants group in the Black Country.

FOCUS

HOUSING ASSOCIATION

the TENANTS' CHARTER

We will make it easy to apply for a Focus home.

We will operate a Fair Housing Policy, giving priority to those people most in
need of somewhere to live, especially the homeless.

You have the right to remain in your home for as long as you wish,
provided you keep within the terms of your Tenancy Agreement.

We will tell you how we set your rent.

We will keep your home in good repair.

We will make it easy for you to contact our staff, and we will respond
to your queries or complaints promptly and effectively.

We will provide information about your tenancy and about Focus.

We will consult you about our housing service.

We will consult you about any changes to our service.

We will encourage and support tenants' organisations.

If we fail to meet any of the commitments in this Charter, the Director of
Housing Services will investigate and ensure that appropriate redress is made.

TENANTS'
CHARTER

Focus' Tenants Charter, approved at the Annual General Meeting in 1993.

The New Deal

By 1994, Focus had considerably improved its tenant representation in decision-making forums and it had provided more opportunities for tenants to affect the policies and practices of the association. Some 29 tenants became shareholders in 1994, as part of a wider review of shareholding. These tenants were mostly representatives from tenants groups. Gillian Saunders became the first tenant to be elected by fellow tenants onto the management committee. She highlighted the main changes she had noticed:

> 'The tenants associations have access to the resources of regional offices, which makes the organisation more approachable. During the last year tenant involvement has taken off. People feel more confident about joining regional committees and the Birmingham regional forum meets every month' (Annual Report 1997).

'The New Deal' for tenants was launched at the 1996 Annual General Meeting and included a range of important pledges from Focus to its tenants about service delivery and representation.

Focus' New Deal for Tenants 1996

- £5 million to be spent annually on home improvement for ten years with around 450 homes improved each year;

- Creating employment and training opportunities for tenants, with Focus contractors being encouraged to employ tenants and training/apprenticeships being provided;

- Providing of a fairer and more affordable rent system with rent increases pegged to inflation with some rents actually reducing;

- Improving tenants' rights in the management of the association, including becoming shareholders and committee members;

- The new regional structure of the association moving decision-making closer to tenants with regional Tenants Forums established;

- Faster responses to repairs requests with routine and priority repairs dealt with in five days and emergency repairs undertaken within 24 hours;

- Introducing an improved complaints procedure with enhanced rights to appeal;

- Reviewing the Tenants Guarantee with increased rights of tenancy.

The Tenants Forum was reconstituted in 1998, with elections for representatives held in the tenants newsletter and in individual housing projects. The purpose was to ensure that the Forum was broadly representative of tenants as a whole. Later that year, Focus' first conference for tenants was held at Birmingham's Centennial Centre. Tenants were 'bused-in' from outlying areas and creche facilities were made available to make the conference family-friendly. Workshops were held on a range of housing policies, such as rents, complaints and neighbourhood nuisance. Guest speakers spoke on subjects such as credit unions, fuel and money advice. Chairman of the conference was Peter Davies from the Birmingham Tenants Forum.

Some indication of Focus' achievements in more actively involving tenants was provided by a survey in Shelter's Roof magazine in 1997 and by Focus' inclusion in the Housing Corporation's 'Tenants In The Lead' initiative (see page 201). The Roof survey had asked the top 50 housing associations to publish the proportion of tenants on their management committees. Focus came 'top of the league' at 40 percent, compared to Liverpool Housing Trust (at 23 percent), Circle 33 (at 20 percent) and North British (at 17 percent).

Structure Of The Tenants Forum

TENANTS FORUM

Tenants Groups
2 representatives from each tenants' group (number of places variable according to number of groups)

Tenants Newsletter Elections
Individual tenants elected via tenants newsletter (22 places)

Supported Housing

Mental Health schemes	2 representatives
Single Homelessness schemes	2 representatives
Womens' Refuge schemes	2 representatives
Learning and Disabilities schemes	2 representatives

Using 'consumerism'

At the same time as these initiatives to involve the more active tenants in its formal governance, Focus also began to adopt a more systematic approach to finding out the views of the 'silent majority' using market research and consumerist approaches we would expect to find in any modern customer-driven business. Copec had previously carried out a tenant satisfaction survey in 1989 (Gulliver). But after the formation of Focus, two major tenants satisfaction surveys were launched in the 1990s (Gulliver 1993, Brockehurst 1997) asking tenants about their homes and the services they received. In addition, a new tenants satisfaction survey was introduced in 1992 (Gulliver) to provide an ongoing assessment of how new tenants felt about their homes and how well their housing applications were administered. Tenants surveys also set about discovering how well tenants thought they were consulted, how much they were involved in the association's management, and in what ways they would like more input. Surveys provided baselines against which future performance and improvements could be measured. Both qualitative and quantitative evidence was provided as the following examples show:

'When you phone up they say that someone is coming out today.....you wait all day..... nobody comes out.....I dislike it when repairmen don't keep appointments.....Focus has improved a lot with repairs over the last year or two.....before that it was bad.....why do inspections take so long?.....respond to complaints quicker.....more vetting of contractors.....they are not clearing up the grass from the garden properly.....very good when they turn up.....I think that you should think about changing the cleaning contractors.....my view is that security should be altered.....bin-room is not cleaned and rubbish is left on the floor.....I find that all services are good' (Brocklehurst 1997).

Table (16) – Copec/Focus Tenants Satisfaction With Key Service Areas (%)			
Tenants Satisfaction Areas	**1989**	**1993**	**1997**
Satisfaction with the home	52	73	76
Satisfaction with the main heating system	46	68	75
Satisfaction with state of repair and decoration	61	69	71
Satisfaction with quality of repairs work	54	75	77
Satisfaction with repairs service	46	69	74
Friendliness/politeness of housing management staff	93	74	86
Association always/usually keeps tenants informed	74	77	80
Association always/usually consults tenants	75	60	69
Tenants wanting more control over association	45	45	35
Tenants willing to form constituted groups	31	35	39
Rent represents good value for money	57	74	73
Satisfaction with association as social landlord	68	84	84

Table (14) shows how tenants' satisfaction increased over time. Satisfaction with the home and the repairs service increased appreciably. The proportion of tenants wanting more of a say in the management of Focus also showed marked increases. In the 1997 tenants survey, questions about 'social investment' were asked to gauge how much tenants wanted Focus to get involved in community regeneration work (in 2000, Focus is planning a new survey, with core questions developed by its trade association the NHF, and a greater range of questions designed to discover tenants' views about their neighbourhoods).

Using research as a means of tenant involvement took a further step in 2000 when Focus was invited to become part in a national survey of tenants. The 'Tenants In The Lead' research aimed to include tenants in setting service standards for housing associations (see over).

Focus tenant committee members, Gillian Saunders of Birmingham and Coventry's Colin Spalding, at a meeting of the Housing Association Residents and Tenants Organisation of England (HARTOE), hosted by Focus.

Tenants in the lead

As part of Focus' approach to implementing Best Value, Focus agreed to take part in a Housing Corporation-sponsored programme in 1998 to develop tenants participation for planning service delivery. Called 'Tenants In the Lead', the initiative was paid for by an Innovation and Good Practice Grant from the Corporation. Alongside five other housing associations in different parts of the country, Focus became involved in the project as part of its commitment to involving its tenants more in the management of their homes and determining the services they receive. The service area which Focus chose as its part of the national project was service charges.

The project was managed by a joint tenant/staff working group called the Tenants Central Consultative Panel. The chairs of each regional Tenants Forum plus two other tenants from each region, met during six months in 1999 to oversee and direct the project. The basis of the approach was to challenge the organisational culture of officer-led views. Focus sought tenants' views about service charges by:

- producing a newsletter explaining the project which was sent to every tenants paying a service charge;

- surveying 5,000 service charge payers and obtaining views from 1,600 of them;

- producing a follow-up newsletter outlining the findings of the survey was produced and distributed;

- setting-up a local joint tenant/staff working party in each Focus region to examine local issues emerging from the survey;

- asking each regional working party to respond to issues raised about quality and the specifications for the services.

The Black Country Tenants' Forum members being shown a Copec house, which was turned over to the local police as a base in the Steelhouse Lane area of Wolverhampton. Trevor Stanley, Chair of the Forum, is shown in the middle of the picture.

Stakeholder networks

Networks of people and organisations have always been sought by Focus and its forebears. Two contrasting examples illustrate the use of networks to secure resources and to enhance accountability.

Involving the 'Great and the Good'....... and the city council

From early days Copec cultivated its 'natural' networks of the 'great and the good?, mainly important Birmingham families, local clergy and members and officers of Birmingham City council. Fenter (1960) remarked on the significance Copec's management committee placed on these networks, including professional people on committees and their relationship with the city council:

> 'A word of counsel given to those wishing to form a housing society – include the following on the committee: an architect, a surveyor, a solicitor, an accountant, as well as those versed in business methods'.

> 'The importance of a close liaison between the local authority and a voluntary body in matters such as housing cannot be over-estimated. The committee has always had one or two councillors among its members. Their presence has allowed for comment upon Copec's proposed schemes from the city's point of view and from differing political angles, and conversely for interpretations of our aims in the council chamber'.

The influential networks cultivated by Copec in its first three decades, and reviewed in Chapters 2, 3 and 7, were impressive. There were close links with the Chamberlains, with wealthy individual philanthropists such as Dame Elizabeth Cadbury and the Sturge family, and with the wider religious and social action networks (such as the Birmingham Settlement) within which many of these individuals operated. All of these individuals and groups were close to Copec and supportive of its work. The need to incorporate 'the great and the good' in this era can be explained by the dependency of the organisation on individual charity and local philanthropic networks (Annual Reports 1920 and 1930s).

A new era was marked by the birth of the Birmingham Housing Trust in 1965, which merged with Copec in 1970, and with it a change in the networks used. There was an even closer engagement with Birmingham City Council as a key 'stakeholder'. As chapter 4 indicates, BHT was linked to the city council through its first manager, David Mumford, who was a senior local councillor. A tactic of BHT, emulating Copec's approach of some years earlier, was to obtain support from the city council via the informal connections of individuals. For example, BHT listed amongst its supporters the Lord Mayor of Birmingham and two prominent councillors. A more formal linkage was developed between Copec, BHT and other local housing associations with the city council in 1969 when the Birmingham Housing Associations Liaison Committee (BHALC) was established. Developed 'under the wing' of the NFHS and in conjunction with Shelter, BHALC was formed to negotiate on behalf of associations with the city council. The importance of these local networks together with national policy networks based around the National Housing Federation (the 1996 successor to the NFHS and NFHA) and the Housing Corporation can be explained by the shift in resource dependencies to public funding after 1974. Even after the development of mixed funding in 1988, it was still the ability to secure public funding that was the main influence on housing associations' ability to grow. However, private financial institutions were obtaining a greater say in the development of housing associations. An example from Focus' recent history shows this well, when the association sought and obtained permission from its private lenders about its proposed transformation into a 'Social Investment Agency' (Annual Report 1998).

Focus' management committee – the association's constitution was changed to enable tenants to become shareholders and committee members. Shown on the back row are Colin Spalding, David Corney (Treasurer), Peter Mortlock, Richard Clark (Chief Executive), Peter Knight (Chairman), Tony Jones, Basil Clarke, Ken Spencer and Keith Suthern. On the front row are Trevor Stanley, Cynthia Bower and Margaret Bannon.

Enhancing accountability to local communities

'Stakeholding' when applied to public policy emphasises a reciprocal relationship between policy-makers, organisations delivering services within policy frameworks and the role of those who receive services (Hutton 1995). A frequently neglected 'stakeholder sector' in the work of housing associations have been black and minority ethnic communities. As we have seen in chapters 5 and 6, these communities significantly affected the shape of the Focus service and came to account for close to half of all its tenants. Here we look at how these communities were regarded as increasingly important 'stakeholders' by Focus.

Chapter 3 shows how Copec responded to immigration from Eastern Europe and the new commonwealth in the early post-war period, including support for a new association, Birmingham Friendship (now Housing and Care), whose main founding purpose was to welcome new migrants. However, the housing market was often much less welcoming

(Rex and Moore 1967), and housing associations themselves soon became implicated in the institutionalised racism faced by BME communities. A range of research (Karn 1983, Niner 1985) in the 1980s demonstrated that housing associations (and indeed, local authorities) in Birmingham as in other cities had practices which discriminated directly or indirectly against ethnic minority groups. Copec faced such an accusation in 1981, and following investigation of a complaint to the Commission for Racial Equality (CRE), Copec was served with a statutory notice under the 1976 Act. Copec responded by introducing a range of initiatives. Ten years later, the CRE's research into housing associations (1992) (see chapter 5) commented:

> 'Focus, formerly Copec, has had an equal opportunities policy since 1981. Progress on implementation has been good. The association has carried out extensive monitoring and analysis of its performance in service delivery and employment. There is extensive staff training on race equality issues'.

Over the years, Copec and later Focus began to involve more people from black and minority communities in its work, either as committee members, as shareholders, as staff or as partner agencies. The proportion of committee members from a black and minority ethnic background has varied since the 1970s until the present day from around 10 percent to 25 percent at various times. Considerable effort was made in the 1980s and 1990s to attract more black and minority ethnic applicants for job vacancies through pro-active initiatives. For example, advertising in specialist newspapers such as the Afro-Caribbean and Asian Times. This approach enabled the association to increase considerably BME representation in its staff (from 14 percent in 1985 to 30 percent in 1999).

Copec, Shape, Hestia and Focus worked in partnership with BME agencies from the 1960s onwards, sometimes supporting the development of new institutions run by and for BME communities. However, as discussion of the Black Star merger in chapter 8 indicates, such partnerships need to be constantly worked at, particularly where there are significant power imbalances between partners.

Relationships with BME community agencies have also been vital to developing Focus' own business, as its current customer profile indicates. Many BME community agencies became key in how the association let homes. They were major sources of referral of BME applicants. Examples of agencies working with the Focus associations over the years in this capacity are Birmingham agencies the AK Centre and Saltley Action Centre, the Handsworth Law Centre, the Asian Resource Centre, and the Ockenden Venture and the Crypt in Wolverhampton. Other initiatives managed directly by Copec working with BME communities included the short-lived Inner City Contracts established after the Handsworth disturbances (see chapter 5).

More collaborative ventures have included the use of management agreements to enable BME community organisations to manage Focus housing stock while providing culturally sensitive support services to residents. Various housing projects have been undertaken with BME housing organisations, such as Ashram, OSCAR, SADAHHA and latterly Black Star (now part of 'Prime Focus'). In addition, BME agencies have assisted the Focus housing associations with various training programmes over the years. For example, the Birmingham Racial Attacks Monitoring Unit (BRAMU) designed racial harassment training for housing officers in the 1980s. As BRAMU manager Amma Owusu- Atuahene stated in 1992:

'We have been working with Focus and Copec for some time now. With the massive rise in racist attacks nationally and in Birmingham any assistance is welcome. The association has provided a place to which we can refer victims of racially-motivated attacks in an emergency. We have held discussions with Focus about the possibility of establishing a 'safe-house' in one of their properties. We have also designed the association's in-house training for housing officers in how to respond to victims, how to gather evidence and how to involve other agencies, such as the police'.

Community Relations Councils also assisted with racism and cultural awareness training (Annual Reports 1980s and 1990s). Today Focus is looking to take part in the CRE's 'Leadership Challenge' and has been shortlisted for the 'Race and Diversity Awards' established by the NHF and the Federation of Black Housing Organisations. While Focus would acknowledge that it is still learning how to deploy its resources to work in genuine partnership with BME communities, there have been many examples of success on which future practice can be modelled.

At the launch of Inner City Contracts (Handsworth) Limited – a black and minority ethnic-led organisation to provide employment opportunities in inner city areas. From left to right are David Mumford (Copec), Kwasi Ofei (ACAFESS), Chris Wadhams (Shape), Julie Clark (Birmingham Friendship), Godwin Adeogba (Handsworth Employment Scheme) and James Wilson of Bournville Village Trust. All of Copec's traditional and contemporary influences on shaping its housing service approach are shown here.

75 years: lessons learnt

Focus and its forerunners' approach to governance and accountability has largely reflected trends in the voluntary housing movement, although in each era Copec and Focus have offered their own distinctive approach. For much of the period from the 1920s to the 1960s, Copec was similar to most housing societies in that it did not include tenants in its formal governance arrangements at all. From 1970 onwards the merged association tried to involve tenants more and for its day was quite innovative but, like most associations, it made only incremental moves to full participation.

The association's approach to other stakeholders has for much of its history been geared to securing resources, first from private charity and philanthropy, later from the state. The 1980s and 1990s have seen more meaningful attempts to widen the shareholding membership to include tenants, and the stakeholder base to involve community agencies, such as black and minority ethnic community agencies more fully in the affairs of the association. It has also been recognised that as consumer orientated businesses, housing associations should be using market research techniques to ensure that all customers have a voice in driving the business. It is only in recent years, however, that the association has really begun to tap the potential for tenants and community stakeholders to shape its service.

10

Influencing opinion: campaigning

Devoting a chapter of the history to how Focus and its forbears campaigned for better housing conditions may seem to be out of place amongst all of the important contributions made since 1925. But throughout their histories, the housing associations that joined together to form Focus (especially Copec, Birmingham Housing Trust and Shape) were involved in campaigning and advocacy alongside people in housing need. For Copec, campaigning and influencing the opinions of the public and policy-makers alike was 'part-and-parcel' of its work. Both Copec and the Birmingham Housing Trust (BHT) campaigned with Shelter in the 1960s and 1970s. Copec continued its campaigning work throughout the 1980s. After the Focus merger in 1990 the association opposed cuts in housing budgets, highlighted the plight of homeless people and supported organisations representing housing associations in their campaigning and lobbying work. Shape developed a distinctive campaigning role in the 1970s and 1980s, advocating new ways for housing associations to meet needs through urban renewal and helping to build communities. So a chapter on campaigning is not out of place in this history. Indeed, some might argue that this has been one of the most important contributions Focus and its forerunners have made to the development of housing policy since 1925.

While the Focus housing associations have seen housing management and development as their main activity, the importance of campaigning has rarely been forgotten. However, it is difficult to gauge how effective campaigning has been over the 75 year history. Over the years some within these housing associations have been sure that campaigning has resulted in changes in housing policy: either as part of wider campaigns or through individual efforts.

> 'An important part of Copec's effort has been to try to guide and educate public opinion in housing matters. Publicity work was always regarded as being of great importance. Copec can claim to have had some influence in the city of Birmingham.....in no small measure we helped to prepare the way for the tremendous effort made by the city council after the last war to deal with the central areas of Birmingham, and, whether or not credit is given for this, Copec has had the satisfaction of knowing that many of the measures it recommended have been adopted' (Copec/BHT Merger Agreement 1970).

Judging whether this is so is problematic. Nevertheless, this history reveals that the Focus housing associations have mounted some impressive campaigns, have often been prepared to challenge housing policy-makers and have cultivated networks of influential people and organisations. In these ways they have followed the types of strategy used by most organisations (whether public or private) to increase control over their operating environment (Mullins and Riseborough 2000a). From early days, Copec had a line in its accounts to record spending on 'propaganda'.

The sort of housing conditions against which Copec campaigned throughout its history.

Some of the changes for which the Focus campaigns have lobbied have come about, although it is certain that these changes were associated with larger shifts in public opinion and policy.   However, from the perspective of many involved in the history of Focus considerable battles have been won.

This chapter seeks to shed light on the approaches adopted since 1925. It does this by looking at six identifiable campaigning themes:

Exposing the evils of unhealthy housing – focuses on publicity material issued by the Focus housing associations to highlight housing problems.

Exhibitionism: demonstrating housing needs – shows the use of exhibitions to raise public awareness.

Using networks to influence – describes the networks used by the associations over their history, and demonstrates how AGMs were used to focus public opinion on social issues.

Research as a campaigning tool – provides key examples of how research was used to demonstrate housing needs from an empirical perspective.

Pressing for change – the use of local and national media.

Influencing policy – the associations were often asked to contribute evidence to key policy forums.

Networks of the 'great and the good' were used to expose the 'evils of unhealthy housing'. This is such a gathering for the opening of a Copec scheme in the 1950s.

Exposing the evils of unhealthy housing

The importance of campaigning against poor housing was indicated by two Copec chairmen, separated by half a century. First, in 1926, Professor Frank Tillyard, Copec's first Chairman recognised the need to influence public opinion if the fight to eradicate the slums was to be won. Second, John Duncan, the first Chairman of Birmingham Housing Trust and later chairman of both Copec and Focus, confirmed the commitment to campaign in 1986.

> 'Copec's management committee soon found that to own slum property gave an urge for reform not felt before. They became convinced that more must be done by local and central government, that they must expose the evils of unhealthy houses and help to create an informed public opinion' (Fenter 1960).

> 'Copec is part of the Shelter family – we are a campaigning organisation' (Annual Report 1987).

Focus and its forbears wished to expand their work and used a range of approaches to inform public opinion and thereby generate support from individuals and groups (such as churches) in the 1920 and 30s. While Garside (2000) has stated that housing societies 'retreated to lobbying, advisory and propaganda activities' after the Housing Act 1935

Publicity put out by Birmingham Housing Trust in the late 1960s and early 1970s in partnership with Shelter. BHT regularly issued leaflets and publicity material to demonstrate the housing problems of local people.

excluded them from any significant role, Copec had always seen publicity activities as part of its core work. Copec, and those housing associations with which it was to merge, later turned their attention to building social action networks and campaigns to secure public funding in the 1960s and 70s. Focus today still tries to inform public opinion about contemporary housing problems and draws on its past to achieve this end. Much of the campaigning work of the Focus' forebears was concerned with demonstrating the need for better housing. Two examples are now given to demonstrate how this was achieved in two eras: the 1920-39 period and during the 1960s.

Publicising social need

A simple and effective way in which Copec in its early days influenced public opinion was by issuing pamphlets, coupled with appeals for financial support. In later years, particularly in the 1960s and 1970s, Copec and Birmingham Housing Trust issued leaflets in conjunction with Shelter with pictures of families living in poor housing conditions, designed to shock and provoke action. The first and possibly the best example of a pamphlet issued by Copec was called: 'The Central Slums Of Birmingham – A Call To Christians To Become Slum Landlords', which launched Copec and began its campaign for donations from the public in Birmingham. This pamphlet was published by Copec itself and incorporated facts and figures about the housing situation in the city. Written by Chairman Professor Frank Tillyard, it said:

> 'The problem of the housing of the poorest members of our community is one that strikes directly at the root of national-wellbeing. Interwoven with the condition of our slums at the present time are the great problems of health and sanitation. It is hardly too much to say that crime is largely due to bad housing. So, too, is disease, not only of the body but also of the mind'.

At the same time, an appeal was launched with local church congregations and other interested friends of the members of the Copec committee to become donors or become share and loan capital holders in the Copec initiative.

A 'Ten Years Retrospect' was published in 1935, with a sketch of Gee St, Aston drawn on the cover by Christopher Parkes, later to become a Copec committee member. The retrospect outlined the achievements of Copec for its first ten years and was also the basis for a new appeal for funds. Two years later, Bournville Village Trust published a larger pamphlet, written from a mainly architectural standpoint, called 'Reconditioning The Slums'. The pamphlet described the various types of schemes undertaken by Copec, especially the reconditioning of 'back-to-backs' as a means of improving housing in Birmingham's central wards. This pamphlet was a major success and was republished over the next two years. Professor Tillyard had a clear view of the impact that publicity and demonstration project could have on long-term public opinion when he wrote that 'public reforms have always come in the wake of private experiments' (Tillyard 1926).

Shock tactics

The 1960s saw a renewal of public interest in housing problems partly as a result of the graphic images of the plight of the homeless and poorly housed people used by the new Shelter campaign for the homeless to put across its message. In the Black Country, Wolverhampton Housing Association Chairman David Gregory had written a number of articles for national and local papers about the problems of minority ethnic communities obtaining housing in the private rented sector. He had also assisted in the making of a 'World In Action' programme about the repercussions for minority ethnic communities in the aftermath of local MP Enoch Powell's views on immigration.

The newly formed Birmingham Housing Trust (BHT) said that it would consult publicity experts before the launch of its fundraising appeal. It copied the fundraising techniques pioneered by Notting Hill Housing Trust, which were adopted by Shelter in 1966. A Shelter memorandum (1989) retrospectively explained that these techniques included:

> 'The use of professional advertising agencies, mass-advertising through the press, powerful photographs of people in bad housing conditions, and a simple formula converting a gift of £x into a home for a pensioner or a small family'.

Shortly after its launch, BHT followed Shelter's example by publishing a leaflet called: 'X Certificate: Not Fit For Children (Nor For Adults)', showing a family with four children living in one room. David Mumford said in the 'Birmingham Evening Mail' that BHT's advertisements – 'would be designed to bring home the full horrors of overcrowded living'. The leaflet included an appeal for funds for BHT and a list of current sponsors, such as the Lord Mayor of Birmingham, the Vice-Chancellor of Birmingham University, local MP's and clergymen. Also obtaining considerable coverage in the 'Birmingham Post' the leaflet was a major success and provided an initial stream of donations for BHT. The 'Post's' editorial at the time commented:

> 'Shock tactics are being used by a newly-formed housing association in Birmingham to focus attention on squalid and degrading housing conditions in which thousands of the city's population have to live. A leaflet asking for funds has a photograph of a young couple and their four children crowded into one room where they live, eat and sleep'.

A second leaflet issued by the newly merged Copec and BHT in 1972 used a similar approach. Called: 'Are You Aware Of This Little Chap's Plight?' and showed a small boy in a rundown street. The leaflet drew attention to the continuing housing problems faced by Birmingham's inner city population. The leaflet used slightly less graphic imagery and concentrated on the achievements which were possible if donations were made. BHT's leaflet also tried to dispel any lingering stereotypes of the homeless and poorly housed people somehow being to blame for their housing circumstances. The leaflet said:

> 'Its not their fault. The situation is not of their making, they are not lazy or unwilling to improve their conditions. Their predicament is simply that Birmingham, at this time, has insufficient good accommodation for those unfortunates who cannot obtain a mortgage or do not qualify for a council house. Such people are trapped and are calling for someone's help'.

In the light of its small impact on housing problems at the time, campaigning was seen as a key contribution which Copec could make to changing housing conditions. Its campaigning ethos was further developed by the merger agreement between Copec and BHT (see chapter 8):

> 'One of the contributions which a housing association can make is to use its expertise of housing conditions in a particular field to influence public opinion. The merged association, when it comes into being, intends to support and encourage progressive plans of area improvement in Birmingham' (Copec/BHT Merger Agreement 1970).

The 1980s and 1990s saw a less dramatic approach (public opinion had grown more accustomed to shocking images, particularly of famines in Africa) and housing in England had become less of an issue of public concern. However, Copec and later Focus publicised housing needs by other means, particularly research (see later in this chapter).

These two photographs show a Copec exhibition at the 1933 Trade Exhibition at Bingley Hall, Birmingham.

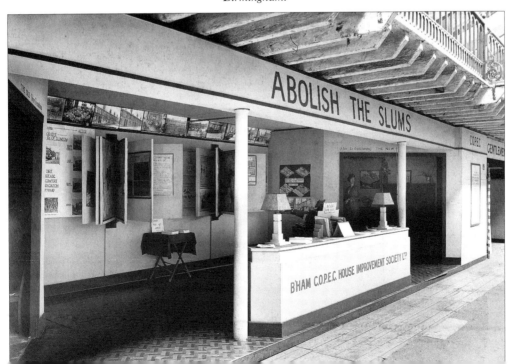

Exhibitionism: demonstrating housing needs

Exhibitions were used extensively from early days to demonstrate needs. In March 1932, a 'New Homes For Old' exhibition was held at the Birmingham central art gallery with the support of the city council's Health and Public Works departments and the committee of the art gallery. Part of the exhibition was borrowed from the London Voluntary Housing Societies' exhibition at the Building Trades Conference. It also included various models, charts and plans, some of which were lent by Birmingham City Council and the Bournville Village Trust. The exhibition illustrated progress made in improving Birmingham's housing. There were photographs of Copec's improved properties. Mr C. B. Parkes, the chief architect at the Bournville Village Trust, mounted many of the charts, plans and photographs on behalf of Copec. The exhibition was well visited and the Copec committee thought that this was a good approach to promoting its work, showing what could be done to improve slum housing in the city.

The Copec 60th anniversary exhibition was not only used to celebrate achievements but also to show the continuing problems of homelessness and poor housing.

A more ambitious exhibition was built for the Bingley Hall Trades Exhibition in 1933, at the invitation of the promoters. Under the title 'Abolish The Slums', it had two rooms in a 'before and after' format. The 'after' room showed what a reconditioned home looked like. The centre of the stand was occupied by a stall for Copec literature, large-sized photographs and a small projection lantern. While the exhibition was welcomed by many visitors to Bingley Hall, some slum landlords were antagonistic and were quoted as saying in the local press coverage of the Trades Exhibition that reconditioning was a waste of money as tenants would soon return them to slum condition. Fenter (1960) commented that the Copec exhibition generated several new investments in the association's housing. In addition, the exhibition went 'on tour' to many of the city's study groups and societies.

Copec's 60th anniversary in 1985 was celebrated with a special exhibition depicting the association's 60 year fight against housing problems in the West Midlands. Under the heading 'Caring In Action' the exhibition had a written commentary explaining the association's roots, its development and plans for the future. Photographs of key schemes, 'before and after' rehabilitation of older properties and examples of the people who had been assisted by the association were displayed alongside facts and figures, charts and trend graphs. The exhibition was sent 'on tour' of shopping centres in the West Midlands, including the New St centre in Birmingham, the main shopping centre in Sandwell and the Manders' centre in Wolverhampton. The exhibition was also displayed in the foyers of libraries, civic centres and theatres throughout the region.

Sponsored by the United Nations, 1987 was declared the International Year of Shelter for the Homeless (IYSH). Copec produced the exhibition for the local campaign which was circulated throughout the West Midlands. The British launch of the campaign was held in early 1987 with the Chairman of the conference, Lord Scarman, introducing a year which was to place a spotlight on the needs of homeless people throughout the world. Lord Scarman, who had been the Chairman of the commission which reported on the disturbance in inner city communities in 1981, said:

'Unless something is done in the next few years, by the year 2000 we could be facing a new generation of slums with all the human misery and degradation that implies'.

Using networks to influence

The Focus housing associations have developed extensive networks to influence public opinion and policy-making. They had always plugged into local elites and policy makers, using the social links of committee members and the efforts of managers to communicate their views and lobby on behalf of the housing association movement. The most important period in which local elites were utilised was in the 1925 to 1950 period when Copec had close links with many prominent families in Birmingham, including the Chamberlains, the Cadburys, the Sturges and the Barrows. This was crucial when most funding came from individual philanthropy. Later on, representative bodies, such as the National Federation of Housing Societies, local authority liaison groups and Shelter, became increasingly important, as associations sought to influence national and local government as major funding sources. For example, Focus and its constituent housing associations have been key contributors to local and national networks involved in promoting housing associations' activities. Locally, the constituent housing associations have contributed to the work of housing association and local authority liaison committees in all areas in the West Midlands. Focus has often led these groups (for

An early Copec Annual General Meeting.

example Chief Executives David Mumford and Richard Clark were both Chairmen of the influential Birmingham Social Housing Partnership in the 1980s and 1990s respectively). Nationally, Copec was a founder of the National Federation of Housing Societies in 1935 and has been an active member of this trade association and its successor organisations (the NFHA and the NHF) over the last 65 years. Also nationally, David Mumford, Chief Executive of Copec and Focus until 1994, was a Housing Corporation Board member for many years. Today, Richard Clark is a member of the Executive Council of the National Federation of Housing Associations.

Meetings as campaigning forums

Annual General Meetings have been used throughout Focus' history to promote the housing association's work and to draw attention to social issues. For example, Copec extensively used its AGMs for this purpose, and, although they received wider coverage in the press in those days than more recently, the practice has persisted up until the present day. From the start, Copec had an excellent working relationship with the two Chamberlain brothers, sons of Joseph Chamberlain, who had been Lord Mayor of Birmingham in the 1870s and had been the chief architect of the city's first housing improvement scheme. Austen Chamberlain was the elder brother, becoming Liberal Member of Parliament for West Birmingham in 1914 until his death in 1937. Neville Chamberlain, the youngest of the two sons, was elected Lord Mayor of Birmingham in 1915 and became a Conservative Member of Parliament for Ladywood, Birmingham from 1918 until his death in 1940. In a letter to the Copec secretary, Frank Hickinbotham in 1928, Neville Chamberlain, who was Minister of Health (including housing) at the time, said:

'I should like to send you my congratulations upon the achievements of the Copec House Improvement Society and my best wishes for your further success. From the point of view of the housing reformer, the benefits conferred from your scheme are numerous and important. You are demonstrating the worth of a method of dealing with unhealthy house property which has long commended itself to me, and which I hope to find it possible to expand into a scheme of general application before I leave my present office'.

Austen Chamberlain later addressed the Copec AGM in 1933. He accepted the offer by stating that it was a way in which he could discharge Birmingham's debt to Copec. He had made an impassioned speech in the House of Commons earlier in 1933, when he had led a debate on the persistent slum conditions in Britain's cities and large towns. His address paid tribute to Copec and he summarised his position:

'I believe in order to reach a true solution to the slum problem you will have among other things to encourage the formation of something in the nature of Public Utility Societies, not formed for profit in the ordinary sense of the word, with a strictly limited rate of interest allowed on their capital and with other precautions taken to hold these properties, and to provide for them that skilled and sympathetic management known in the housing world as Octavia Hill management. I should like to see Public Utility Societies subject to registration, limited to a fixed, modest dividend, employed in the management of this property'.

Father Basil Jellicoe, founder of St. Pancras Housing Association, with friends in the 1930s.

Other key speakers at AGMs 'targeted' by the Copec committee fell into three groups – local Members of Parliament, key city council decision-makers, and opinion formers in general society, such as senior clergymen and academics. Birmingham MPs Lt-Colonel Freemantle (1928) and Robert Bernays (speaking about the Housing Act 1935) made early contributions. Sir Herbert Manzoni, Birmingham's Chief Engineer and Surveyor, spoke about town planning and housing standards in 1943, and Mr. Neville Borg, another senior city official, spoke about Birmingham's redevelopment scheme in 1954.

AGM addresses by clergymen included the Reverend Basil Jellicoe of the St Pancras Society in 1929, a leading campaigner for housing societies (Malpass 2000), and Bishop Barnes in 1930. Other telling contributions were by Lord Balfour of Burleigh, later a leading figure in the NFHS (Malpass 2000) in 1934, Paul Cadbury (who spoke about post-war housing in 1942), and Seebohm Rowntree (who reviewed the Nuffield survey of old people in 1947) and later gave his name to a major report of social services in 1968. Another key speaker was Sir Parker Morris, Chairman of the Council of the Federation of Housing Societies who, in 1959, outlined his thoughts on the contribution of voluntary housing societies at the time:

'The story of the work of Copec provides one of the best and most exciting illustrations of how voluntary bodies have shown the way for social reform in the country. During a period of serious unemployment and low wages, Copec showed by the Second World War that even modest works of reconditioning, with better sanitary provision, demolition of buildings gravely obstructing light and air, provision of quite limited space for gardens, and relief from overcrowding, coupled with enlightened yet efficient and businesslike management ….do much to ameliorate the awful conditions in back-to-back houses and generally raise the whole standard of areas'.

Jim Coulter, Chief Executive of the National Housing Federation addressing a Focus meeting. The NFHA, and its forerunners, the NFHS and the NFHA, have all been important partners in Focus' campaigning work. Copec was a founding member of the NFHS in 1935 and one of only three housing societies at that time to remain major voluntary housing organisations today.

Two years later, an influential report 'Homes For Today And Tomorrow', chaired by Parker Morris, set standards for all new housing which remained mandatory for local authorities until 1981 (the so-called 'Parker Morris' standards'). During the 1950s and early 1960s, AGMs declined in importance as key arenas for highlighting the work of Copec. However, with the emergence of BHT and its 1970 merger with Copec, AGMs once again became opportunities to publicise the need of local people and the response of housing associations. Up until the present day, AGMs have been important mechanisms to promote the association and to cement links with partner and representative organisations. Key speakers during the last thirty years have included Richard Best of the Joseph Rowntree Foundation and Sheila MacKechnie and Chris Holmes, Directors of Shelter in the 1980s and 1990s. Speakers with links to the Church have continued to be prominent (eg the Right Reverend Mark Santer, the Bishop of Birmingham), maintaining the organisation's links with its Christian founders.

Research as a campaign tool

There has been a strong vein of research activity in Focus' history. Research has often been used as a tool to highlight housing problems, to show the needs of local people, to promote changes in housing policy and practice wherever possible. In addition, research, and monitoring, has been used to ensure that equal opportunities in housing allocation is being provided, particularly with regard to race. From 1925 onwards, a key network developed with local academics who could advise on research matters and issues of national housing policy. This network has proved successful and enabled key research to be carried out in partnership between the Focus housing associations and academic institutions. Certainly the major academic institution close to Focus over the last 75 years has been the University of Birmingham, and in particular the Centre for Urban and Regional Studies (CURS).

Copec's first Chairman, Professor Frank Tillyard (the 'poor man's lawyer') (Glasby 1999) was a senior academic in the Commerce Faculty at the University. Links have continued until the present day. Professor Barry Cullingworth was a committee member of Birmingham Housing Trust in the late 1960s and a Copec committee member after the first merger in 1970 (see chapter 8). Cullingworth was the first Director of CURS and undertook research for the landmark Cohen Committee in 1968 (see chapter 4). Other members of the University of Birmingham who have been close to Focus and its forebears were CURS academic Valerie Karn, later a Professor of Social Policy at Manchester University (a committee member in the 1970s), Professor Ken Spencer (head of the School of Public Policy and still a committee member since the 1980s) and current CURS director Professor Alan Murie, who assisted Focus with development of its social investment work in the late 1990s. Another key Birmingham University academic with close links to Focus or its constituent associations was Rick Groves (previously Chairman of Shape and a member of Focus' Birmingham regional committee from 1995 onwards).

Copec played a key part in the report of the Commission set up by the Bishop's Council of the Diocese of Birmingham. Entitled 'Faith in the City of Birmingham' (1998) the report was one of a range produced by the Church of England in response to its concern about the country's inner cities. Copec Chairman John Duncan and

Secretary Hazel Wright were key members of the Commission. Professor Ken Spencer, also a management committee member and linked to the University of Birmingham, was the report's Research Officer. Copec also drafted part of the report which concerned housing associations in the city.

The 'Rhombus' research project is a joint effort between Focus and three other housing associations representing different parts of the country. In the middle is Richard Best of the Joseph Rowntree Foundation, which is sponsoring the project. Richard Best has been a key supporter of Focus over the years, in both his present capacity, and as Director of the NFHA in the 1980s.

Measuring housing needs

The earliest example of Copec-sponsored research to measure housing needs was in 1929. A major research project was carried out called '500 Birmingham Homes: Report On Housing Conditions'. Two property surveyors undertook the study which reviewed the types of homes available and their state of repair in Birmingham's central areas. The extent of furnished lodging houses, the access of the poor to this housing and problems of overcrowding were all addressed. The report concluded:

> 'Salient features brought to light by the survey are the very bad state of repairs and the overcrowding of bedrooms, often due to the attic being unfit for use. As a whole, the survey reveals once again the deplorable conditions under which many of our fellow citizens are still obliged to live. It presents a strong case for continued house building in these areas accompanied by adequate provision for social amenities; reconstruction in these areas; prevention on the part of landlords of the wasteful deterioration of property due to neglect of ordinary repairs; and, better management' (Barclay and Perry 1929).

Copec also played an active part in the Bournville Village Trust survey of 1941 'When We Build Again: A Study Based On Research Into Conditions Of Living And Working In Birmingham'. Copec had representatives on the study's steering group and supplied photographs of its housing to illustrate the research report. This extensive survey looked at conditions in various parts of the Birmingham, including the central wards, the approach of the city council, population densities, rents and tenants' ability to afford them, and the characteristics of households living in the central areas, middle rings and peripheral housing estates.

Further needs assessments were undertaken in the 1970s and 1980s, with the Birmingham Housing Aid Service (BHAS), which was financially supported by Copec, undertaking a range of assessments. Maintenance of detailed records of its client group showed that BHAS had received 1,220 written enquiries and 6,291 telephone enquiries in 1986. During the same year BHAS undertook 1,344 interviews with clients of whom 23 percent were homeless or facing eviction and 17 percent were living in poor or overcrowded housing conditions.

In the 1990s, Focus carried out, usually in partnership, research into a number of issues relating to housing needs including:

- the housing needs of older people with the National Federation of Housing Associations (NFHA) regional office (1993);
- a review of the effects of changes in the Housing Needs Indicator (HNI) on the West Midlands region with the National Housing Federation (NHF) and CURS academic Pat Niner (1998);
- the health, accommodation and social care needs of older Irish men in Birmingham with the Birmingham Irish Community Forum (Williams 1998);
- housing and social exclusion in the Midlands, undertaken by Professor Alan Murie and Peter Lee at CURS, as a follow-up for their national study of poverty, housing and social exclusion issues for the Joseph Rowntree Foundation (Lee and Murie 1998, 1999) – Focus held a conference at Aston Villa leisure complex to launch the report.

The Housing and Social Exclusion Conference in the West Midlands in 1999. Focus commissioned research from the Centre of Urban and Regional Studies at the University of Birmingham in 1998. Professor Alan Murie and Peter Lee undertook a major study which was launched at a well-attended conference. Seen here are local policy-makers Heather Mytton-Sanneh, Director of the West Midlands Region of the Housing Corporation, and Phillipa Holland, Director of Regeneration at the Government Office for the West Midlands.

Pressing for change

Copec, Shape and Focus have all used articles in the national and local papers, trade journals and Christian outlets to underscore the needs of tenants, homeless people and the poorly housed, and to advocate solutions and approaches to meeting need. A series of examples below shows how different eras have called for different approaches to press campaigning.

Dungeons.

It is no exaggeration to say that it would be more healthy to live in a modern prison than in some of our 70 to 100-year-old derelict houses.

This photograph shows some typical back houses. Overshadowed and enclosed with ugliness, deficient in ventilation, surrounded by squalor and dirt, depressed by disease and tales of disease, what chance can there be for a woman to show her glorious pride and privilege of motherhood and homecraft?

The Water Supply.

In many yards, one tap is the sole source of supply for all the houses. Possibly as many as twelve houses draw from the one tap.

Every drop of water has to be carried. There is no running supply for washing up, no sink, no sculiery.

Near the common tap is usually the common drain, liable to be choked with its common collection of potato parings and vegetable refuse.

In this photograph the water tap for this yard is attached to the black post to the right of the bucket.

Note the crumbling brick-work (involving internal dampness).

W.C's.

This yard shows dustbins exposed to weather, and an accumulation of refuse amongst which the children play.

The photograph also shows the w.c. accommodation.

Generally speaking, there is one w.c. to every two houses. Sometimes there are three houses to one w.c. When in a yard there are frequently houses containing two families, the position is positively disgusting and indescribable.

Little imagination is needed to realise the situation at the weekends, when the wage-earning members of the families are also "at home."

Divided responsibility regarding cleanliness of w.c.'s, brew-houses, dustbins, drains, water taps, is naturally the cause of much quarrelling between neighbours in the same yard.

Each house should have its own w.c., with as much privacy as possible.

The Brew-house.

The brew-house or wash-house is to the right.

The brickwork is in good condition as far as brew-houses are concerned. Windows are replaced by wooden strips and the woman washing would be exposed to the vagaries of the weather, especially with the defective roof letting in the rain.

In the corner is the w.c. used by the families in the yard.

Note the defective downspouts, creating damp and crumbling walls, also note how potential disease is encouraged by the proximity of garbage, w.c. dampness, darkness, cat, bad drain, and, in due course, flies.

These plucky little children ask us—
"What about our JOURNEY'S END ?"

"*Take heed that ye despise not one of these little* "*ones; for I say unto you, That in heaven their angels* "*do always behold the face of my Father which is in* "*Heaven.*

"*Even so, it is not the will of your Father which is* "*in heaven, that one of these little ones should perish.*"

PREPARED FOR THE BIRMINGHAM CRUSADE, 1930, BY COUNCILLOR A. F. BRADBEER.
J. PATRICK, TYP., PERSHORE ST., B'HAM

The 'Crusaders' pamphlet in 1930. Photographs and text were supplied by Copec. Photographs showed the living conditions in Birmingham's central areas.

Crusading

An early example of the use of an article to galvanise support for Copec and its work was placed in the 'Crusade' Journal in 1931. Frank Tillyard produced an article called: 'Social Conditions In Birmingham'. In the twelve page article, Professor Tillyard outlined the slum conditions in the city, the nature and level of unemployment, the extent of Poor Law relief and reviewed what had been achieved in the central areas of the city. A second article by him appeared a year later in the 'Congregational Quarterly' entitled 'Developments And Experiments: The Birmingham Copec House Improvement Society'. This article, which was so popular a 1,000 copy reprint was undertaken, reviewed Copec's achievements up until that date and set out the housing problems still to be tackled. Tillyard commented about Copec's achievements:

'It should be pointed out that the Christian public of the city have not merely contributed money; they have also rendered much personal service. If the present day Church in Birmingham is asked for a 'monument', it might do worse than point to the Birmingham Copec House Improvement Society'.

Highlighting inner city problems

Using articles in this way was not repeated extensively by Copec or Focus until closer to the present day. David Mumford, in particular, wrote a number of articles, mainly for the housing trade press. One notable example was an article in 1983 in 'Housing Associations Weekly', which covered the problems of inner urban areas and promoted housing associations as potential key regeneration agents. The article came soon after the disturbances in inner city areas and dwelt on the consequences of economic recession, which David Mumford attributed to the government's monetarist policies. He said:

'Today within the inner urban areas of Britain, lie major social problems, which, if not tackled urgently, could lead to serious consequences for the whole community. Economic insecurity, racial discrimination, perceived deprivation and enforced idleness due to high unemployment levels lead inevitably to crime, vandalism, tenant damage and other anti-social behaviour. Housing associations have the ability to make a major contribution towards tackling these grave social problems, but although their work is supported by all major political parties, insufficient of the available funding is channelled into high stress areas. In the long run, the cost of neglecting the problems or our inner cities will be substantially greater than the cost of tackling them. Either because of conscience or because there is no other way of achieving an orderly society, action is essential now. Give us the tools.....'

Chris Wadhams, the Chief Executive of Shape and a key architect of the association's approach to community renewal in the 1980s and 1990s, produced an article for 'Housing Review' in 1990 outlining to a greater extent the role of housing associations in neighbourhood renewal. Called: 'Catalysts For Change?', the article examined how housing associations could become more involved in renewal programmes, particularly people-led programmes, and reasons why this was a policy worth pursuing. Highlighting the track record of community-based housing associations, their entrepreneurial skills, their commitment to the long-term, their flexibility and their closeness to tenants and communities, Chris Wadhams concluded:

'The community-based associations set up in the 1960s and 1970s have areas of activity which correspond well with inner city areas where neighbourhood renewal is necessary. They are almost neighbourhood renewal chameleons, having links to a wide variety of organisations. They are flexible organisations and appropriate in size for the job in hand. Most have offices in or nearby the areas they serve. Because they are not motivated by profit, their investment decisions are more stable, and they can be relied upon to stick around'.

A 'birds eye view' of Sparkbook in Birmingham. The area is one of the country's most disadvantaged. Shape campaigned widely for housing associations to take on a wider role in urban renewal, to the extent that it 'declared' Sparkbrook an urban renewal area, alongside partner Friendship Housing Association, and set about tackling its problems in the 1980s.

Using the national and local press

Focus and its antecedent housing associations have obtained press coverage in the national and local media on many occasions. From its beginnings in 1925, Copec used the local press extensively, with all of its AGMs reported in Birmingham's 'Post', 'Mail' and 'Gazette' on numerous occasions in the 1920s and 1930s. More than 200 articles and reports relating to Copec's work were published in these influential, local papers between 1925 and 1939 – that's one every three and a half weeks. A good example of the coverage obtained by Copec was the 'Birmingham Gazette' story of June 1929 when Bishop Hamilton Baynes said about the early Copec achievements:

> 'The people are proud of their better homes, and show themselves most anxious to maintain the state of their houses. I think that it has had an effect on private landlords too'.

Another tribute was covered by the 'Post' in 1934 when the Lord Mayor of Birmingham, Alderman S. Grey, commented:

> 'The Copec Society is a great organisation, and has done splendid work in dealing with the slum problem, and has made definite contributions towards social and philanthropic objects in the city'.

During the war, newspaper coverage of Copec's work fell away, understandably, as there were greater media priorities. However, coverage in the local press did not pick up in the 1950s to any great extent. This may have been because Copec was not seeking the level of publicity for its work previously sought and had 'relaxed' its earlier campaigning instincts. In addition, because of post-war reconstruction and the renewed emphasis on the provision of council housing by both the Labour and Conservative governments of the period, the work of Copec and similar Societies, was not seen as so newsworthy as in previous decades.

Press coverage in the 'Shelter' years

Media interest was renewed in the 1960s and 1970s with the launch of the Shelter campaign and a renewed interest in the country's housing problems. There were major features about the formation of Birmingham Housing Trust in July to October 1966. One feature said about BHT:

> 'Its principal aim is to rehouse families from overcrowded homes all over the city in converted properties. To help it start, BHT has been offered £3,000 by Notting Hill Housing Trust'.

Both the BHT third anniversary in 1969 and the BHT/Copec merger in 1970 were covered extensively. In Wolverhampton, the establishment of the Wolverhampton housing association was reported in the 'Express and Star' (October 1969):

> 'The association is a registered charity with about 50 members. Many of them are connected with the Wolverhampton Shelter Group, the Wolverhampton Council of Churches and the Wolverhampton Council for Community Relations'.

The merger between WHA and Copec was also reported widely. During the 1970s, Copec continued to receive some coverage, especially in relation to its work in Housing Action Areas. By the late 1970s, however, interest had again waned and this together with an absence of positive promotional activity appears to have continued through the 1980s.

A renewed campaigning approach

After 1994, Focus made a concerted attempt to re-ignite the public's interest in housing problems and made major contributions to the housing debate, despite social housing being relatively low on the nation's agenda in comparison to health, education and the economy. The use of press releases and letters by Focus and the adoption of a modern approach to public relations, enabled the association to score some considerable media successes in this period. Some of the best examples of its campaigning approach were demonstrated in connection with the substantial cuts in public grant in the mid-1990s in the last years of the John Major-led Conservative government. In two articles in the 'Birmingham Evening Mail' and the 'Express and Star' in March 1995, Focus hit out at the budget by Chancellor Kenneth Clarke when he cut £300 million from funding to housing associations. Headlines for the articles were 'Sharp Fall In Homes To Rent' and 'Housing Group Slams Budget', respectively. Richard Clark was quoted as saying:

> 'More than £16 million in the form of building grants has been taken away from the local community. When the money which housing associations invest themselves is added to the Government grant, more than £55 million has been taken out of the Birmingham economy – representing £55 for every man, woman and child in the city'.

In the following year's budget, which cut a further £350 million from housing association programmes, John Duncan, Focus Chairman, had a letter published in the 'Guardian' which said:

> 'What Kenneth Clarke calls a virtuous Budget, I find to be a betrayal of the poor and the homeless. Have we honestly become so poor a society that we cannot afford to house all of our fellow citizens adequately?'

Other articles were carried by the national and local press on rent rises, changes to housing benefit, rising housing vacancy rates and ethnic minority target setting.

Chief Executive Richard Clark with Shelter Director Chris Holmes marking the opening of a jointly funded housing advice service in 1996. The new advice service was marked by attendance of Environment Minister James Clappison MP. This is the latest chapter in Focus' partnership with Shelter, which goes back to 1966.

Influencing policy-making

There are numerous examples when Copec and later Focus have been invited to contribute evidence on the future of housing policies. An early example was evidence given to the Beveridge Committee, the architects of the post war welfare state. In the postwar period, evidence was also provided to range of other important advisory committees. The impact of such responses on subsequent policy making is always difficult to interpret. However, the importance attached to taking part in such consultation processes by the staff and committees of organisations like Copec should not be underplayed.

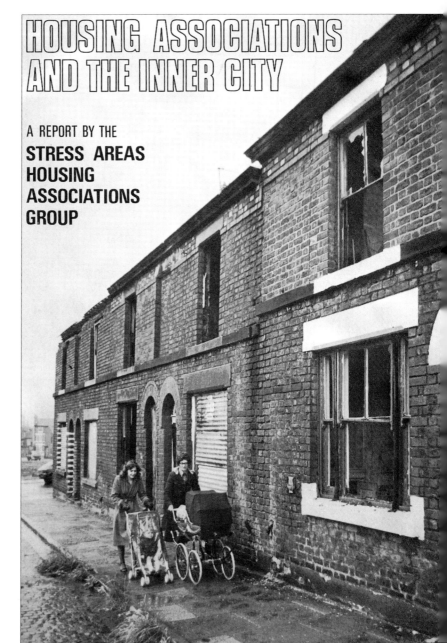

Stress areas report in 1982 – Copec was a leading housing association in the group.

Advisory Committees Receiving Evidence From Copec

- The Central Housing Advisory Committee on design of houses and flats;
- The Committee on Damaged Licensed Premises and Reconstruction;
- The Scottish Housing Advisory Committee on design and furniture;
- The Nuffield Reconstruction Survey for the Beveridge Committee on social insurance;
- Voluntary Social Organisation.
- The Cohen Committee.

Source: Annual Reports

Coming closer to the present day, Focus' current chief executive, Richard Clark, also used a series of articles to demonstrate the wider housing concerns which affect associations and their tenants, and to put forward ideas on how the housing association agenda can be developed to take account of current realities. In two articles in 1995 for 'Inside Housing' and 'Business West Midlands' he outlined various aspects of the Focus philosophy. In the first, 'Shaken But Not Stirred', he said:

'Focus belongs in the inner city, doing urban regeneration. We need to hit priority areas, and put enough resources to make a visible impact'.

In the second, 'Safeguarding The Future As Focus Partners Big Business', Richard Clark explained why neighbourhood renewal agents required the financial strength to make a material difference:

'Associations now have the capacity to contribute to the cities and towns where they work. We are in contact with local communities and sensitive to local needs but can at the same time deliver in a businesslike way. We are capable of doing a lot more than we used to do'.

In a further article for the 'Parliamentary House' magazine in 1990, entitled: 'Affordable Rents: The Way Forward For Social Housing', Richard Clark summarised the debate on rental affordability:

'The transfer of public subsidy from the cost of building and renovation of homes to rents should be reversed as much as possible. If rents in the social housing sector could be frozen or increases kept below inflation, the money saved on housing benefit could be used to build thousands of new homes for people who need them. Incentives to tenants to take up employment opportunities would also be improved'.

In 'Housing Today', later that year, he put forward his views about the way in which associations are managed – 'The Future In Our Own Hands':

'Following Nolan, many associations have extended their accountability to tenants, local authorities and communities. Nevertheless, the charge of unaccountability which can be made against us is strong. All associations, no matter what their strategic direction, must make themselves more accountable to the people they serve. Tenants must be brought centre stage, with associations directly recruiting tenant shareholders and committee members'.

Focus' staff raise funds for Homeless International. The association is increasingly involved in 'reciprocal philanthropy' – campaigning and fund-raising on behalf of partner organisations.

Campaigning in perspective

This chapter does not claim that the housing associations which came together to form Focus played the major role in affecting housing policy in this country. However, they all placed campaigning at the heart of their strategies and can demonstrate a number of aims that were achieved. An example is the early campaign by Copec to promote action to improve housing in Birmingham's central areas, which was seen to have been successful in securing a response by the municipal authority in the postwar period. Both Copec and BHT played a major part in Shelter's campaign in Britain's second city of

Birmingham. Their committees later celebrated the resulting impact on the national conscience. It can be argued that the campaign led to the major public funding for housing associations and their work in inner city areas and the introduction of the homelessness legislation in 1977. In more recent history, both Shape and Focus have played major parts in forging a 'housing plus and social investment' role for housing associations which is now an accepted feature of the housing policy consensus.

The Focus housing associations have contributed to these changes by campaigns in the media through their networks of the 'great and the good', and via their trade organisations. They have also used opportunities to contribute to national debates as mechanisms to get across their key messages. These messages have highlighted the changing housing problems faced by different generations living in the West Midlands from 1925. The Focus associations can claim some success in demonstrating to the public and policy-makers alike that many local peoples' lives have been blighted by poor housing, and the positive contribution which associations can make to alleviate such problems.

Focus' Chief Executive Richard Clark chairing a meeting to discuss 'homelessness and rooflessness'. Focus also took part in the rough sleepers' count of 1998 and today provides 500 bedspaces for homeless people in the region.

11

Looking to the future

'It is always easier to describe the achievements of the past than to forecast future developments. This is especially true in the sphere of voluntary housing as so many unknown factors affect the trend of events.....but there is still much to be done and the influence of good housing has never been more recognised than today.....it would be surprising if the voluntary society with experience and resources had no part to play'.

This is how Margaret Fenter, Copec's first housing manager from 1926, opened the final chapter of her history of the organisation in 1960. I think that it is as good a summary, in many ways, of where Prime Focus is today as it was for Copec all those years ago. I have also borrowed her chapter's title to conclude this history of the association 40 years down the line. It is perhaps worthy of note that when she wrote her history of Copec, the association managed less than 2 percent of the housing managed today (see the table at the end of the chapter). She would not have believed the tremendous changes which occurred in the intervening period. It is worth recapping that the Housing Corporation had not been established. There was no substantial public funding for housing associations, and local authorities reigned supreme as social housing providers. Housing associations were on the periphery of housing provision and it seemed likely that they were going to stay there. The previous 40 years had seen many achievements of voluntary housing organisations like Copec. But there were many more disappointments as committee members and staff saw the housing world pass them by as seemingly out-dated relics of a by-gone philanthropic age in the face of public provision 'from the cradle to the grave'.

She could not have envisaged the scale and scope of the association as it celebrates its 75th anniversary in the millennium year. Yet there are many aspects of today's association which she, and the original Copec committee, would have recognised. The continued commitment to the inner areas of the West Midlands' cities and towns; the focus on social care and regeneration of communities as part-and-parcel of the association's work; the place of Christian members on the management committee, and the continued importance attached to links with local authorities would all translate today's world to her. Perhaps the continuing need for housing organisations such as Prime Focus to tackle persisting housing and community problems might have surprised her.

Her predictions for the future of voluntary housing organisations are perhaps worth recalling. Margaret Fenter thought that housing associations would become more involved in providing housing for special needs groups. Today Prime Focus is one of the largest providers of such schemes in the voluntary housing sector. She predicted that housing associations would convert large, former 'grand' houses into flats for single people. Focus and its forerunners spent the 1965 to 1988 period concentrating on this work. She thought that associations would increasingly provide housing for marginalised groups, 'voluntary migrants and unfortunate refugees' as she put it. Close to half of Focus' tenants are from an ethnic minority group and the association continues to house refugees from around the world. She speculated that large municipal landlords would become remote from their tenants. Many local authorities have decentralised their housing services (Focus has had a decentralised structure since the 1970s). She believed

The 'wheel turns'. Garrison Lane flats in Bordesley Green – 'The Mansions' – the first purpose built flats by Birmingham City Council in 1925, the year Copec was established. Seventy years later, these 180 flats were refurbished by the housing association in consultation with tenants.

that housing associations would increasingly provide a mixture of new and reconditioned homes. Focus, like most associations, provided newly built homes alongside refurbished homes throughout the late 1980s and early 1990s. She foretold that housing associations might one day take over from the municipal sector as major providers of social housing saying that 'one day they may become the heirs and assigns of the local authorities'. Today is planned the largest transfer of housing from local authorities to 'registered social landlords', and Birmingham City Council itself may no longer be a landlord in a few years time. She predicted that housing associations might refurbish commercial properties such as shops. Focus has been providing housing over shops and managing commercial property for some years.

If here today, how would Margaret Fenter view the new group structure of Prime Focus, the latest in a long line of organisational transformations? The long series of mergers, the establishment of a range of satellite organisations, the bewildering range of regulatory frameworks and the place of tenants and communities in decision-making might all have astonished, but delighted her. So what has the history of the last 75 years got to teach the association as it looks to the future?

The book has shown, I think, that Focus and its forerunners, particularly in the 1925 to 1988 period, and since 1994, have been about tackling social problems. Focus and its antecedents have tried to meet housing need, although this became a secondary concern in the expansionary period following the Housing Act 1988. The Focus associations have always used the opportunities open to them to expand their work (such as the provision of housing outside of the West Midlands region in 1988 to 1994), even if these opportunities have sometimes been a distraction from their core work in inner cities. Copec, and then Focus from 1991, continued to learn from merger partners, such as Shape, which helped Focus develop its current approach as a Social Investment Agency from 1994. Above all, the social concern of the early Copec has always been a distinguishing characteristic.

Yet social enterprise has also been a constant theme. It is not something which has developed recently as housing associations have become Pat Garside's 'commercial philanthropists' (2000). Paying due regard to the financial underpinnings of the association was evident from the start with 'every penny counting'. In 2000, Focus had around £140 million of loans, which it has invested alongside public grants in a range of housing for people in the most disadvantaged circumstances. This level of loans is not that different, proportionate to activity, to that carried by Copec in the 1920s and 1930s (although interest rates were lower!) Like the early Copec, the association is constantly seeking to become more efficient and minimise its costs to reduce the poverty trap for tenants (there was a rent freeze in 2000). Enterprise is about more than money. During its history, Focus has always been an enterprising concern. It has thrived on networks, and used them judiciously to obtain maximum benefits for the association and its tenants. New ways of working, risk-taking, developing experimental housing projects, providing services beyond traditional housing management have all been tried. Like a tree 'bending with the wind' when necessary, while retaining deep roots in soil of the organisation's values, have been enterprising aspects. The establishment of Prime Focus as a modern social enterprise, built on social concern, is the latest variant of the entrepreneurial spirit shown by the Copec pioneers. The new group structure, which has evolved from some quite deep 'organisational thinking' since 1994, should stand the association in good stead for the future. It is a flexible and welcoming structure, built on partnership and the shared goals of its members. It is certain that other 'men and women of goodwill' as Margaret Fenter put it will wish to join Prime Focus in the coming years, as they have done the past.

Table (17) – Growth In Focus Housing And Key Factors Over The 75 Years			
Year	**Key Drivers**	**Stock Developed/ Acquired (1)**	**Stock Owned**
1925	● Fundraising, personal donations	19	19
	● Bequests, donations from charitable trusts		
1930	● Issue of loan and share stock	224	243
1935	● Grants under 1933/1936 Housing Acts	49	292
1940		47	339
1945	● Homes lost in World War Two	−11	328
	● Grants under Housing Act 1949		
	● Stock lost through compulsory purchase by Birmingham City Council in the redevelopment of central areas		
1950 1955	● Municipal housing growth reduces need for association contribution	-114	214
1960	● Shelter grants provided to Copec and Birmingham Housing Trust	−2	212
1965	● Copec and Birmingham Housing Trust merge in 1970	−2	210
1970	● Support from Birmingham City Council	31	241
1975	● Foundation of public funding regime for housing associations	109	350
1980	● Copec and Wolverhampton Housing Association merge in 1976	989	1339
1985	● Support from local authorities through stress areas programmes	2001	3340
	● Housing Act 1988 enables private finance to be used for housing association investment	1089	4429
1990	● Copec merger with Hestia/St Chad to form Focus adds 2,500 homes – expansion into rural areas	3804	8233
	● Approved Development Programme (ADP) doubles in early 1990s –		
1995	● Recession reduces ADP by 60% but Housing Market Package adds 570 homes	1161	9394
	● Mergers with Shape and Harambee housing associations add 1,000 homes to stock		
2000	● Stock growth through estate regeneration	2553	11947
	● Prime Focus formed		

(1) – Stock developed (ie renovated or newly built), stock acquired in lettable condition (ie the Housing Market Package) and stock acquired through merger.

Bibliography

Alder J & Handy C (1985) Housing Association Law. London. Sweet & Maxwell.

Alder J & Handy C (1997) Housing Associations: The Law of Social Landlords. London. Sweet & Maxwell.

Asch B (1932) Translation of an article appearing in an unknown German periodical. Berlin.

Barclay I & Perry E (1929) 500 Birmingham Homes: Report on a Survey of Housing Conditions. Birmingham Printers. Birmingham.

Briggs A (1952) The History of Birmingham Volume VII. Oxford University Press.

Bournville Village Trust (1941) When We Build Again: A Study Based on Research into Conditions of Living and Working in Birmingham. London. George Allen and Unwin.

Brion M (1995) Women in the Housing Service. London. Routledge.

Brocklehurst R (1997) Focus Tenants Satisfaction Survey. Unpublished. Focus Housing.

Brown C (1984) Black and White Britain. Policy Studies Institute.

Brown T (ed) (1999) Stakeholder Housing: A Third Way. London. Pluto Press.

Clapham D (1997) hort History. Studley. Brewin.

Chinn C (1999) Homes for People: Council Housing and Urban Renewal in Birmingham 1949-1999. Studley. Brewin.

Commission for Racial Equality (1994) Investigation into Housing Associations. CRE.

Commission for Racial Equality (1996) Code of Practice in Rented Housing. CRE.

Cope H (1999) Housing Associations: The Policy and Practice of Registered Social Landlords. Basingstoke. Macmillan.

Copec (1925-1990) Annual Reports and Newsletters.

Cullingworth J (1979) Essays on Housing Policy: The British Scene. London. George Allen & Unwin.

DETR (1998) Housing and Regeneration Policy: A Statement by the Deputy Prime Minister and Secretary of State for the Environment, Transport and the Regions. London. HMSO.

Department of the Environment (1971) Report of the Cohen Committee. DoE.

Diocese of Birmingham (1988) Faith in the City of Birmingham: An Examination of Problems and Opportunities Facing a City. Exeter. The Paternoster Press.

Empson D (1983) nthropy: William Sutton Trust 1900 2000. London. Cambridge University Press.

Giddens A (1998) The Third Way: The Renewal of Social Democracy. Cambridge. Polity Press.

Gibson M & Langstaff J (1982) An Introduction to Urban Renewal. London. Hutchinson.

Glasby J (1999) Poverty and Opportunity: 100 years of the Birmingham Settlement. Studley. Brewin.

Groves R (2000) Renovating the Urban Fabric of our Cities: An Evaluation of 25 years of Renewal and Regeneration in the City of Birmingham.UK. Unpublished and Forthcoming Conference Paper.

Gulliver K (1989) Copec Tenants Satisfaction Survey. Unpublished. Focus Housing.

Gulliver K (1992) New Tenants Survey. Unpublished. Focus Housing.

Gulliver K (1993) Focus Tenants Satisfaction Survey. Unpublished. Focus Housing.

Gulliver K (1999) Various Reports on Voids. Focus Housing.

Harrison M (1999) Bournville: Model Village to Garden Suburb. Chichester. Phillimore.

Hestia (1989-1990) Annual Reports and Newsletters.

Hillman J (1994) The Bournville Hallmark. Brewin. Studley.

Hood M P (1999) 'Tenants As Stakeholders' in Brown T (ed) Stakeholder Housing: A Third Way. London. Pluto Press.

Housing Corporation (1996-1999) Annual Reports.

Housing Corporation (1997) A Housing Plus Approach to Achieving Sustainable Communities.

Housing Corporation (1998) Regulatory Guidance on Constitutional and Structural Partnerships.

Housing Corporation (1999) Best Value - Guidance for RSLs.

Hutton W (1995) The State We're In. London. Vinatge.

Karn V & Henderson J (1987) Race, Class and State Housing: Inequality and the Allocation of Public Housing in Britain. Birmingham. Gower.

Kenrick B (1963) Come out of the Wilderness. Taking the Gospel to a Notorious Slum. London. Collins.

Lee P & Murie A (1998) Housing, Poverty and Social Exclusion. Joseph Rowntree Foundation.

MacArthur A (1996) Housing Associations and Neighbourhood Initiatives: The People for Action Initiative. York. Joseph Rowntree Foundation.

Maclennan D et al (1988) The Effectiveness of Housing Management in England. Glasgow University/DoE.

Malpass P (1998) Housing, Philanthropy and the State: A History of the Guinness Trust. UWE.

Malpass P (1999) The Work of the Century: The Origins and Growth of the Octavia Hill Housing Trust in Notting Hill. Octavia Hill Housing Trust. London.

Malpass P (1999) ssociation Limited. Newcastle upon Tyne. Home.

Malpass P & Jones C (1996) Extending the Hand of Friendship: The first Forty Years of the Friendship Group. Birmingham. Friendship.

Malpass P & Murie A (1994) Housing Policy and Practice. Basingstoke. Macmillian.

Mantle J (1995) Every Change is a Challenge: The Story of Paddington Churches Housing Association. London. James & James.

Morris J & Winn M (1990) Housing and Social Inequality. London. Shipman.

Mullins D (1999) ns. Voluntas 11(3).

Mullins D (2000b) Constitutional and Structural Partnerships: Who Benefits? Housing Research at CURS paper no 8. Birmingham.

Mullins D & Riseborough M (2000a) What are Housing Associations Becoming? University of Birmingham, Housing Research at CURS paper no 7. Birmingham.

Mullins D & Riseborough M (2000b) Non profit Housing Agencies: using Federation (1998) Code of Governance. London. NHF.

National Housing Federation (1998) Regeneration and Communities: A New Role for Housing. London. NHF.

National Federation of Housing Associations (1985) Jubilee Album 1935-1985. London. NHF.

National Federation of Housing Associations (1993) The Needs of Older People in the West Midlands. NFHA W. Mids.

Nevin B (2000) The Changing Policy Framework for Housing Providers in the West Midlands: A Discussion Paper for Focus Housing Group. CURS.

Niner P (198 Second Report on Standards in Public Life. London. HMSO.

Paris C & Blackaby B (1979) Not Much Improvement: Urban Renewal Policy in Birmingham. London. Heinemann.

Parker T and Dugmore K (1976) Colour and the Allocation of GLC Housing, GLC Research Report No. 2. London. GLC.

Platts Y (1995) Looking Forward - Looking Back: A Report on the Experience of Shape. Unpublished. Focus Housing.

Policy Agenda in Harris M and Rochester C (2000) Voluntary Organisations and Social Policy. Basingstoke. Macmillan.

Randolph nd Conflict: a Study of Sparkbrook. Oxford University Press.

St. Chad (1989-1990) Annual Reports and Newsletters.

Silverman J (1986) Independent Inquiry into the Handsworth Disturbances September 1985. Birmingham City Council.

Skipp V (1980) A History of Greater Birmingham: Down to 1830. Studley. Brewin.

Social Exclusion Unit (1998) Bringing Britain Together: A National Strategy for Neighbourhood Renewal. London. HMSO.

Sutcliffe A & Smith R (1974) Birmingham 1939-1970. Oxford University Press.

Thomas M (1985) Copec - 60 Years Caring in Action: The Story 1925-1985. Focus Housing.

Tillyard F (1926) The Central Slums of Birmingham: A Call To Christians To Become Slum Landlords. Copec.

Tillyard F (1932) Social Conditions in Birmingham. Crusade/Congregational Quarterly.

Upton C (1997) A History of Birmingham. Chichester. Phillimore.

Urban Task Force (1999) Towards an Urban Renaissance. London. HMSO.

Wadhams C (1990) 'Catalysts for Renewal?' in Housing Review, Vol. 39, No. 1 (Jan/Feb 1990).

Williams P (1998) The Social Care Needs of Irish Men in Birmingham. Irish Community Forum.

Committee members of Copec and Focus

The committee members below are those for the governing body (ie management commitee) of Copec from 1925 to 1990. From 1990 to 2000, committee members are from the Focus governing body. Because of the number of housing associations which merged with Copec over the 1925 to 1995 period (ie Birmingham housing trust, Wolverhampton, Hestia, Shape and Harambee housing associations, and St Chad housing society) there are too many members of these former housing associations to list accurately. Consequently, only those committee members 'transferring' to the merged housing association in each case have been included. Members who did not sit on management committees of the resulting housing associations have been excluded. However, many of these committee members can be seen in the text boxes in various chapters throughout the history. To those individuals not listed below, many apologies.

In addition, members of the various housing associations which now make up Focus but who sat on sub-committees but not the various governing bodies over the years, are also excluded for reasons of space. These individuals have also carried out stirling work and apologies to them for their exclusion. Only sub-committee members within Focus from 1990 onwards are included.

The dates in brackets after committee members' names are their dates of office within Copec and Focus but do not usually include their committee service in their 'original' housing associations:

Achurch, G. Philip (1941-54)
Margaret Barron (1999-)
Bassral, B. M. (1987-)
Barlow, F. R. (1934-79)
Barrow, F. M. (1925-)
Barrow, G. Corbyn (1925-28)
Batty, G. F. (1934-48)
Baynes, Bishop A. Hamilton (1925-37)
Berry, K. (1979-1991)
Billingham, F. T. (1967-72)
Blunt, T. (1991-)
Bower, C. (1998-)
Bradbeer, N. (1954-55)
Brown, C. (1979-1991)
Broughton-Taylor, J. (1982-87)
Clark, H. (1991-)
Clarke, B. (1994-)
Clutton, A. E. (1965-1979)

Collinson, The Reverend N. (1977-1979)
Coffey, F. W. (1925-33)
Copeman, W. M. (1962-1965)
Corney, D. J. (1977-)
Cox, J. A. (1991-)
Craig, J. M. (1945-52)
Crooke, J. A. (1994-)
Crosskey, J. H. (1928-70)
Cullingworth, Professor J. B. (1968-70)
David, J. (1930-35)
Dickinson, P. (1991-)
Dixon, P. (1996-)
Duncan MBE, The Venerable J. F. (1965-99)
Evason, C. (1965-91)
Evason, M. (1965-74)
Fitzpatrick, P. (1996-)
Fryer, J. (1930-43)

Fysh, D. (1988-1991)
Garner, M. R. (1991-)
Groves R. (1995-)
Gosling, H. W. (1938-57)
Goitein, Professor H. (1933-37)
Gregory, D. (1976-1991)
Hardy, Councillor W. (1991-)
Harvey, R. R. (1953-65)
Hewitson, J. (1976-1995)
Hickinbotham, F. J. L. (1925-41)
Hillsdon, M. E. (1925-35)
Hobbs, N. (1998-)
Josan, Councillor S. (1991-)
Jones, J. (1997-)
Karn, Professor V. (1974-1978)
King, D. (1991-)
Keep, H. F. (1925-37)
Kenny A. (1965-1970)
Keys, B. S. (1966-82)
Keyte, J. (1925-39)
Knight, P. (1991-)
Leake, B. (1984-1992)
Liddell, D. (1967-73)
Lidderdale, N. B. (1927-39)
Linton, E. (1991-)
Lloyd, Councillor B. (1991-)
Lockley, F. (1976-1990)
Longden, S. G. (1991-)
Loose, P. (1965-73)
Lowe, D. P. S (1950-66)
Luteman, H. (1991-)
McGowan, The Venerable H. (1938-45)
McKeown, Professor T. (1947-48)
McLatchie, T. (1991-)
Massey, H. (1978-1999)
Mathews, R. St. J. (1933-52)
Maule-Ffinch, J. (1991-1992)
Miller-Yardley, R. (1991-)
Mitchell, F. L. (1991-)
Morris, The Reverend R. Morris (1983-)
Mortlock, The Reverend P. (1991-)
Muirhead, W. (1970-1982)
Murray, D. (1991-)

O'Connor, M. (1991-)
O'Shaughnessy, O. E. (1957-60)
Page, D. (1970-1974)
Parkes, C. B. (19491955-)
Parsons, G. (1980-19982)
Patterson, C. (1984-1999)
Potter, M. (1985-1999)
Powell, Bishop W. (1996-)
Priestley, Sir R. (1942-46)
Pritty, M. (1996-)
Randall, J. (1997-)
Reardon, R. P. (1965-1975)
Reddy, A. (1965-73)
Robinson, A. E. (1925-27)
Russell, V. (1965-1973)
Saunders, G. (1996-)
Schofield, H. (1991-)
Scott, D. G. (1991-)
Shipway, S. (1926-29)
Skinner, J. (1994-1997)
Snell, H. (1935-67)
Spalding, C. (1997-)
Spencer, Professor K. (1977-)
Southall, P. R. (1950-72)
Stanley, T. (1998-)
Suthern, K. (1994-)
Sykes, S. E. (1940-1970)
Tallis, M. (1991-)
Taylor C. B. (1929-73)
Terleski, P. (1991-)
Thorley, The Reverend B. (1982-83)
Tighe, Professor M. (1996-)
Tillyard, Sir F. (1925-1972)
Turner, P. (1978-1980)
Vincent, E. (1926-29)
Wiener, P. (1970-1979)
Wilcox, E. G. (1965-70)
Williams, G. (1992-)
Willmot, J. E. (1926-31)
Wilson M. L. (1925-43)
Wood, D. (1996-1998)
Wood, W. (1991-1995)
Wright, H. (1985-1992

Table – Changes In Voluntary Housing And The Responses Of Focus

External Environment	Voluntary Housing Responses	Focus And Its Forebears' Responses
Pre-industrial rural poverty • Law, workhouses, charitable foundations	• Bedehouses (from the Crusades) • Almshouses (from Elizabethan times)	
18th & 19th Century: • Industrialisation and Urbanisation • Slums and poor sanitation • Beginnings of philanthropy and social reform • Enlightened capitalism	• Endowed Housing Trusts • Subscription charities • Model Dwellings Companies (5% philanthropy) • Over 40 providers in London by 1890s	• Forerunners of Copec pioneers in Birmingham - Christian radicalism - Unitarians (eg the Chamberlain Nettlefold and Martineau families) and Quakers (eg the Cadbury, Sturge and Barrow families)
1890-1920s: • Contest between Philanthropic and Municipal solutions • Emerging state responsibility for urban and housing conditions - Housing and Town Planning Act 1909 enables I&P Societies to borrow from PWLB • Liberal government reforms - First World War ends • Housing and Town Planning ('Addison Act') 1919 introduces public funding for housing associations for first time	• Trusts and Model Dwellings Continue with some merging or transforming into commercial landlords • Workers housing, co-partnership and garden cities models developed • PUSs build 4,500 homes under the Housing and Town Planning Act 1919 • Complementary role to local authorities in reconditioning slum housing pioneered by PUSs	• Christian Conference on Politics, Economics and Citizenship (COPEC) in 1924 inspires foundation of the Birmingham Copec House Improvement Society in 1925 - Quaker inspired • Copec becomes a PUS and raises funding by the issue of shares and loan stock at 3-4% - campaigns against slum conditions - receives charitable donations • Copec reconditions 202 properties in Birmingham's central areas by 1929
1930s: • World wide depression and large-scale unemployment(poor housing conditions persist and slum clearance policies begin) • Moyne Committee (1933) recommends expanded role for housing associations but Housing Act 1935 keeps them in subsidiary role to local authorities • Charitable action remains important, especially by church-based groupings	• Major housing societies formed in the north-east as part of regional policies • Over 200 recognisable housing societies by 1935 • National Federation of Housing Societies (NFHS) founded in 1935 - 75 societies join, mainly new societies	• Copec introduces 'housing plus' activities • Copec becomes founding member of NFHS in 1935 • Copec raises funding in its traditional way between shares and loan stock and donations from wealthy benefactors linked to Church - continues to recondition properties in central areas - (339 homes by 1939).

External Environment	Voluntary Housing Responses	Focus And Its Forebears' Responses
1940s And 1950s:	• Some housing associations obtain charitable status to gain tax advantages under the War Restrictions Acts	• Copec changes from PUS to an organisation (I&P Society) with charitable status - the association was a forerunner of others which changed in wartime - Copec changes to avoid income tax and to more accurately represent its philanthropic roots and objects
• Labour Government post-war reconstruction - housing seen as part of the new Welfare State - later, Conservative government continues with municipal housing 'numbers game' and partial de-regulation of private renting	• Little state support for housing associations, but large number of new specialist associations formed (eg for older people, self-build and workers)	
• Pre-eminence of municipal authorities confirmed in housing construction - large volume building required	• 490 associations belong to NFHS by 1950	• Copec relinquishes major property holdings through Compulsory Purchase Order by Birmingham City Council for municipal redevelopment of central areas
• Housing associations differentiated from the private rented sector	• 638 associations belong to NFHS by 1959	• Copec becomes a managing agent for the city council and begins to specialise in special needs housing (often newbuild) for older people, women workers and refugees from Eastern Europe
1960s:	• 'Not-For Profit' housing association model emerges	• Copec manages 241 properties in 1960 - undertakes small no. of refurbishment and newbuild schemes but is still reliant principally on philanthropy - grows slowly throughout the decade
• 'Rediscovery' of poverty/homelessness		
• Housing Acts in 1961 and 1964 promote new tenure forms for middle income groups through 'new-style' housing societies - Housing Corporation founded in 1964 to promote cost-rent and co-ownership initiatives	• Cost-rent and co-ownership societies formed with more commercial ethos and management	
	• Largest ever rise in number of housing associations	• Birmingham Housing Trust (BHT) formed in 1965 - linked to Birmingham University City Council - campaigns and sees rapid growth
• Social reform: churches active in forming new wave of housing associations	• NFHS membership 1,948 by 1969	
	• Values-based urban rehabilitation - housing associations, particularly those inspired by Shelter, begin to work increasingly in 'twilight' or 'stress' areas	• Copec and BHT become sole recipients of Shelter donations in Birmingham - Wolverhampton Housing Association formed in 1967 - Copec and BHT merge in 1970 - become the Birmingham Copec Housing Trust - 500 homes owned.
• Shelter established in 1966 by Notting Hill Housing Trust and housing charities		
• Shelter promotes and finances housing associations in inner city refurbishment work (aided by Housing Subsidies Act 1967 - public subsidy for refurbishment)	• Housing associations increasingly involved in campaigning activities	

External Environment	Voluntary Housing Responses	Focus And Its Forebears' Responses
1970s:		
• Housing Finance Act 1972 introduces fair rents and a new subsidy system for housing associations	• Public sector era for associations - high growth rate in number of association homes: 185,000 built or refurbished between 1974 and 1979 (three quarters of all association homes at this time) but associations sacrifice their independence - NFHS becomes National Federation of Housing Associations in 1973	• Foundation of Shape, Hestia, St. Chad and Harambee Housing Associations in early 1970s - Shape undertakes shortlife housing/establishes training schemes for disadvantaged groups - the others form in response to availability of public funding - Harambee founded as community response to ethnic minority housing needs
• Housing Act 1974 introduces more generous public subsidy regime for associations - Housing Association Grant for capital projects and Revenue Deficit Grant as deficit funding for housing association running costs	• Housing Corporation funding and regulatory regime 'incorporates' existing housing associations and creates new associations - differences between associations reduce:	• Copec and Wolverhampton Housing Association merger in 1976 - drops 'Birmingham' from name and expands out of the city into Sandwell
• The 1974 Act also extends regulatory and supervisory powers of the Housing Corporation	• Housing associations become active in GIA and HAA regeneration programmes	• Copec takes advantage of 1974 Act - involved in rehabilitation work and increasingly provides housing for special needs groups
• Homeless Persons Act 1977 introduces statutory definition and places limited duty on local authorities to assist	• Municipal housing growth 'tails off' in late 1970s due to economic crisis	• Copec grows significantly (3,000 homes by 1979) - involved in GIAs and HAAs in Birmingham, Wolverhampton, Sandwell
• Introduction of area-based renewal as response to previous slum clearance programmes - General Improvement Areas and Housing Action Areas - DoE Circular 14/75 outlines important role of associations in 'stress' areas	• Associations primarily undertake rehabilitation work for general needs and for 'special needs' groups	• Hestia and Shape also grow - Hestia provides 500 homes in north Birmingham - Shape becomes more involved in community renewal - St. Chad remains small rural association
• Economic crisis in late 1970s - 1979 Conservative Government starts to 'roll back the state' - end in growth of municipal housing	• Cuts in public funding for housing association development due to overall tightening of public expenditure	
	• Housing associations receive £590 million in public investment by 1979	
1980s:		
• Housing Act 1980 introduces Right To Buy for council tenants - enables association involvement in provision of low cost home ownership via subsidiaries	• Housing associations begin to take on mainstream role - 2,000+ associations by late 1980s with 600,000 homes	• Copec and Hestia form group structures with home ownership subsidiaries - Copec Two/Three and Hestia Homes - servicing companies introduced - Inner City Contracts provides work for BMEs
• Public housing funding declines - rent subsidies to tenants grow	• New associations continue to be formed in response to community (eg 20 rural, 60 BME registered with the Corporation)	• Shape develops social business approach

External Environment	Voluntary Housing Responses	Focus And Its Forebears' Responses
1980s (cont'd):		
• Mainstream role established for associations which become the 'independent rented sector' with private landlords	• Low-cost home ownership subsidiaries established within new group structures	• Copec pioneers the Government's 'Challenge Funding' - a pilot programme for the introduction of private finance in 1988 - Copec builds a scheme with only 30% public funding
• Care in Community	• Housing associations begin to borrow large tranches of private finance, move from deficit to surplus and establish business culture models of development and management	• Copec, Shape and St. Chad increase special needs provision
• Community drivers - BME, rural needs and cooperatives		• Formation of Focus 'umbrella' incorporating Copec, Hestia, Midland Area, St Chad Housing Associations in 1989 - Shape and St. Basils also apply for membership but withdraw when the Housing Corporation encourages a full merger in 1990
• Some associations experiment with private finance to 'stretch' public subsidy, but public sector era continues until 1988	• Housing associations assist municipal authorities with their duties to house homeless people and people discharged into the community for care and support	
• Housing Act 1988 introduces private finance for housing associations	• Local authorities trade nominations rights for land as housing associations develop main role in the provision of new social housing	• Copec 'goes for growth' after 1988, increasingly providing housing outside of inner city areas - pecial needs schemes become a major area of activity
• Increased emphasis on home ownership provision role for associations		
• Major financial institutions begin to lend to housing associations - Housing Corporation and municipal authorities fund public element		• Business planning techniques and long-term financial planning introduced to meet the demands of private finance and surplus management
• Compulsory Competitive Tendering of municipal services attracts some housing associations		
1990s:		
• Privatisation/mixed economy of welfare/competition for regeneration funding (eg City Challenge, Single Regeneration Budget)	• Strong housing associations grow rapidly with increased competition for resources within the voluntary housing sector	• Focus becomes a unitary housing association by merger of three of the original partners - Midland Area does not go ahead
• Housing Act 1996 fails to allow private sector to compete for subsidy but relabels housing associations and other 'Not For Profits' as Registered Social Landlords	• Mergers and lower number of new associations keeps total number of associations static	• Merger produces the largest housing association in the West Midlands - 8,000 homes in management including some stock transfer (eg tower block in Wolverhampton)
• 'Housing Plus' introduced	• Housing associations see major growth in early 1990s as the Major government increases funding - 1.9m homes by 1999	

External Environment	Voluntary Housing Responses	Focus And Its Forebears' Responses
1990s (cont'd): • Funding for housing declines after 1993 but transfer of municipal stock, primarily in rural areas, becomes a major source of growth • Issues surrounding housing association governance gain prominence (eg the Nolan Committee) • Labour Government places housing in context of social exclusion/regeneration policies - SRB and introduction of New Deal for Communities (NDC) • Capital Receipts Initiative (CRI) - phased release of RtB receipts • Best Value (BV) replaces CCT • NFHA succeeds in branding stock transfers and traditional associations as NFP sector, excluding private competition • New organisational forms enabled - Housing Action Trusts, Local Housing Companies, PLCs • Resources for housing remain low despite release of funds accumulated by local authorities through the Right To Buy (the Capital Receipts Initiative) • A new regeneration role for housing associations is developed through the SRB and NDC • Economic/value drivers for diversification	• Large new housing associations formed via Large Scale Voluntary Transfer (LSVT), Housing Action Trusts and Local Housing Companies - existing housing associations also receive stock transfer from local authorities- 350,000 homes transferred from councils • The Housing Corporation and NHF push for greater accountability in housing associations' governance structures • NFHA becomes National Housing Federation (NHF) in 1996 • Strong pressures for mergers and group structures - economies of scale, introduction of performance management Housing Corporation introduces new Performance Standards and Best Value • Housing associations increasingly become involved in regeneration and 'Housing Plus' activities • Housing associations diversify across a broad spectrum - 'social investment agencies', social care, social businesses, conglomerates, PLCs • The Labour Government encourages greater diversity in social rented sectors and promotes stock tranfer in urban municipal areas	• Copec home ownership subsidiaries taken into the merged association (Focus Two and Focus Three) - St. Chad provides rural dimension - expansionism increases - Focus receives 14% of total Housing Corporation capital programme in the West Midlands - increase in newbuild development in rural areas and outside the West Midlands (eg Milton Keynes, West Midlands) • Shape subsumed into Focus in 1994 - brings experience of community renewal, social investment, prestigious housing schemes (eg the Foyer) and makes Focus a major provider of supported housing • Focus incorporates Harambee stock in 1995 - creates new BME association (Black Star) • Focus revamps its approach to governance (adopts a new constitution and increases formal tenant involvement on management committees) • Focus retracts operations outside region • Community regeneration becomes core activity in 1995 - involved with HAT, estates action, SRB, area renewal, home improvement - Social Investment Agency created in 1997 - 13,000 homes managed - Focus charitable group structure developed in 1999/2000 - Prime Focus is head of a group of housing associations and related organisations

Source: Adapted from Mullins D (1999) using material from Cope H (1999), Malpasss P (2000) and Garside P (2000).

INDEX